Making Choices About Conflict, Security, and Peacemaking

Part I: Personal Perspectives

A High School Conflict Resolution Curriculum

by
Carol Miller Lieber

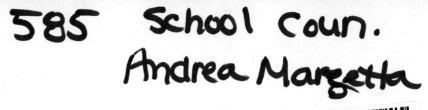

EDUCATORS
for
SOCIAL
RESPONSIBILITY

23 Garden Street
Cambridge, MA 02138
(617) 492-1764

585 School Com.

Andrea Margarta

Making Choices About Conflict, Security, and Peacemaking

Part I: Personal Perspectives

Making Choices About Conflict, Security, and Peacemaking Part I:
Personal Perspectives, A High School Conflict Resolution Curriculum
by Carol Miller Lieber

Lieber, Carol Miller

Inquiries regarding permission to reprint all or part of *Making Choices About Conflict, Security, and Peacemaking* should be addressed to: Permissions Editor, Educators for Social Responsibility, 23 Garden Street, Cambridge, MA 02138.

Editor: Laura Parker Roerden
Production Editor: Jeremy Rehwaldt-Alexander

Cover design by Karla Tolbert.

Table of Contents

Chapter 4: Resolving Interpersonal Conflict 181

Chapter 5: Dealing with Anger and Violence 233

Chapter 6: Perspectives on War and Peacemaking 287

Chapter 7: Tools for Participation, Decision Making, and Problem Solving 345

Introduction

Why Was This Book Written?

For the most part, learning about the world we live in and learning how to get along in it, are separate experiences in school life. In secondary schools, practical tools for dealing constructively with interpersonal conflicts, cultural differences, and the violence embedded in our social fabric, are rarely integrated into a student's day to day classroom experience.

Making Choices About Conflict, Security, and Peacemaking, Part 1, is an attempt to provide secondary teachers and students with an interdisciplinary, systematic approach to exploring conflict, security, and peacemaking issues from an interpersonal perspective. The curriculum integrates academic study and interpersonal skill-building emphasizing critical thinking skills, personal problem solving, and group decision making. Through the activities in this book,

- Students explore security and conflict, and peace and violence from a personal perspective to discover how the presence or absence of these conditions affects their own lives, their relationships with others, and the well-being of their local communities.

- Students develop a "conflict tool box" of practical communication, problem-solving, and peacemaking strategies. Through practice, reflection, and feedback they gain greater confidence and self-awareness to choose the "best tools" to work together effectively as they learn how to manage and resolve their own interpersonal conflicts.

Effective teaching about conflict, security, and peacemaking must begin with students where they live. Students need first to think about how conflict, violence, and the need for security affects their own lives. They know what it means to feel safe or insecure. They will gladly tell you about incidents of injustice or situations in which they have felt powerless and bullied. They've been hurt by "fighting words" and know firsthand about the small confrontations that lead to explosions of anger and violence.

Adolescents often experience conflict without a clear understanding of its sources or the means to resolve their problems effectively and nonviolently. Their attempts at peacemaking are often artless. What students rarely learn is a systematic way of thinking about conflict and a tangible process for handling conflict that can become integrated into their everyday experience. Although conflict is a normal, natural part of daily living, we usually perceive conflict as a negative experience, not as an opportunity for personal growth. We cannot eliminate conflict, but we can change how we deal with it.

This curriculum gives students the opportunity to learn how to negotiate their own relationships, resolve their own differences more peacefully, and build more effective ways to live and work together. It explores the connections between what's personal and what's public, what challenges our intellect and what engages our social conscience, what we learn in a classroom and what we experience in real life. This personal perspective provides limitless opportunities for self-reflection and observation, writing, reading, discussion, and skill building. Learning more about interpersonal conflict becomes a powerful tool for learning more about ourselves.

After students gain a greater understanding of interpersonal and intergroup conflict, they are more likely to link insights gained from their own personal perspectives to an understanding of the wider world. *Part 2* of this curriculum, *Local to Global Perspectives*, (to be published in 1995) will focus on community disputes, controversial public issues, national security, and international and global conflicts, providing opportunities for students to extend and apply the skills and concepts presented in *Part 1*.

Making Choices About Conflict, Security, and Peacemaking is a modest effort to develop curriculum that connects what students learn to how they choose to live. Yet, if we want students to truly use these peacemaking tools in their own lives, as teachers, we need to strengthen our commitment to model and practice these skills on a daily basis in our own classrooms and school communities. We hope this curriculum can be a starting point for you and your students to build more peaceable relationships and a more peaceful world.

4

Who Is This Book For?

High school educators who teach social studies, English, health education, intergroup relations, or interdisciplinary elective courses will find this book most useful. Counselors, youth service providers, and trainers in conflict resolution and leadership development will also find activities that they can use with the young people they work with. This curriculum will be of special interest to secondary educators who are seeking new materials and activities that

- Explore issues of peace, conflict, and violence from the perspective of students' own lives and communities.

- Help students refine and practice nonviolent communication skills, conflict resolution, and problem-solving strategies.

- Develop a sense of community among students through team building exercises, interactive dialogue, and cooperative learning.

- Can be integrated into interdisciplinary units on the themes of war and peace, conflict, and violence.

- Use real life issues to help students develop and practice the "democratic arts" of citizenship.

Some Learning Principles and Practices That Frame the Curriculum

Although teachers may find the content of conflict, security, and peacemaking issues compelling, students may not be so ready to "jump in." The challenge is to present lessons in ways that are both meaningful and engaging to the students we teach.

These are the guiding "rules of thumb" we used in developing activities for this book:

- We try to balance emphasis on content and process, integrating *what* students learn with *how* they can learn successfully.

- Activities incorporate both the *learning and practice of social skills and academic skills*.

- The curriculum provides opportunities for *students to take active responsibility for their own learning*, from helping to set agendas to developing their own assignments and projects to assessing what they have learned and experienced.

- Students are invited to *"feel, see, think, and do"* as they engage in the activities. In other words, the curriculum encourages teachers to use a variety of approaches to build on the motivations, interests, and learning styles of students.

- The curriculum encourages *voluntary student participation* and provides extensive opportunities for students to *create and make choices*.

We believe that this curriculum works best in a ``safe`` and caring classroom.

In "safe" classrooms students feel okay about expressing their feelings and concerns. They know they can make mistakes without ridicule, deal with their differences constructively, and disagree respectfully. The activities in this book work best in a classroom where each student can develop her or his own voice and where listening to peers matters as much as listening to teachers.

In a safe classroom everyone participates and everyone feels that they belong. Students know that their individual and cultural differences will be accepted and valued as much as the things they share in common. Teachers show students that everyone counts by balancing the emphasis on personal achievement with a commitment to the well-being of the whole classroom community.

Students seem more likely to risk "stretching" intellectually and socially when they know that they can practice newly learned skills and receive concrete feedback about how they're doing. We notice that teachers who practice "partnership learning" through shared goal setting and assessment, joint decision making and planning, seem to diffuse the adversarial (Us vs.Them) relationships so characteristic of secondary schools.

We believe in a learning process that's student-centered and integrates multiple ways of knowing and learning.

The latest learning research tells us that children "actively construct their own knowledge in very different ways, depending on what they already know or understand to be true, what they have experienced, and how they perceive and interpret new information."[*] This curriculum emphasizes a student-centered approach that follows students' thinking and concerns in ways that build on their own knowledge and connect their life experiences to what's happening in the larger society.

Most students learn best when we use an active, experiential teaching approach. Students are more inclined to listen to instructions and retain information if they know they will be expected to "do something" with it. We also know that students are more willing to read, write about, and discuss "what other people say" if they also have time to share their own ideas, opinions, and experiences. In this curriculum, students have opportunities both to work in groups and to try things out by themselves. We need to ensure that students who are "watchers" get to "do and perform" while students who are "hands-on" learners have opportunities to think and reflect!

Step-by-step lessons are always written at the risk of sounding too "canned." We invite you to revise and modify lessons in ways that fit your students and the knowledge that they bring to your classroom. You know best what thought-provoking question, story, or anecdote might "hook" your students when introducing a new concept or activity.

---

*Darling-Hammond, Linda, "Reframing the School Reform Agenda", Phi Delta Kappan, June, 1993

We believe in a learning process that *complicates* thinking.

Real-life questions rarely have "yes" and "no" answers. Rather, the issues and conflicts presented in this book often encourage students to complicate their thinking in ways that look beyond simplistic solutions and easy answers. Discussion strategies and open-ended questions invite students to tackle tough problems and controversial issues in nonpolarizing ways.

Activities encourage students to consider multiple perspectives and seek a deeper understanding and knowledge of the unfamiliar and "the other." Many activities allow students to try on different roles and perspectives and then reflect on the values, beliefs, and attitudes that influence their own points of view.

We want to help develop students' capacities to be flexible thinkers and creative problem solvers as they practice informed and responsible decision making and consider the consequences of different choices. Students get to practice the messy process of democracy as they gather information, analyze a problem, talk through their disagreements, compromise and negotiate, and finally reach agreement as a group.

Case studies of current conflicts often challenge students to consider how issues of justice, equity, human rights, development, and environmental stewardship impact policies and potential solutions. Students are asked to think about how all peoples and the planet Earth are affected by decisions that individuals, groups, and governments make.

We believe that learning becomes a powerful experience when students have the opportunity *to follow their interests and act on their concerns.*

Learning more about the troubling world we live in can easily lead students to the "So What" syndrome: "So what if this is happening...I can't do anything about it!" Students need to meet and learn about adults and young people who are making a difference in the world. They also need to know that their participation (in school councils and public meetings, in elections and local referendums, in public awareness campaigns, legislative lobbying, volunteer service, and action research projects) can bring about positive change in their own schools and local communities. Students who develop a public voice in adolescence are more likely to become lifetime participants in public culture.

How To Use This Book

The final publication of *Making Choices About Conflict, Security, and Peacemaking* will includes two sections, *Part 1, Personal Perspectives*, and *Part 2, Local to Global Perspectives*. Together, they will form a curriculum easily adapted to a semester or quarter course format for elective courses variously described as "Conflict Resolution", "Peace and Conflict Studies", "Conflict and Peacemaking", "Communities in Conflict", or "Communication and Intergroup Relations".

The lessons and activities in the pilot version of *Part 1, Personal Perspectives*, can be used to supplement any core curricula in a variety of ways:

A Two to Threee Week Unit on Interpersonal Conflict Resolution

Selected activities from Chapters 3, 4, and 6 can form a two to three week unit on "Interpersonal Conflict." Look for the ✔next to selected activities.

``Pick and Choose`` Chapter Essentials

If you are interested in selecting activities from the whole book, the ✱ indicates activities that are essential to understanding the basic concepts or theme presented in each chapter.

Activities That Are Academically Challenging

These activities will probably work best with older students who are comfortable with more sophisticated reading and more abstract analysis. Look for the 📖 next to selected activities.

Activities Which Build Community in the Classroom and Promote Positive Intergroup Relations

Look for the ☺ next to selected activities that are highly interactive and encourage students to find out more about each other, exchange ideas and experiences, work together cooperatively, and reflect on how they build a real community in the classroom. These are ideal activities to use at the beginning of a school year.

Ten Experiential Activities that Teachers and Kids Like the Best

The ☝ identifies activities that kids like because they're fun and teachers like because they make difficult concepts concrete and understandable. Enjoy!

Eight Approaches To Integrating Conflict, Security, and Peacemaking Concepts into Your Curriculum and School Community

We know that a lot of teachers like to take ideas and suggestions from a curriculum and adapt them to create their own lessons. The curricular approaches in this section offer eamples of lessons, activities, and mini-units that integrate concepts of conflict, security, and peacemaking across the curriculum. They can be simplified or complicated, broadened or narrowed, depending upon the age, interests, and abilities of your students, and your course requirements, instructional goals, and time limitations. Many of the suggestions presented here are expanded into complete lessons in *Part 1* and *Part 2* of this curriculum. Curricular approaches include:

1. Examples Of Primary Lessons That Can Be Integrated Into Traditional Courses.

2. Examples of Self-Contained One to Two Week Units

3. Two Examples of Interdisciplinary Units in the Humanities

4. Using A Thematic Focus Throughout The Year

5. Examples Of A Learning Strategy Approach

6. Example Of A Skill-Centered Approach

7. School Wide Conflict Resolution Programs

8. Examples Of Conferences, School Wide Projects, and Special Events

1. EXAMPLES OF PRIMARY OR SUPPLEMENTARY LESSONS WITHIN A SPECIFIC COURSE CONTENT

LITERATURE
● Examining the theme of personal security in a literature unit about children from around the world. (See Chapter 1)

● Reading selections about American and global peacemakers whose life work has made a positive difference for others and made the world a better place. (Eleanor Roosevelt, Cesar Chavez, Mary McLeod Bethune, Ralph Bunche, Jane Adams, Anwar Sadat, Bishop Desmond Tutu) (See Chapter 6)

● Reading about children (fictional and biographical) who, through courage and determination to survive, confront conflicts not of their own making. (Examples: Farewell to Manzanar; Stand Up Lucy, A Frost in the Night, Sadako and the Thousand Cranes)

MATH
● Manipulating decimals and percentages to create bar and circle graphs that compare and contrast vital statistics which reveal the security of children in various nations.

CIVICS
● Exploring the tools of public policy and political pressure that are employed at local, national, and international levels.

● Studying state and federal legislation or international policies aimed at increasing children's security; taking a position, and working for passage or rejection of legislation or recommendations.

INTRODUCTION TO THE LAW
● Exploring the "tuna fish" controversy (drift net fishing) and the Law of the Seas as a way to understand the impact of change in the law on local & national economies and international relations.

● Examining the competing interests between policies that promote and protect national interests and efforts that increase international security.

WORLD GEOGRAPHY
● Examining geo-political factors that contribute to a nation's relative strengths or weaknesses within a region or the world.

● Comparing data profiles of different nations to identify how geographic features influence economy and quality of life.

AMERICAN HISTORY
● Examining the values and competing interests of groups in conflict in the making of the U.S. in the 17th and 18th centuries.

● Studying the successes and failures of international peacekeeping in the 20th century specifically contrasting the League of Nations and the United Nations.

● Discussing under what conditions students would "go to war". Comparing "just war" criteria to U.S. rationales for various wars and interventions.

ECONOMICS
● Comparing and contrasting the strategic value of different country's natural resources and products in the world market place and examining how that market value affects the economic well-being of each nation's citizens.

● Investigating the impact of defense spending on local economies.

SCIENCE
● Introducing the concept of global ecology by examining "trans-national" environmental problems that require international cooperation.

WORLD HISTORY
● Examining the role of military expansion and arms technology in the building of empires and their decline.

● Exploring how the "settler state" mentality and "manifest destiny" promoted the policy of 19th and 20th century American imperialism.

2. Examples Of Self-Contained One To Two Week Units

SCIENCE/SOCIAL STUDIES

● Examining the multiple causes and the environmental implications of rain forest destruction, as well as the economic, cultural and political consequences of deforestation for 1st, 2nd, and 3rd world nations. (Three resources which tackle the complexities of this issue are the video *Spaceship Earth* from WorldLink; *Vanishing Rain Forests* from World Wildlife Fund; and *Global Resources: Opposing Viewpoints* from Greenhaven Press.)

SOCIAL STUDIES

● Exploring conditions that make your family, your local community, and your nation more secure. Developing a security survey for your own community. Identifying obstacles to meeting security needs. Thinking through policy choices that provide greater security at all levels. Examining whether policies that make a nation-state more secure clash with policies that make people more secure.

LITERATURE/ LANGUAGE ARTS

● Exploring cross-cultural differences among people in the U.S. through poetry, plays, short stories, and autobiographical accounts. Practice perspective taking - seeing, believing, feeling from another's point of view. How do assumptions and miscommunication escalate conflict among different groups? Invite people from different cultural perspectives and traditions to talk with your class. Have students imagine being a person whose traditions and experiences are different from their own. Ask them to respond to various situations from that person's perspective through discussion and writing.

MODERN HISTORY, GOVERNMENT, CONTEMPORARY ISSUES

● Exploring the variety of ways nations respond to international conflict from total war to non-violent resistance and non-cooperation, closely examining the conditions which lead to a decision to use force or a decision to use other means to defuse or resolve international conflicts (See SPICE publication, *Choices in International Conflict;* Dushkin publication, *Clashing Views on Controversial Issues in World Politics;* Greenhaven Press, *War and Peace in the 20th Century;* and New Society Publication, *Alternatives to Violence.)*

● Looking back at the Cold War and national security policies from 1945-1990 and looking ahead at emerging threats to America's security in the 1990s and the 21st century

WORLD GEOGRAPHY

● Selecting a region (South or Southeast Asia, the Middle East, Southern Africa, Eastern Europe) where there is a long history of conflict within and among nations, for comparative study examining the geo-political, cultural, economic, and governmental factors that reveal the relative security, wealth, and power of one nation in relation to another, and illuminate the sources of deep seated conflicts in the region

● Exploring the value tensions between ethnic/ tribal identity and nationalism vs. the competing economic, political, and environmental forces that reflect increasing global interdependence and the need for international cooperation

3. EXAMPLES OF AN INTERDISCIPLINARY HUMANITIES APPROACH

DRAMA AND CONFLICT: AN INTEGRATED EXPERIENTIAL LEARNING UNIT

I. AN INTRODUCTION TO CONFLICT:
What is it? Who is it between? What's it over? How do people respond to conflict? Why is conflict a key dramatic element?

II. WATCH AND LISTEN FOR CONFLICT:
Identify conflicts in video clips and dramatic excerpts

III. WRITE ABOUT CONFLICT:
Write about conflict from slides, photographs, memories, observations
Write conflict stories and dialogues

IV. PRACTICE COLLABORATIVE PROBLEM-SOLVING SKILLS
Introduce exercises in which students practice conflict resolution skills and WIN-WIN solutions
Write two part scenarios (Part 1 - The Conflict and Part 2 - The Resolution)

V. MAKING GLOBAL CONNECTIONS
Global conflict analysis
Write global conflict scenarios involving different groups and nations that remained unresolved

VI. PRODUCE A PLAY INCORPORATING PERSONAL AND GLOBAL CONFLICT SCENARIOS AND DIALOGUES, **"BIG TROUBLE ON MOTHER EARTH"**
Students representing individuals, groups, and nations role play unresolved conflicts while others kick and bash a big earth ball. Mother Earth appears, tired and battered. Conflict continues, and she dies. Students share what they would miss on earth and ask audience how they can bring back Mother Earth. Then replay some of the interpersonal and global conflicts, this time working out WIN-WIN solutions. Mother Earth revives and urges students to think about the words of peacemakers who have made the world a better place. (Contact author for script outline.)

VII. PERFORMANCE OF PLAY FOR PEERS OR YOUNGER STUDENTS

WAR AND PEACE IN ANCIENT GREECE AND THE TWENTIETH CENTURY

Selections From:

Greece:	*The Iliad*
Greece & 20th C.:	*The March of Folly: From Troy to Vietnam*, Tuchman
Greece & 20th C.:	Films: *The Warriors, Cry, Freedom, An Essay on War*
Greece:	*The Peloponnesian Wars*, Thucydides
20th C.:	*The Good War: An Oral History of World War II*, Terkel
Greece:	*The Trojan Women*, Euripides *The Melian Dialogues*, Thucydides
20th C.:	*Children of War*, Rosenblatt *Sad Song of Yellow Skin* (Film about Saigon after Vietnam War) *Women on War*, Daniela Gioseffi (Anthology of women's writings from around the world)
Greece:	*Greek Lyrics* and *Epitaphs*, Lattimore
20th C.:	*Peace and War: Poems*, Harrison *The War Prayer*, Twain
Greece:	*Lysistrata*, Aristophanes
20th C.:	*Sticks and Bones*, Rabe
Greece & 20th C.:	Depictions of war and peace in friezes, sculpture, vases, modern painting

4. A Thematic Focus Throughout The Year

SPOTLIGHT ON PEACEMAKERS

Use readings, videos, correspondence, interviews with local individuals, and print media to highlight people (known and anonymous) who spend their lives working to make the world more peaceful and just for all people. Among the list — writers, philosophers, religious leaders, Presidents, diplomats and negotiators, Nobel Peace Prize winners, military officers, organizations, local community workers and mediators, international leaders, scientists, grassroots organizers, and young people. (See Chapter 6)

Teachers and students can plan a calendar of presentations. Students might choose to interview or write individuals, or invite them to class. Students may want to research or write for information about organizations that work on peace and justice issues.

FOCUS QUESTIONS might include:

Why do you do what you do? What is your vision of peace?

How has your work made your life different?

What are the obstacles to realizing your vision of the world? What are three steps that would help your vision come true?

What kinds of contributions and participation from citizens help make your vision a reality?

JOURNAL AND DIALOGUE REFLECTIONS might include:

What questions would you like to ask this individual or organization?

What attitudes, personal characteristics, and commitments do these individuals have in common?

Do their visions sound idealistic, realistic, achievable, impossible to you? Why or why not?

Are their perspectives exclusive or inclusive? absolute or conditional? adversarial or invitational?

What were new ideas, information, insights for you?

Are the means which shape their work consistent with the ends they wish to achieve?

5. Examples Of A Learning Strategy Approach

USING A MICRO-LAB where small groups of students generate a list of universal rights and needs of children and then determine the five most important concerns on their list.

USING PROBLEM SOLVING STRATEGIES
● Predict how a conflict might be resolved in a play or story. Students or teacher read only to the point where a conflict is revealed and then students work in small groups, writing various ways that the conflict might be settled.

● Explore "social studies" topics by transforming bland text book material into case study problems which students analyze. After exploring the conflict, students divide into groups to propose solutions that would meet some of the interests of various constituencies involved in the conflict. Then have students compare their solutions to what actually happened. (For example, create a case study about conflicts among farmers, native Americans, ranchers, business-people, and the U.S. government in the settlement of the American West.)

USING ROLE PLAYS to help students appreciate the number of different groups and individuals affected by a fictional, historical, or current conflict to better understand the competing interests which may make a problem more difficult to solve. (Some good conflict case studies: *Eastern Europe Series*, SPICE; *Contrasting Urban Lifestyles in Brazil*, SPICE; *Cultural Conflicts- Case Studies in a World of Change*, J. Weston Walch. Sources for simulations: Center for Teaching International Relations, Denver; American Forum for Global Education, N.Y.; Interact, Lakeside, CA; and SPICE, Palo Alto, CA)

USING A "FISHBOWL" to discuss how students perceive and feel about the tensions among various groups at school

USING COLLABORATIVE PROBLEM SOLVING to investigate and suggest solutions to various community conflicts.

USING DECISION TREES to explore alternative responses to a current conflict. (See Chapter 7)

USING "REAL LIFE" SITUATIONS TO ENGAGE STUDENTS IN CONFLICT ANALYSIS (See Chapters 3 and 7)

USING HISTORICAL & CURRENT CASE STUDIES THROUGHOUT THE YEAR TO EXAMINE CONFLICT
● World History - African resistance to European colonial rule; the struggle for Indian Independence in 1947; the 12th Century crusades.

● U.S. History - Gunboat diplomacy and American intervention in the 19th and 20th centuries.

● Economics - The success and failures of economic development in a 3rd World nation.

USING SIMULATIONS to explore divergent viewpoints and competing interests which shape a nation's conception of security, and it's responses to international conflict. These events provide opportunities for students to participate in a decision making body which would consider:

● Appropriate U.S. responses to the crisis in former Yugoslavia

● The use of the Monroe Doctrine in Nicaragua in the 20th century

● The U.S. Declaration of War against Germany in WWI

● Trade talks among the "Big Seven" nations

● Federal Budget priorities in the 1990s

● Conditions for U.S. withdrawal from Vietnam

USING JOURNALING to reflect on the violence students experience personally and observe in the media and "on the street" within a week.

6. Example Of A Skill Centered Approach
IMPROVING WRITTEN AND ORAL COMMUNICATION SKILLS

A composition or English class provides excellent opportunities to include discussion and exploration of controversy surrounding issues of war, aggression, peace, and security as an integral part of developing speech and writing skills. Writing classes allow time for students to research and discuss issues, assess information, and finally develop informed opinions based on careful analysis. When students care about what they write or say, their "public voices" usually become clearer and more authentic. Another benefit of addressing controversial issues is the opportunity to create an environment where students can safely raise questions, respectfully disagree, struggle to clarify their positions, and even leave room for their opinions and beliefs to change during the process of investigation and dialogue.

Students can begin by turning general topics of war, peace, aggression, and security into controversial statements. For example:

Conflict: | Groups with opposing goals and viewpoints can never really resolve a conflict.

Human Aggression: | Humans are innately aggressive and violent.
Humans are aggressive and violent through conditioning and socialization.

World Government: | World Government is unmanageable and unenforceable.

Foreign Aid: | The U.S. should stop handing out foreign aid and invest that money here at home.

Arms Proliferation: | All weapons of mass destruction should be eliminated.

Peace: | Peace among nations and peoples is possible if and when more resources are spent on human development and less on preparing for war.

A range of reading, writing, research, and discussion activities emerge from placing controversy at the center of a writing program:

- Examining the differences between persuasion and propaganda .

- Reflecting on what influences you to change your mind (experiences, facts, the opinion of someone you trust, reflection overtime, etc.)

- Think/Pair/Share exercises in which students get to try out their own positions or take on another's perspective in a conversation with one person.

- Reading opinion and persuasion pieces; identifying what makes some voices more convincing than others; developing criteria for effective persuasive writing.

- Choosing controversial issues to research in small groups; preparing a presentation for the rest of the class that includes multiple perspectives on the issue.

- Building dialogue skills by talking, listening and questioning through an issue after students have read about it and have heard presentations; practicing the facilitator role in a discussion.

- Writing letters to key national and international leaders, writing "op-ed" pieces, persuasive essays, analysis, and reflective journals.

16

7. School Wide Conflict Resolution Programs

- Involve training faculty, support staff, administration, parents, and students

- Teach students collaborative problem solving, negotiation, and mediation skills and provide opportunities for practice.

- Build more effective non-violent communication skills and more effective intergroup relations.

- Acknowledge the value of dealing with differences and conflicts as part of day to day school life.

- Infuse conflict analysis and problem-solving into the academic curriculum.

- Encourage students and teachers to participate in solving school, community, and classroom conflicts.

- Provide opportunities for students to practice personal, social, and civic responsibility within the school community.

- Implement a conflict resolution management model within individual classrooms where teachers and students develop class rules and guidelines for participation: where students and teacher negotiate assignment choices and projects; where students are expected to responsibly participate in resolving their conflicts.

- Provide key students and faculty with conflict resolution training as a way to begin school wide efforts toward community building, prejudice reduction, and violence prevention.

- Establish mediation programs in which mediators are trained to deal with peer conflicts within the school community.

- Train students in conflict resolution as part of health education and communications courses.

CONFLICT RESOLUTION AND VIOLENCE PREVENTION PROGRAMS:

1. Children's Creative Response to Conflict Program (CCRC), P.O. Box 271, Nyack, NY,10960.

2. Committee for Children, 172 20th Ave., Seattle, WA 98122

3. Conflict Resolution Resources for Schools and Youth, The Community Board Program, 1540 Market St., Room 490, San Francisco, CA 94102.

4. Educators for Social Responsibility, 23 Garden St., Cambridge, MA, 02138.

5. Peace Education Foundation, PO Box 19-1153, Miami, FL 33139

6. Institute for Peace and Justice, 4144 Lindell Blvd. #400, St. Louis, MO 63108

7. NAME (National Association for Mediation in Education), 425 Amity St., Amherst, MA 01002

8. Resolving Conflict Creatively Program (RCCP), 475 Riverside Dr., Room 450, New York, NY 10115.

8. EXAMPLES OF CONFERENCES, SCHOOL-WIDE PROJECTS AND SPECIAL EVENTS*

- Organize an Earth Summit researching issues and presenting policy recommendations to peers and adults.

- Organize an assembly on the rights and needs of children for HUMAN RIGHTS DAY. Have students prepare presentations for their peers and community audiences.

- Organize a U.N. SUMMIT on The Security of the World's Children in which students represent various countries and recommend programs and policies that would benefit children around the world.

- Have each class at school identify programs and projects that increase the security of children (locally and globally). Each class selects a project to support or the entire school chooses one or two projects to support after hearing recommendations from each class.

- Sponsor an intra- or inter-school federal budget committee simulation in which students defend increases or decreases in federal allocations according to a program's impact on the nation's security.

- Sponsor monthly dialogues about controversial national and global conflicts. Students can take responsibility for inviting people with different perspectives on the issue to join student dialogues.

- Sponsor a day long conference for peer mediators and mediation advisors from middle and high schools in the area. Students from different schools trade" shop talk" about their mediation programs and school wide efforts to reduce prejudice and prevent violence. Students and teachers also participate in workshops to improve their skills and address issues of common concern.

- Organize or become a part of a local Model United Nations and participate in General Assembly, Security Council, and World Court proceedings.

- Sponsor a negotiation conference in which students receive background information on a specific conflict and hear speakers with differing positions and perceptions of the problem (U.S.-Japan trade, toxic and nuclear waste management, immigration and refugee policies). Students are then assigned to negotiating teams to prepare their strategies for an actual negotiation session.

- Have students identify local citizens whose commitments and know-how have been crucial in addressing community conflicts. Create an awards ceremony to honor problem-solvers and peacemakers. Another option is to honor students whose work in the local community has made a positive difference in the life of others.

- Sponsor a half day conference on "Community in Conflict" for Law, Civics, Government, and Contemporary Issues classes. Choose speakers to introduce three local public issues on which there is deeply divided opinion. Then students sign up to explore one of three issues in depth with a panel of people who are affected by the conflict and those who are trying to resolve it. Give speakers with differing positions and perceptions of the problem an opportunity to identify common concerns. Afterwards, students can work in small groups to choose "next steps" that would enable disputing groups to resolve conflict. Finally groups report back to larger assembly and panel members respond to student recommendations.

All of the activities cited have been implemented in St. Louis. Contact the author for further information about any of these programs.

18

TEACHING STRATEGIES

We know that all students have different "best" learning styles and most teachers use instructional approaches that reflect their own philosophy and "comfort zones." The teaching strategies briefly described below actively engage students in the learning process and seem particularly suited to teaching about conflict, security, and peacemaking. We hope this curriculum provides opportunities for you and your students to try out some new ways of learning, knowing, and making meaning.

1. Quick Starts and ``Hooks``

"Quick starts" and "hooks" are introductory activities that shake things up — that give students a reason to get involved, to get excited, and to want to find out more. Some examples include: using controversial quotes by controversial people that spark immediate discussion; video clips, news stories, or anecdotes that give abstract issues a concrete context; role plays that students can act out to illustrate the conflict or problem; challenging students to consider, "What would you do?" after hearing a brief case study of a current or historical conflict; using a "moving" opinion poll" asking students to physically place themselves along a continuum from one end of the room to the other according to their opinions (from "Strongly Agree" to "Strongly Disagree").

2. Generative Thinking

To introduce a hot topic, new concept, or problem, use group brainstorming, "webbing." or open-ended questions to assess what kinds of knowledge, perceptions, and understanding students bring to the issue.

3. Written Reflections and Journaling

Reflective writing is a good way to begin a lesson to find out what students are thinking, to take time out in the middle of a lesson to get some feedback, or check out what's going on in students' minds at the end of a lesson. It gives students an opportunity to think about what they've seen, heard, read, or experienced. This kind of quick reaction writing also has the power to connect a student's own thinking to the issue you are studying, answering the question, "What does this have to do with me and my life?"

4. Interactive Dialogues and Peer Listening

Good listening and discussion skills are crucial if we want students to personally connect to the content they are studying and together discover new insights, questions, and emergent truths which deepen understanding and increase the chances for creative problem solving. Students in secondary schools are most familiar with "one-way listening" (the teacher talks and students listen) and "one-up talking" (my argument's better than yours, so I'm right and you're wrong!). The following strategies help develop and refine peer listening.

- **Pair-share dialogues** between two students who exchange ideas, information, and experiences or talk through a problem or question until they reach agreement with each other.

- **Small group "go-arounds"** in which each student responds to a question without being interrupted by others. Only when each student in the group has had his/her say does the "go-around" shift to "back and forth" conversation.

- **Micro-labs** in which small groups of students talk with each other—responding to questions and sharing insights and experiences that connect to the topic or issue being presented.

- **"Fishbowls"** in which a small, intentionally diverse group of students have an extended dialogue in a circle in the center of the classroom while the rest of the class listens.

5. Perspective-Taking Through Role Plays & Simulations,

The capacity to take on another's perspective — to "step into another person's shoes" and see and feel problems as others do — is a key step to understanding the complexities of conflict. Perspective-taking also enables children to develop greater empathy for those who are different — to "be with" and identify with the feelings, thoughts, and beliefs of another.

Perspective-taking activities enable students to increase their understanding of people and conflicts in several ways. First, these activities raise a student's awareness of another's situation — students gain a deeper intellectual understanding of distinct conditions and cultural, political, economic, and/or social experiences which influence an individual's or group's beliefs and behavior. Second, as students make decisions and face problems from another's point of view, they experience how that individual or group feels in a given circumstance.

Finally, through debriefing discussions and writing after perspective-taking exercises, students can take a fresh look at an issue as they explore possible solutions. This process invites students to rethink their original positions and opinions and be open to changing their minds.

6. Examining Language That Frames Our Public Talk: Checking For Bias and Propaganda

Information and facts rarely come in packages that are truly "objective." The selection of information that teachers present in class is inherently biased; it is never complete and it is never completely balanced. We struggle with this issue daily as we decide what sources to use, what content to emphasize, and what issues to play up or down. How can we help students through the maze of contradictory facts and opinions they face every day? When we study controversial public issues we often focus on a critical analysis of the <u>content</u>. Yet, critically analyzing the <u>package</u> in which the content is presented can be a powerful lesson in itself. Examining the biases, assumptions, propaganda, and persuasion devices embedded in "public talk" can help students become more aware of their own biases and help them appreciate how the use and misuse of language can influence what we think.

7. Cooperative Learning

Emerging research in the fields of cognitive science and social and moral development confirms the social nature of the learning process and the benefits of thinking out loud and reasoning together in a group. *Cooperative learning is an intentional restructuring of the learning process.* In addition to being asked to complete an academic task--the "what" of the activity--students are given guidelines on "how" to do it using the skills and resources of the group.

Students have a common purpose in aiming to complete tasks in ways that include every group member. In traditional individualistic and competitive school settings, children rarely experience "*positive interdependence*"—situations in which one student's success is linked to the success of others. Students who work together are learning how to get along together. As human beings we are constantly applying our collective intelligence to accomplish group goals.

Cooperative learning activities also give teachers an opportunity to observe how groups are working and affirm behaviors that enable students to interact positively with each other. These activities give students a chance to reflect on the group process itself and become more aware of individual roles and responsibilities that help groups work effectively.

8. Collaborative Problem Solving

Collaborative problem-solving engages small groups of students in the process of
- defining a problem
- gathering information and assessing the steps necessary to solve the problem
- generating alternative solutions
- selecting the means and resources to solve the problem in a way that factors in constraints and meets some interests of everyone in the group and
- implementing the plan or solution.

One of the benefits of open-ended problem solving is presenting students a challenge to which there are a number of approaches and solutions. Debriefing problem-solving activities is an excellent opportunity for students to reflect on how they think through a problem and decide what to do.

9. Conflict Analysis

Chapters 3 and 7 present several models for conflict analysis ranging from a simplified form for recording firsthand observations of an interpersonal conflict to an in depth step-by-step analysis of domestic and international conflicts which require investigative research. We have also provided some "in between" models that help students get to the heart of public policy disputes and global conflicts in one class period.

10. Peacemaking Strategies

Throughout the curriculum, students are introduced to a variety of peacemaking processes—from active listening to effective questioning to negotiation and mediation. Students put their new "tools" to use when they participate in mock negotiations and role plays and when they apply their peacemaking skills to real problems in their schools and communities.

11. Community Action Projects

Community action projects provide students with an opportunity to systematically investigate, research, and take action on real problems or deeply felt concerns that emerge from their studies. Students may wish to work by themselves or in small groups and use a variety of media to document their work.

Although this type of activity requires significant chunks of time and commitment, the benefits far outweigh the aggravations! Students experience the pleasure of designing a project from scratch and they meet the challenges of applying their new tools and skills.

12. Developing a Public Voice Through Civic Writing and Civic Participation

Many activities in the book that highlight current conflicts and public crises offer suggestions for how students can make known their opinions, solutions, and concerns by writing letters to newspapers and public figures, supporting specific legislation and participating in public meetings and conferences. We often overlook how relatively easy it is for students to actually participate in community affairs and underestimate the positive power students experience through civic participation.

Project History

In the fall of 1988, through the support of the Joyce Mertz-Gilmore Foundation, the Center for International Studies at University of Missouri-St. Louis, St. Louis Educators for Social Responsibility, and local educators developed an educational project with a security and peacemaking focus that would bring information and resources as well as practical expertise to local school districts and educators who were interested in teaching more thoroughly and effectively about conflict, security, and peacemaking.

In 1990, the United States Institute of Peace funded a week-long graduate institute on "Emerging Issues in National Security and Peacemaking" for 25 St. Louis educators and continued to support the project as teachers piloted and refined curricular units and lessons. The Center project staff published a draft resource guide and workshop manual, and conducted workshops and demonstration lessons throughout the St. Louis educational community.

I want to thank Dr. Joel Glassman and Kathy Cochrane at the Center for International Studies for their continued support and the many teachers who participated in workshops and institutes, who tried out new activities, and who gave me invaluable feedback on what worked and what didn't.

I am delighted that Educators for Social Responsibility has chosen to revise and publish a more comprehensive version of the resource guide that the Center originally developed. The publication of this curriculum has been generously supported by the Ploughshares Fund. I want to thank especially the National ESR staff and the incredible network of ESR program leaders for their inspiration, suggestions, and friendship throughout this project.

Carol Miller Lieber

The Conflict Resolution Connection

Why Is Conflict Resolution Needed in School Communities?

The changing diversity of our communities, the pressures on school staffs to "teach everything" and "be everything" for children, and the alarming increase of violent and aggressive behaviors among our students all place new demands on us to improve our capacities to work together effectively to manage conflict and differences in our schools.

We hear a lot of teachers say, "I spend too much time disciplining the same students who don't listen, don't work, and constantly make life difficult for others." The resulting tension often creates a cycle of student misbehavior, teacher frustration, and ineffective attempts to control and punish children that improve neither children's behavior nor their attitudes. When classroom relationships become adversarial, teaching becomes more stressful and the learning climate turns negative. Everyone loses.

Conflict resolution provides tools and strategies that help us create pro-social school cultures in which we can negotiate our relationships with students in ways that benefit everyone. The more teachers model conflict resolution and problem-solving strategies with children, the more likely school staffs will use these same strategies to effect change and resolve differences in the larger school community.

Yet, even our best intentions to create positive, peaceable classrooms aren't enough for some students who don't come to school with the ability to get along or the readiness to learn. Too often these children lack the security, confidence, and skills to trust others, to cope with change and disappointment, and to develop healthy social relationships. Specific skill development in interpersonal communication and problem-solving helps all kids; for students who really struggle, these tools can make the crucial difference between dropping out and getting "hooked" on school.

We are painfully aware of the dramatic increase of violence among children and adolescents. For many young people, physical aggression and intimidation are the first responses to interpersonal problems and disagreements. Sadly, for many children, fighting may be the only response they know.

The *Harvard Education Letter* (July-August 1991) cites recent studies showing that aggressive youth are more "likely to attribute hostility to others. . . [they] search for few facts in trying to understand a situation and have difficulty envisioning alternative solutions, especially nonviolent ones." These are children who are likely to say, "I had no other choice but to fight." Aggressive children also seem to unable to express their feelings and have little awareness of how their behavior affects others; they "tend to ignore or deny the suffering of the victim." In other words, these kids are disconnected from what it feels like to be on the receiving end of verbal and physical violence.

This "wake-up call" sends a clear message to educators. *First, we need to think about how we can help students develop a greater capacity for empathy with others. Second, we need to teach students a repertoire of communication and problem-solving tools that they can choose to use when they experience conflict.*

Deborah Prothrow-Stith, author of *Deadly Consequences*, notes that American children grow up in a world where interpersonal and institutionalized violence are not only tolerated but sold as entertainment. Her violence-prevention work emphasizes the importance of engaging students in "safe" experiences and conversations which can provide them with the skills and insights to change what they think and believe about violence and aggression as they "learn nonviolent means of getting what they want and need."

How can schools reinvent themselves so that they can become places where children learn how to get along peacefully? We must ask ourselves whether our school cultures actually help students develop the skills and attitudes which enable them to form caring relationships with others, to work effectively with all kinds of groups and individuals, and to participate responsibly in public and private life.

The Resolving Conflict Creatively Program, developed by Educators for Social Responsibility (ESR) in New York City, and the Child Development Project in the San Ramon Valley, California, are compelling reminders that comprehensive efforts to develop *intentional pro-social school cultures and pro-social curricula* can make significant differences in students' lives without diminishing academic achievement.

What is Conflict Resolution Education?

Conflict is a natural and essential part of living. Yet, we usually perceive conflict as negative rather than as an opportunity for change and growth. Through training and practice, both students and teachers can build a repertoire of skills to manage and resolve interpersonal conflict. Conflict resolution education emphasizes systematic ways of thinking about conflict and provides us with tools and strategies which can help us respond skillfully and creatively to conflicts and differences of all kinds.

Conflict resolution is both a *process* and an *outcome*. It involves a *step-by-step process* which teachers and students can use to negotiate and mediate their relationships with each other. Conflict resolution education can also help people communicate more effectively and treat each other with greater care and sensitivity. When we make a commitment to practice conflict resolution, we invest in an *outcome* that

- Ensures the safety of children and adults involved
- Enhances student learning, skill development, and responsible decision making
- Empowers each person to seek a mutually satisfactory solution that is nonviolent (physically, verbally, emotionally) — a solution that meets some important needs and interests of everyone involved (We call this a WIN-WIN approach to problem-solving)
- Strengthens relationships and enables all persons to preserve their dignity and self-esteem in the process of working things out.

Obviously, not all conflicts can be resolved in a way that meets all of these outcomes; some conflicts can only be managed or defused. Yet, aiming for these *outcomes* is the goal of conflict resolution, nonetheless! Active listening, the ability to see situations from other points of view, and an analytical understanding of conflict itself are integral elements of the conflict resolution process.

Conflict resolution is neither adversarial nor coercive—it is a voluntary partnership process. It is not a discipline system which produces compliance or obedience. Rather, conflict resolution education gives students opportunities to take responsibility for their choices as they become more socially skillful and learn new strategies to deal with interpersonal conflicts and differences. Finally, this work is about our own courage and capacity to change—we cannot expect our students to change and grow if we are not willing to do the same.

ESR's Approach to Conflict Resolution: What Makes It Different from Other Programs?

ESR's approach to conflict resolution is comprehensive, student centered, and classroom-oriented. Effective teaching about conflict begins with students' experiences of conflict and their own questions and concerns. It addresses the conflict and violence in young people's lives and helps them make connections between their own lives and the larger world as they apply new understandings to conflicts outside their immediate experience.

A comprehensive approach to conflict resolution education involves classroom teachers in the application of concepts and skills at three levels:

- *Through classroom management*, which may involve developmental discipline, class meetings, and community-building activities; by implementing a collaborative curriculum that incorporates student choice and decision making and reflects students' needs and interests; and by negotiating the ways in which students and teachers interact and learn together.

- *Through direct instruction and practice of conflict resolution skills in the classroom* by teaching active listening, perspective-taking, conflict analysis, anger management, cooperative problem solving, negotiation, and peer mediation and by practicing these skills in the process of dealing with everyday conflicts in the classroom and school community.

- *Through curriculum infusion* using literature, historical and current conflicts, personal experiences, and controversial public issues to explore multiple points of view and seek a deeper understanding of the scope and range of conflicts we face—in our personal lives, in our communities, and in the larger world. Perspective-taking and conflict analysis give students the tools to think critically about both the sources of conflict and potential solutions to problems.

Although peer mediation is a valuable experience for many young people, ESR believes that school mediation is best implemented as part of a larger effort to train staff and students in conflict resolution. While third party mediation is an important tool for resolving disputes among students, it does not necessarily develop students' abilities to resolve interpersonal differences on their own.

Key Conflict Resolution Concepts

1. Affirmation—Affirm the dignity and value of every individual and acknowledge each other's concerns, interests, and needs.

2. Building Community—Create a safe, trusting, comfortable environment in which all individuals participate and care about the well-being of the group and the individuals in it. Build a pro-social community in which each voice is heard and the group's efforts are celebrated.

3. Responsible Decision Making—Ensure that people affected by decisions are involved in making decisions. Practice a decision-making process in which people consider the consequences and implications of choices before making a responsible judgment.

4. Cooperation and Collaborative Problem Solving—Practice cooperative learning and collaborative problem solving in ways that make each person's contribution integral to achieving the goals of the group.

5. Accepting and Dealing With Differences—Respect and value individual and cultural differences. Teach tolerance, bias awareness, and prejudice reduction. Develop the capacity for empathy through perspective-taking and the inclusion of multiple points of view.

6. Expressing Feelings—Make time for expressing and responding to feelings appropriately. Encourage people to acknowledge their own feelings and the feelings of others as a first step toward problem solving.

7. Caring Communication—Practice non-violent communication skills. Encourage active listening and open, honest dialogue. Make room for ways to respectfully disagree and hear other points of view.

8. Learning and Practicing Skillful Resolution of Conflict—Create a "toolbox" of choices you can use to respond to conflict peacefully and creatively. Prevent, manage, and resolve conflicts through the day-to-day practice of problem solving, negotiation, and mediation.

These concepts are emphasized throughout the curriculum. When working with secondary students, we have found that it is essential to lay the "groundwork" before teaching specific conflict resolution skills. For us, this means focusing on the kinds of agreements, learning strategies, and interactive experiences that help students and teachers build a caring and respectful community.

Implementing Conflict Resolution Education Step by Step

1. Think about what skills you would like your students to have learned and practiced by January—then work backwards! Conflict resolution education is an evolving process which requires time, attention, and intention. Go slow! The beginning of the school year is a time to build community, affirm the learning power and potential of each student, get to know each other well, and make agreements about the ways in which you and your students want to work together and care about each other. It's the time to change "my" classroom to "our" classroom.

   Let students know from the beginning of the year that *how* you live and learn and work together is as important as *what* you learn. Develop social contracts and agreements. Ask them what kind of classroom is safe for them, what a "good teacher" does and says, how they would like to be treated. Emphasize activities that reflect these goals.

2. Try not to make assumptions about what social skills and work skills students have when they walk in your door. You may have students who have never worked cooperatively, whose voices and ideas have rarely been heard, who have never had opportunities to make learning their own, who have rarely participated in the give-and-take of shared decision-making and shared responsibilities. Find out what experiences they *have* had.

   Design activities that let you observe and assess what kind of social and work skills individual students have and do not have. Then prioritize the social, work, and academic skills that you think are most critical to making conflict resolution a successful experience in your classroom, skills that reflect your commitment to creating a pro-social environment. Pick two to five skills you want to focus on. Don't try to focus on too many things at once.

3. Introduce activities that emphasize conflict analysis and problem solving across the curriculum and incorporate key conflict resolution concepts in to day-to-day learning experiences.

4. Although you may want to introduce ideas and questions about handling conflict in informal ways from the beginning of the school year, wait awhile to do direct conflict resolution instruction (learning and using a

variety of tools and techniques to respond to different conflicts appropriately, managing and defusing anger, and learning and practicing negotiation and mediation skills). You need to feel comfortable that students are "skillful enough" to make the process and the practice effective and meaningful.

When you do introduce direct instruction of conflict resolution skills, try to include several extended periods of time within a couple of weeks. Learning and practicing on a once-a-week basis, for example, makes it difficult for students to see how all the pieces fit together. Spreading the work out also doesn't provide you with opportunities to give students immediate feedback and intensive practice.

5. Make time for students to use their new skills in group problem solving situations, in interpersonal conflicts, and during class meetings that are a natural part of everyday school experience. Be mindful of "teachable moments."

variety of tools and techniques to respond to different conflicts appropriately, managing and defusing anger, and learning and practicing negotiation and mediation skills). You need to feel comfortable that students are "skillful enough" to make the process and the practice effective and meaningful.

When you do introduce direct instruction of conflict resolution skills, try to include several extended periods of time within a couple of weeks. Learning and practicing on a once-a-week basis, for example, makes it difficult for students to see how all the pieces fit together. Spreading the work out also doesn't provide you with opportunities to give students immediate feedback and intensive practice.

5. Make time for students to use their new skills in group problem solving situations, in interpersonal conflicts, and during class meetings that are a natural part of everyday school experience. Be mindful of "teachable moments."

A Sampling of Secondary Conflict Resolution and Violence Prevention Programs and Projects

The chart on the page 30 offers concrete examples of ways to incorporate and infuse conflict resolution education into classrrom and the larger school community.

High School Conflict Resolution & Violence Prevention Program Options

Student Leadership Options

1. **Peer mediation programs** (overview for whole staff, 15 hour training for 25-30 students per year; 15 hour training for several staff; 3 or 4 staff advisors who coordinate program)

2. **Student facilitators** who conduct interactive programs for their peers on issues like violence awareness, interpersonal conflict resolution, diversity and prejudice reduction (15 hour training for students, at least two staff advisors who coordinate program)

3. **Peer helpers** who do one-to-one listening and problem-solving with peers (20 hour training for students, at least two advisors)

4. **Conflict resolution interns** who develop programs and activities to conduct for elementary and middle school students (20 hour training for students, at least two advisors)

Staff Initiated Options

1. **Semester or year long electives** in social studies or English (**Conflict, Violence, and Peacemaking - From Personal to Global Perspectives or Conflict, Diversity, and Communication**)

2. **Developing the "Peaceable Classroom Community"** that incorporates community building, active listening skills, negotiation, student choice and voice, problem-solving, collaborative decision-making into the daily teaching/learning process.

3. **Incorporating conflict resolution, violence prevention, and intergroup relations curriculum units** (10 to 15 sessions) into health education, social studies, or English classes.

4. **Incorporating conflict analysis and problem-solving** as well as role-playing and perspective-taking into the study and discussion of literature, current issues, and history.

5. **Incorporating conflict resolution skill-building into advisory periods**

6. **Student action projects** which investigate youth issues and community conflicts

Partnership Options (Students, Parents, and Staff)

1. **Safety and violence prevention committee** comprised of staff, students, and parents that is a sounding board for on-going concerns and can make recommendations for programs and policies at school

2. **School climate committee** that becomes the "eyes and ears" of the community, for the purpose of establishing a more positive "pro-social" culture for the 85% of kids who are not highly aggressive and hostile. This is the place to get a "reality check" on what the school is doing to promote positive social values, positive student empowerment and participation, positive experiences that help students develop a sense of connectedness and community.

3. **Student-teacher mediation teams** who mediate student-teacher conflicts

4. **Interactive parent-student-staff programs** that focus on family conflict and keeping the peace at home.

School-Wide Projects and Programs

1. **"Peace Keepers"** (Development of teams of staff and students who help "Keep the Peace" and can facilitate discussions with student body around issues of violence, school policies, safety, rumors, and other issues of concern. Students can also represent the school at community and school meetings, contributing input to community efforts to reduce violence and increase safety.)

2. **"Peacemaking" Awards Dinner** (Students identify peacemakers for the school and the community and give annual awards to highlight positive contributions of people who make a difference.)

3. **Model United Nations** experiences in which students actually negotiation, consensus-building, and problem-solving skills to deal with international conflicts.

4. Development of a school **constitution or an agreement of rights and responsibilities** for staff and students in the school community.

5. **Martin Luther King (Center for Non-Violence) Support Group** that organizes and coordinates special programs and projects which promote non-violence, peacemaking, and human justice.

33

Chapter 1: Security In Your Life

Activity 1:   Writing and Talking About Personal Security

Activity 2:   Defining Personal Security

Activity 3:   How Secure Do You Feel

Activity 4:   The Luck of the Draw; Who's Secure in America

Activity 5:   The Rights and Needs of Children

Activity 6:   How Secure Are American Kids

Activity 7:   How Secure Is Your Community

ACTIVITY 1: Writing and Talking about Personal Security

OBJECTIVE: Students will reflect on their own experiences and concerns in order to personalize the concept of personal security.

LEARNING STRATEGIES: Reflective writing and whole group discussion

TIME: One class period

MATERIALS: Paper and pencils

SUGGESTED INSTRUCTIONS:

1. Ask students to write their personal reflections on security. Use any of the following journal suggestions to help students connect their own experiences and feelings to the concept of personal security.

   a. Write about what it means to have personal security. Would your definition be the same as your parents'? Why or why not?

   b. Write about a time when you experienced complete safety and security. What was special about this experience? What made it so safe and secure?

   c. Write about an experience in which you felt completely unsafe. What made it so unsafe? Was there anything you could do to reduce the danger? What happened? How did you "come out of it" okay?

   d. Think about what a child needs most to feel secure growing up. What would be on your "top ten" list?

   e. What kinds of situations or conditions create the most insecurity for young people?

   f. What conditions in your neighborhood or community threaten your security the most?

2. Invite students to either read from their journal entries or discuss the journal questions that interested them the most. Compare and contrast student responses.

ACTIVITY 2: Defining Personal Security ✱

OBJECTIVES:

1. Students will help develop a definition of personal security and examine various aspects of personal security.

2. Students will identify how different aspects of security (physical, emotional, cultural, economic, etc.) affect personal well-being.

LEARNING STRATEGIES: Brainstorming, reading for understanding, whole group discussion

TIME: One class period

MATERIALS: Newsprint, markers, **Handouts 1:2A and 1:2B**

SUGGESTED INSTRUCTIONS:

1. Brainstorm words and phrases that will help define the meaning of personal security. Select the three or four most important points that students think should be included in a definition.

2. Pass out **Handout 1:2A: "The Concept of Personal Security."** Read it together as a class, highlighting new vocabulary words as appropriate and soliciting examples from students to illustrate each point. Check back and identify where there is overlap between your students' definition and major ideas included in the handout.

3. Put the word "security" on the board with a blank in front of it (_____ security). Ask students to think of words they would place in the blank. They will probably mention job security, social security, or national security. Explain to students that *other aspects of personal security can be as important as physical and emotional security*.

4. Pass out **Handout 1:2B: "Aspects of Personal Security."** The first three aspects on the list are described in **Handout 1:2A**. Read through rest of the list with the class and discuss how these other aspects of security directly impact on people's personal lives. Solicit examples to illustrate differences in the degree of security people feel, given the conditions in which they live. Some discussion openers follow:

- Do few, some, or most Americans have all these security needs met? Explain your reasoning. Which aspects of security do Americans need to worry about the least? the most?

- For what groups would a specific aspect of personal security be hardest to achieve, here in the United States or in other countries? For example, you might explore the *cultural security* of the Tibetan people whose very existence as a unique culture is seriously threatened under Chinese occupation.

☞ **Going Further:** Ask students to bring in newspaper and magazine articles to illustrate an individual's need for a particular aspect of personal security or successful attainment of a particular aspect of security.

THE CONCEPT OF PERSONAL SECURITY

- **Security Is a Feeling**—Our experiences and knowledge can inform and even alter our perceptions, but each of us ultimately responds in a given situation according to *how secure or safe we feel.*

- **There Is a Developmental Basis to Personal Security** — The most basic definitions of security refer to "the absence of threats to survival or freedom from fear, anxiety, danger, and uncertainty." For children, a feeling of security is critical. Think about the kind of security you needed as a child.

  Children need *physical security* (nourishment, protection from the elements and disease, remedies for illness), *safety* (orderliness, protective rules, and consistent protection from physical harm, abuse, violence, and terror) and *affection* (attachment to at least one parent who provides love, nurturing, acceptance, comfort, and a stable and constant presence). According to Abraham Maslow's "hierarchy of needs," children need all three of these things in order to grow and develop into healthy adults.

- **Relative Security Is Defined by the Degree of Relative Uncertainty** —Our feelings of uncertainty and unpredictability often shape our responses to new situations. These feelings can determine whether we trust others to consider and provide for our own safety, security, and well-being in a given situation. The more we feel that our own interests are not considered or valued by another person, the more we distrust her or his actions. Saying it another way, the more threatened we feel, the less likely we are to place our trust in others.

- **The Degree of Autonomy and Power We Have Affects Our Sense of Security and Our Ability to Increase Our Security**—If individuals believe, "There's nothing I can do," there probably isn't. When individuals feel that their security is totally controlled by others or that they are powerless to change a situation, it becomes very difficult to act in ways that actually help us feel more secure.

  People can become so overwhelmed by a threatening situation that they become paralyzed, unable to act, and their fear and despair simply deepen within. Others may become so accustomed to a threatening situation that they become desensitized to it, passively accepting what may be unacceptable. Some people may become so frustrated by a loss of control and powerlessness that the only acceptable alternatives become acts of intimidation and violence.

Aspects Of Personal Security

- **Physical Security** — nourishment; clothing and shelter that; provide protection from the elements; protection from disease; treatment for illness

- **Safety Security** — orderliness, protective rules, and consistent protection from physical harm, abuse, violence, and terror; the certainty that your basic needs will be met

- **Emotional Security** — a sense of belonging and being loved and cared for; feelings of acceptance from others; healthy interpersonal relationships with family, friends, adults, peers, and coworkers

- **Developmental Security** — access to education; the opportunity and freedom to learn, achieve, and contribute to society

- **Cultural Security** — affirmation of cultural identity, values, and traditions; tolerance and legal protection of a person's ethnic, racial, religious, and gender identity; freedom to participate as full partners in society regardless of cultural identity

- **Political Security** — the degree of protection and safety that a government provides its citizens within a nation; protection from threats beyond a nation's borders; the quality and degree of citizen rights and civic participation in decision-making

- **Economic Security** — access to training and the development of useful skills; access to jobs and wages which provide a decent standard of living; provision of benefits for the aged, the sick, the differently abled, and children

- **Environmental Security** — protection from environmental hazards and toxins; provisions for safe and clean air, water, and food supplies; provision of a safe, clean habitat

ACTIVITY 3: How Secure Do You Feel?

OBJECTIVES:

1. Students will identify how secure or insecure they would feel in various situations.

2. They will discuss conditions that make them feel least secure and explore how feelings of security or insecurity affect their own attitudes and behavior.

LEARNING STRATEGIES: Interactive exercise, whole group discussion

TIME: One class period

MATERIALS: Paper signs and **Handout 1:3**

SUGGESTED INSTRUCTIONS:

1. Make five paper signs using these words:

    Very Secure, Moderately Secure, Unsure, Moderately Insecure, and Very Insecure.

    Tape the signs on the floor, evenly spaced across the room from one end to another.   Explain to students that you will read ten statements. Each time they hear a statement, students are to stand by the sign that is the closest to how they would feel in that particular situation.

2. Read statements 1 - 10 on **Handout 1:3: "How Secure Do You Feel?"** After you read each statement and students have placed themselves where they want to be on the security continuum, tally where students are standing. For each situation ask a couple of students why they chose to stand where they are.

3. After students are seated, pass out **Handout 1:3** to each student. Ask students to fill in their responses to statements 11 - 20 on the back side of the handout. When students have finished, tally responses for some or all of the situations by using a show of hands or by collecting sheets for tallying and then returning them to students.

4. Select various situations from **Handout 1:3** to discuss with students. *In each situation, it is critical to explore ways that students can be proactive and take steps that would enable them to increase their own sense of security in a particular situation.* Ask students to identify situations in which they would have *greater* or *lesser* autonomy and power to change the outcome or prevent a situation from becoming more unsafe.

It's equally important to talk about conditions beyond an individual's power or control that make situations more or less secure. Suggested discussion questions follow:

● Were there any situations where almost everyone felt secure? Insecure? How would you characterize the differences in these situations?

● Are there any common factors in situations that gave you a feeling of little or no security? What would you need or what actions would you take in these situations to feel more secure?

● The situations in Part A are paired (1 & 2, 3 & 4, etc.) What factors made the second situation in each pair less secure?

● What aspects of security (safety, economic, cultural, etc.) most directly affect each situation?

● Look at 8, 12, 14, and 19. Why would the degree of security vary so much from person to person? For example, while some people love the risk of being in a situation where much is *unfamiliar*, others only feel safe in situations where everyone and everything are known quantities. The security or insecurity we feel in many situations may depend on our individual skills, abilities, confidence, and previous experiences.

HOW SECURE DO YOU FEEL?

A.	(The first ten situations can be read out loud, or students can record their responses on this handout)	Very Secure/ Safe	Moder- ately Secure/ Safe	Unsure	Moder- ately Insecure/ Unsafe	Very Insecure/ Unsafe
1.	There have been three burglaries in your neighborhood in the last year.					
2.	In the last week there have been three burglaries on your block, including one next door.					
3.	You are driving with a friend, and you have a flat tire near your house at night.					
4.	You are driving alone, and you have a flat tire in a strange neighborhood where the majority of residents are a different race than you.					
5.	You are a member of the Thespian Society and you are trying out for a part in a school play. (You have already appeared in three school plays.)					
6.	You have transferred to a new school in the middle of the year, and you are trying out for a part in the school play.					
7.	You and other students in your French class are going to be living with French families in Quebec for three weeks.					
8.	You are an exchange student and you will be living in Indonesia for a year. You do not know the language.					
9.	One of your parents works for a defense company that has recently laid off 500 workers. Your other parent also works.					
10.	You live with your mom and she has been laid off. Her unemployment runs out this month, and the only job offers she's received are for salaries at half her former income.					

B.	(Students can record responses to the second ten situations on this handout)	Very Secure/ Safe	Moder- ately Secure/ Safe	Unsure	Some- what Insecure/ Unsafe	Very Insecure/ Unsafe
11.	A police officer pulls you over to the side of the road.					
12.	You want to invite a girl/boy you kind of like to a party.					
13.	Your parents argue a lot and threaten to divorce each other.					
14.	It is March 1, and you are waiting for a college acceptance letter due on April 15.					
15.	You've been accepted to college, but you find out there's not enough money in your family's budget to pay for it.					
16.	You are in a class where there are only three other students who are the same race as you are.					
17.	You have a friend whose family are recent immigrants to the United States, and you have been invited to dinner. The food is unrecognizable.					
18.	You live in a neighborhood where drug deals and shootings are common.					
19.	You have a math test tomorrow, and you haven't studied for it.					
20.	You live in a neighborhood that is next to two toxic chemical plants. Chemicals seep into the ground and spill into the river nearby.					

ACTIVITY 4: The Luck of the Draw 1: Who's Secure In America?

PURPOSE: To experience the degree of security or insecurity that various United States citizens might feel depending on their family circumstances, socioeconomic status, and life choices and chances.

LEARNING STRATEGIES: Interactive exercise, whole group reflections and discussion

TIME: One to two class periods

MATERIALS: Handout 1:4, several bags of peanuts in the shell (about 300 peanuts)

SUGGESTED INSTRUCTIONS:

1. Make two copies of the cards in **Handout 1:4**. Cut up cards and place each set face down in a tray or basket.

2. Divide your class into two groups and have each group form a circle sitting in chairs. Ask two students from each group to volunteer to be "game directors." Each pair of game directors will sit on the floor in the center of the circle. One student's task is to pass the basket to each person who chooses a card when it is his/her turn. The other student is the "peanut distributor."

3. Explain to students that they will go around the circle taking turns picking cards and reading them until there are no cards left in the basket. Explain that each card describes a life situation of an individual or a family. According to the card, you will be allowed to receive 0 to 20 treats. The peanut distributor will take your card and give you the number of treats designated on your card. Then the next person picks a card from the basket, reads it, and receives his/her peanut allotment. Let students know that they cannot eat their peanuts during the exercise.

45

As you listen to the stories on the cards, think about the conditions that make life very insecure and risky for families and individuals and the conditions that make family life secure and give people an excellent life chance to become healthy, productive individuals.

4. Debriefing Questions with Whole Class:

   a. Did everyone get the same amount of treats? Why or why not? What seemed to determine the number of treats people received?

   b. Did everyone who got treats earn them through hard work? Should anyone have gotten treats who didn't?

   c. Were there any situations that families faced that were beyond their control? What were they?

   d. What aspects of security seem to greatly improve an individual's life chances? What factors seem to diminish a person's chance of a healthy, productive life?

   e. If we accept that the cards represent a cross section of individuals and families that live in the United States, do all Americans seem to have an equal chance to a good life? Why or why not? Is it possible for all U.S. citizens to have equal life chances growing up here? What would need to change for everyone to have an equal life chance?

⚑ Going Further: Ask how many peanuts you would give yourself if **20 peanuts = complete security and 0 peanuts = no security at all.** Ask students to explain why they chose the number they did. Students might also write down one change they would make in their own lives that would bring them greater security in the future.

✐ Assessment: Ask students to work in pairs and create a case study which describes the relative security or insecurity of an individual given his or her living conditions and life experiences. Include at least five aspects of security in your description. The case study can describe a real or imagined individual. Fictional characters from TV, movies, and literature or people featured in broadcast and print media can provide interesting sources for ideas.

The Luck of the Draw 1: Who's Secure in America?

1. Your house burned down in a fire and your family doesn't have home owners insurance. You lost everything your family owns. Take NO treat.	2. Due to the efforts of the people in your neighborhood, you now have a community garden where neighbors can grow vegetables for their families. You can now afford ONE treat.
3. You just graduated from high school and were lucky enough to get a job. You are saving all your money so that you can train to be an electrician. Take ONE treat.	4. Your Mom got a scholarship to go to college and now has a very good job. Take TEN treats.
5. Your mother worked for the airlines for ten years. During the recession, the airlines had to cut back the number of employees. Your mother lost her job this year. You CANNOT have a treat.	6. Your family owns a small grocery store in the neighborhood. Your parents made very little money this year because they couldn't keep prices as low as the big chain supermarket located one mile away. Take NO treat.
7. Kids are constantly spray painting graffiti on walls and sidewalks in your neighborhood, including the front of your family's garage. You have to spend Saturdays repainting your garage. Take NO treat.	8. Your younger brother and sister both developed lead poisoning from the paint in the apartment you now live in. Your family has no health insurance. Take NO treat.

9. Your father's union just won a wage increase and guaranteed health benefits. You may take FIVE treats.	10. Last spring a volunteer worked with families in your neighborhood to improve basic nutrition. Your family now purchases food with more protein and less fat. You can now afford ONE treat.
11. Your brother receives a scholarship to attend college in another state. Everyone is happy for him, but it means you will have one less working adult to contribute to your family's income. Take ONE treat instead of the TWO you took last year.	12. Your father cannot work because of an industrial accident. Your mother must work at a low-wage job even though she would rather stay home with her young children. Take NO treat.
13. Your family started a small construction company with two other close friends. For the first time in almost ten years your father and older brother have had full-time work all year long. You can afford ONE treat.	14. Your father works for a supermarket chain. He buys fresh produce and sells it to the supermarkets in the county. If the produce has not been sold after three days he buys it back from the county supermarkets and sells it to the supermarkets in the inner city. Take TWO treats.
15. Your Mom works for a business that provides day care for your little sister in the same building where your mother works. The company also encourages secretaries like your Mom to take free classes to upgrade their skills. Take TEN treats.	16. Your parents both work to try to keep up with the cost of living. Your Mom doesn't have to stay home during the day because your brothers are enrolled in a Head Start program. Although your parents' wages are not high, they make sure you get what you need. Take FIVE treats.

17. A chemical company is the major employer in your town. Toxic chemicals have been found in the ground water, and people in your town contract cancer at much higher rates than normal. Most people don't want to make trouble because the company offers good jobs. Take NO treat.	18. Your family has lived in this neighborhood for three generations. Now the city wants to build a highway right through it. If you can't stop the highway, the government will buy your house for less money than it will cost your family to buy another home. Take NO treat.
19. You come from a close-knit African-American family where relatives have always help each other out. Everyone in your family pitches in so that each child has the opportunity to attend college or vocational training. You are very proud of your family's accomplishments. You can take FIVE treats.	20. You have participated in a summer job program in which you helped to rehab ten houses in the neighborhood. Because you were so good at this, you have been selected to participate in a carpenter's apprenticeship program. You can take FIVE treats.
21. Your Mom inherited money from a relative this year, and she invited everyone in your family to decide together what to do with the $25,000 she received. You may take FIVE treats as long as you give THREE of them to people who have none.	22. You live with two sisters who had babies when they were teenagers. They live hard lives, and one has abused her children. You have moved in with an aunt to get peace and quiet. You want to finish high school, but it's scary to think about whether you have a real future. You get NO treat.
23. You were out with friends on a Friday night, and you were wounded in a drive-by shooting. You had been mistaken for a rival gang member. You are now afraid to go outside, especially at night. Take NO treat.	24. Your father is president of a bank in your town. Your Mom is an accountant, and you hardly see her for four months of the year during tax season. You like your big house and all the stuff you have, but you'd like more attention from your parents. They hardly know you're there. Take TWO treats.

25. Your mother and father used to work in a car assembly plant. The company has moved the plant to Mexico where wages are cheaper. Your Mom cleans houses now, and your Dad found part-time work at the local gas station. Your family is under great stress.

Take NO treat.

26. You live in a good home. You go to a good school. You've lived in the same safe neighborhood your whole life. Both of your parents are college-educated, and they both have good jobs. You feel like you can grow up to be anything you want.

You may take TEN treats.

27. Your Mom is a computer operator at night, and your Dad is a union truck driver during the day. Your family schedule is a little crazy, but Mom and Dad share child care and household chores. They make sure that the whole family does something special together every week.

Take TEN treats. You deserve it.

28. Your parents are divorced, but they still fight all the time over money and over you. You feel pulled in two directions all the time. You get depressed and have stopped doing your school work.

Take NO treat.

29. You were born into the Oglala Sioux tribe and live on a reservation. Your family is deeply committed to preserving your tribal heritage and make every effort to honor and celebrate tribal traditions. Although you get bored sometimes, you're also proud of who you are.

Take FIVE treats.

30. Your Dad is Mexican, and your Mom is Anglo. You aren't very dark. You live in the Midwest where your school friends think all Mexicans are lazy, stupid "wetbacks." You're afraid to even mention your family's heritage. You think all the kids will made fun of you.

Take NO treat.

31. Your family's farm has been devastated by the flooding of the Mississippi River in 1993. It will take your family at least two years to bring back the land if that's even possible. In the meantime you're living in a trailer camp without your dog, who got lost in the flood.

Take NO treat.

32. Your parents have good jobs, but they spend all of their extra income on private school fees so that you and your sister can get a good education. Your neighborhood school is not very safe, and it seems like a lot of teachers there have given up teaching real stuff.

Take only ONE treat.

33. You went into the Air Force as an eighteen-year-old. When you left the Air Force, you used money from the G.I. Bill to pursue a degree in engineering. You now own a successful engineering firm. You are married and have two children who do well in school.

Take TEN treats.

34. You are a third-generation Chinese-American. Your parents wanted you to join the family business, and they have had a difficult time accepting your plans to teach English to new immigrants in your community.

Take FIVE treats.

35. Your father works at a printing shop. He and other workers have been asking the company to raise their wages, which have not kept pace with the cost of living. The company says it can't raise wages and will move to another location if complaints continue.

Take only ONE treat.

36. Your grandparents established a trust fund of $500,00 that you will receive when you are 21. You even have people who manage this money so that your trust fund keeps earning more money every year.

Take TWENTY treats.

37. You are a 25-year-old white male who didn't go to college. You know that non--college-bound white males lost more income than any other group in the last twenty years. What's the point of even looking for a good-paying job?

Take NO treat.

38. You have been physically abused at home. You ran away at age fifteen and have lived on the streets for two years. You'd like to get off the streets, but you don't know how, and you have no other place to go.

Take NO treat.

39. You are the only person in your family to ever go to college. You went to the state university and then entered the Peace Corps. You married a native from Thailand and have three children. You now coordinate programs for refugees.

Take TEN treats.

40. You live in a big city. You go to a public school that's old and dirty. Kids fight a lot. You are real smart, but you know it's very "uncool" to like school and get good grades. You don't feel like you can ever really be yourself.

Take NO treat.

ACTIVITY 5: The Rights and Needs of Children

OBJECTIVES:

1. Students will first explore their own ideas about children's rights and needs.

2. Students will examine the United Nations (UN) Convention on the Rights of the Child to broaden their understanding of the rights and needs of children.

3. Students will prioritize rights and needs that are most critical to children's security.

LEARNING STRATEGIES: Brainstorming, independent and small group reading, large and small group discussion, analysis of data, cooperative problem-solving, reflective writing, mime, public speaking, prioritizing and group decision-making

TIME: Two to four class periods depending upon your selection of activity options

MATERIALS: Newsprint, colored markers, adhesive sticker dots, **Handouts 1:5A and 1:5B:** (Optional: art materials for drawings, magazines for collage photographs, camera and film)

SUGGESTED INSTRUCTIONS:

1. In small groups, have students brainstorm a list of rights and needs of children and record their responses on large sheets of newsprint. Post the sheets and have students identify similar responses from various groups. Someone might mark with different colored markers the three most common responses.

2. Then ask each student to star or sticker the three rights among all the sheets that they think are the most important. On a separate newsprint sheet write down the five or six rights that got the most responses.

Keep this sheet to refer back to when students examine the U.N. Convention on the Rights of the Child.

3. Pass out **Handout 1:5A: "U.N. Convention on the Rights of the Child"** or **Handout 1:5B** (a simplified version of **Handout 1:5A**). There are ten basic categories of rights. See if there is any overlap between any of these basic rights and the ones that students selected earlier. Look more closely at the articles and identify the rights and needs most critical to children's security. What kinds of political, economic, and environmental conditions can threaten the basic security of children?

4. Questions for class discussion, small group discussion, or reflective writing:

   • Which rights do you think are easiest to achieve in the United States? the world? Why?

   • Which rights do you think are most difficult to achieve in the United States? the world? Why?

   • What obstacles would make it difficult for countries to comply with the Convention?

   • What articles in the Convention are ones that countries might have disagreements about? (For example, the United States has neither signed nor ratified the Convention because of possible interference with laws of individual states and objections to Convention restrictions on children 15 -- 18 years old in armed combat. Other countries object to articles relating to child labor because their countries are dependent on the labor of children.)

   • Why are children often the last to be protected in a nation? (Although there are fewer senior citizens in the United States than children, 28% of the federal budget is spent on the elderly, while only 8% is spent on children. Think about special interest and lobbying groups that get what they want in Congress: children can't vote and they have little lobbying power.)

☞ **Going Further:**

- Choose an article or basic right to write about. What does it look like and feel like to have that right? How would life change if you did not have that right?

- Have students divide into small groups and choose a particular right to pantomime. Have other students guess which right they have acted out.

- Create a children's rights rap.

- Create a visual display at school that illustrates children's rights:
    Take photographs of students to depict different rights.
    Make a collage of photographs and pictures of children
    to depict different rights.
    Create drawings and paintings of different children's rights.
    Bring in objects which symbolize different children's rights.

- Prepare "Headline News" reports on:
    The story of UNICEF
    The story of the World Summit on Children, September 30, 1990
    Success stories about programs that have improved the health and well-being of children around the world.

Where to Find Out More About Children's Rights Issues:

Defence for Children International, PO Box 88, 1211 Geneva 20, Switzerland

The United States Committee on UNICEF, 333 East 38th Street, New York, NY 10016

UNICEF, UNICEF House, Three UN Plaza, New York, 10017

Amnesty International-USA, Urgent Action Office , PO Box 1270, Nederland, CO 80466

Social Education, Volume 56, Number 4, April/May 1992, "The Rights of the Child"

United Nations Convention on the Rights of the Child*

*Adopted by the U.N. General Assembly on November 20, 1989.
Ratified by twentieth state by September 2, 1990 (Necessary for treaty to become U.N. law)
Has not yet been sent to Congress by the President of the United States.*

A Child means every human being below the age of 18 years unless the child lives in a nation where majority age is attained earlier.

---

1. THE RIGHT TO LOVE, CARE AND UNDERSTANDING

Best Interests of the Child — Article 3
The best interests of the child to prevail in all legal and administrative decisions and to ensure care and protection of children.

Parental Care & Non-Separation — Article 9
The right to live with parents unless proved harmful to the child's best interests; the right to maintain contact with both parents and to provide information when separation results from State action.

Family Reunification — Article 10
The right to leave or enter any country and to maintain contact with both parents.

Parental Responsibilities — Article 18
To recognize that both parents or guardians are responsible for the upbringing of their children; to assist parents or guardians in this responsibility and to provide child care for eligible working parents.

Adoption — Article 21
To regulate adoption (including intercountry adoption), where it is permitted.

Children Without Families — Article 20
The right to receive special protection and assistance when deprived of family environment and to be provided with alternative family care, such as foster placement, adoption or institutional placement.

Standard of Living — Article 27
The right to an adequate standard of living; to assist parents who cannot meet this responsibility.

---

*The standards contained in this Convention do not supersede higher standard contained in national law or other international instruments.

2. THE RIGHT TO ADEQUATE NUTRITION, HOUSING AND MEDICAL CARE

Survival & Development — Article 6
The right to life and to ensure the survival and maximum development of the child.

Health Care — Article 24
The right to the highest attainable standard of health, health education and medical services in order to combat disease and malnutrition health education.

Social Security — Article 26
The right, where appropriate, to benefit from social security or insurance.

Recovery Care — Article 39
To promote the physical, psychological, social recovery of child victims of abuse, neglect, exploitation, torture or armed conflicts in an environment which fosters the health, self-respect and dignity of the child.

3. THE RIGHT TO FREE EDUCATION AND FULL OPPORTUNITY FOR PLAY AND RECREATION

Education — Article 23
The right to education; to free and compulsory primary education, to secondary and higher education and to school discipline that reflects the child's human dignity.

Leisure & Recreation — Article 31
The right to leisure, play and participation in cultural and artistic activities.

4. THE RIGHT TO PROTECTION AGAINST ALL FORMS OF NEGLECT, CRUELTY AND EXPLOITATION

Protection of Privacy — Article 16
The right to protection from interference with privacy, family, home, correspondence, or attacks on honor and reputation.

Abuse & Neglect — Article 19
The child's right to protection from abuse, neglect and exploitation by parents or others, and to create preventive treatment programs for abuse and neglect.

Periodic Review — Article 23
The right to have all aspects of placement (adoption, foster care, etc.) reviewed regularly.

Torture and Capital Punishment — Article 1
The right to be protected from: torture or other cruel, inhuman or degrading treatment; capital punishment or life imprisonment; and deprivation of liberty.

Child Labor — Article 32
The right to be protected from economic exploitation.

Narcotics — Article 33
The right to be protected from illegal drugs and from involvement in their production or distribution.

Exploitation, Sexual — Article 34
The right to be protected from sexual exploitation and abuse, including prostitution and involvement in pornography.

Sale & Trafficking — Article 35
To prevent the abduction, sale and trafficking of children.

Juvenile Justice — Article 40
The right of the accused child to be treated with dignity and respect. To ensure that every accused child is presumed innocent until proven guilty in a prompt and fair trial, receives legal assistance, maintains contact with the family and is not compelled to give testimony or confess guilt; alternatives to institutional care are available.

5. THE RIGHT TO A NAME AND NATIONALITY

Name & Nationality — Article 7
The right to a name and to acquire a nationality; the right to know and be cared for by parents.

Preservation of Identity — Article 8
The right to preserve or re-establish the child's identity (name, nationality, and family ties).

Children of Minorities — Article 30
The right of children of minority communities and/or of indigenous origin to enjoy their own culture, practice their own religion and use their own language.

6. THE RIGHT TO SPECIAL CARE IF HANDICAPPED

Disabled Children — Article 23
The right of disabled children to special care and training to help achieve self-reliance and a full and decent life in society.

7. THE RIGHT TO BE AMONG THE FIRST TO RECEIVE RELIEF IN TIMES OF DISASTER

Refugee Children — Article 22
To ensure protection and assistance to children who are refugees or who are seeking refugee status.

8. THE RIGHT TO LEARN AND TO BE USEFUL MEMBERS OF SOCIETY AND TO DEVELOP INDIVIDUAL ABILITIES

Free Expression of Opinion — Article 12
The child's right to express an opinion in matters affecting the child and to have that opinion heard.

Freedom of Information — Article 13
The right to seek, receive and distribute information through any media.

Media & Information — Article 17
To ensure access to information and material from a diversity of national and international sources.

Education, Aims of — Article 29
To direct education towards: developing personality and talents; preparing for responsible life in a free society; developing respect for parents, basic human rights, personal, cultural, national values and those of others.

9. THE RIGHT TO FREEDOM FROM PERSECUTION AND TO BE BROUGHT UP IN THE SPIRIT OF UNIVERSAL PEACE AND BROTHERHOOD

Freedom of Conscience, Religion — Article 14
The right to manifest religion or beliefs and to respect the rights of parents or guardians to provide direction in the exercise of this right.

Freedom of Association — Article 15
The right to freedom of association and freedom of peaceful assembly.

Armed Conflicts — Article 38
To ensure that no child under 15 takes a direct part in hostilities or is recruited into the armed forces and that all children affected by armed conflict have protection and care.

10. THE RIGHT TO ENJOY THESE RIGHTS
regardless of race, color, sex, religion, national or social origin

Freedom from Discrimination — Article 2
These rights apply to all children without exception and are made to protect them from any form of discrimination or punishment based on family's status, activities or beliefs.

Implementation of Rights — Article 4
To translate the rights of this Convention into actuality.

Parental Responsibility, Respect for — Article 5
To respect the rights of parents or guardians to provide direction to the child in the exercise of the rights in this Convention.

U.N. Convention on the Rights of the Child

Adopted by the U.N. General Assembly on November 20, 1989.
Ratified by twentieth state by September 2, 1990
(Necessary for treaty to become United Nations law)
No U.S. President has sent the Convention to Congress to be ratified.

A Child means every human being below the age of 18 years unless the child lives in a nation where majority age is attained earlier.

EVERY CHILD HAS THE RIGHT TO:

1. Equality, regardless of Race , Color, Religion, Sex or Nationality

2. Healthy Mental and Physical Development

3. A Name and a Nationality

4. Sufficient Food, Housing and Medical Care

5. Special Care if Handicapped

6. Love and Understanding in a Caring Family

7. Free Education, Play and Recreation

8. Immediate Aid in the Event of Disasters and Emergencies

9. Protection from Cruelty, Neglect, and Exploitation

10. Protection from Persecution and a Right to an Upbringing in the Spirit of Worldwide Brotherhood and Peace

ACTIVITY 6: How Secure Are American Kids?

OBJECTIVES:

1. Students will become more familiar with the status and security of children in the U.S., especially in comparison to other population groups.

2. Students will interpret and discuss statistical data related to children growing up in the U.S.

3. Students may choose to investigate specific children's issues in American society and decide as individuals or a class what they might want to do to bring their concerns to the attention of community leaders and lawmakers.

LEARNING STRATEGIES: Reading for understanding, class discussion, micro-lab, investigative research, civic writing and participation

TIME: 1 - 5 class periods depending on your choice of optional activities

MATERIALS: Handout 1:6

SUGGESTED INSTRUCTIONS:

1. Pass out Handout 1:6: "How Secure Are American Kids? Ask students to work in pairs to "guestimate" their answers to the questions. Review the answers with students.
   ANSWERS: 1. children; 2a. 70 billion; 2b. 350 billion; 3. 10 times 4. 25%; 5. 20%; 6. 2 1/2 million; 7. 70%; 8. 40%; 9. 1/3; 10. 7 in 10; 11. 30%; 12. 40% and 20% 13. 22nd

2. Ask students what conclusions they might draw from this statistical data. The following questions can lead to a deeper discussion of the security of children in the United States. Some of these questions may also become starting points for individual or small group investigative research on children's issues:

- What statistics surprised you? shocked you? Why?

- What present conditions that affect children may result in high "costs" to society, government, and the United States taxpayer in your lifetime? How does the health and well-being of children connect to the "health and well-being" of the economy and the nation as a whole?

- Why does the United States spend so much more per capita on the elderly than on children? (Think about who votes - the largest voting bloc is composed of people aged 60 and older. This group also has the highest percentage of discretionary income - money that can support lobbying groups that pressure Congress to maintain programs that provide health benefits, social security, retirement benefits, housing, and food.)

- If you went to lobby in Congress or your state legislature for increased federal spending for children, what points would you emphasize to make your case?

- If you want to increase spending for children it would probably mean less money for the elderly. What would you say to a person over 65 to persuade him or her that spending more money on children and less money on the elderly is a good investment?

- Many people argue that children are solely a parent's responsibility. Do you agree or disagree with this position? If parents cannot provide adequately for their children (physically or emotionally) does the larger community have any responsibility to care for the youngest among us?

- Write the following list on the board: Head Start; Youth Employment; Health Care; Housing and Nutrition; Affordable Day Care; High Quality of Elementary and Secondary Education throughout the U.S.; Foster Care and Adoption Assistance; Juvenile Justice and Rehabilitation; Health, Drug, and Violence Prevention

- If you could *fully fund* only two of these programs in the next decade, which two would you choose? (Full funding would mean that the program would be available to every child who needed it.)

✎ Going Further:

- Keep adding to a clipping file of articles about the security of America's children. This is an excellent way to encourage use of periodical guides on a topic that is of great interest to young people. It is also a topic that has received more in-depth media attention in the last three or four years.

- Have students write news briefs, or reports, or prepare presentations about this topic. Use a conflict analysis (Chapters 3 and 8) or an action research project (Chapter 7) strategy to investigate the most pressing problems for children in your own community.

- Encourage students to recommend policy and program choices that would increase the well-being of children in your community and state. Generate suggestions for student projects that reflect their concerns and recommendations.

- One compelling project can be researching and evaluating state or federal legislation that attempts to increase the security of children (health care, Head Start, education, and child protection initiatives). After students arrive at positions for or against the passage of a bill, students might consider ways that they could further educate their peers on the issue. They might consider holding a "hearing" at school where citizens and experts testify for or against a particular bill. Students could also conduct a letter writing or lobbying campaign to key legislators.

Where to Find Out More About Children's Issues in the U.S.:

Congressional Resources — House Select Committee on Children, Youth, and Families; Chairperson, Patricia Schroeder; phone: (202) 226-7660; Ford House Office Building, 300 D St. S.W., Washington, D.C. 20515.

Statistical Data, Background Information, and Policy Recommendations — Children's Defense Fund; phone: (202) 628-8787; 122 C St. NW, 4th Floor, Washington, D.C. 20001.

State References — Check out resources that the State

Departments of Health and/or Human Services can provide. Identify the state legislative committees that work on child, youth, and family issues.

Local References — Find out whether your local government, mayor's office, or an important citizen's group has a local task force on children and youth issues. Local departments of welfare, health or human services may also provide useful resources.

Readings Which Focus on the Security of America's Children:

Atlantic Monthly, June, 1990, Cover Story: "Growing Up Scared."

Garbarino, James, et. al, *No Place To Be A Child: Growing Up in a War Zone* — extensive documentation and personal narrative describing children's lives in Cambodia, Mozambique, Nicaragua, Occupied Territories in Israel, and Chicago.

Hechinger, Fred, *Fateful Choices: Healthy Youth for the 21st Century* — a call to reexamine our community and educational priorities for adolescents in the U.S.

Kozol, Jonathan, *Rachel And Her Children* — a compelling narrative about children in New York City's "welfare hotels" for homeless families.

Kottowitz, Alex, *There Are No Children Here* — a biographical narrative about two brothers growing up in a Chicago public housing project.

Riis, Jacob, *How the Other Half Lives* and Harrington, Michael, *The Other America* are good historical references that examine the lives of children at the beginning and mid-points of the 20th century.

Time, Oct. 8, 1990, Cover Story: "Do We Care About Our Kids?"

Fortune, August 10, 1992, Special Report: "Children in Crisis" — comprehensive interviews with nine children from across the country and nine adults who have overcome the obstacles of childhood poverty.

HOW SECURE ARE AMERICAN KIDS?

Read each question and make your best guess from the choices given.	Choices	Correct Answer
1. The poorest group in American society are _____.	a. the elderly b. children c. the physically disabled	
2a. The population of children (from birth to age 18, is 68 million. The federal government spends _____ on children. 2b. The population of elderly (age 65 and older) is 32 million. The federal government spends _____ on the elderly.	a. 70 billion b. 100 billion c. 350 billion a. 30 billion b. 100 billion c. 350 billion	
3. The federal government spends _____ times more on the elderly than children per individual (per capita).	a. twice b. five times c. ten times	
4. Almost _____ % of all children under 16 do not have health insurance.	a. 10% b. 25% c. 50%	
5. In 1990, the poverty level for a family of four was an annual household income of $13,359. Over ____ % of U.S. children live below the poverty line.	a. 10% b. 20% c. 30%	
6. About _____ million children are living in a place that they don't call home (in a shelter or institution, or on the street).	a. 1 million b. 2 1/2 million c. 5 million	

7. The graduation rate (Ninth graders who finish high school in four years) is _____%.	a. 70% b. 80% c. 90%	
8. The American work force is shrinking. In ten years the number of young people (18 to 24) entering the work force will shrink by over 4 million (14%). At the same time, over _____% of young adults do not receive adequate job training skills for high wage jobs. They are doomed to a minimum wage ($4.25 an hour) life.	a. 10% b. 25% c. 40%	
9. Nearly _____ of the young work force (18 to 24 years old) in 2000 will be African-Americans, Asian-Americans, Latinos, and Native Americans.	a. 1/4 b. 1/3 c. 1/2	
10. By 2000 nearly _____ in _____ pre-school children will have mothers who work outside the home.	a. 1 in 5 b. 2 in 5 c. 7 in 10	
11. Nearly _____% of children are born out of wedlock. These children will spend most of their lives in single parent families.	a. 10% b. 20% c. 30%	
12. Before the age of 20, ___% of girls get pregnant and ___% bear children.	a. 20% b. 30% c. 40% d. 50%	
13. The U.S. ranks _____ in child mortality rate in the world (the number of children who die before their fifth birthdays).	a. 1st b. 14th c. 22nd	

Sources: *Annual Report Card on Children (1991)*, Children's Defense Fund, *Fateful Choices*, Fred Hechinger, *Fortune Magazine* (August 10, 1992), *Time Magazine* (October 8, 1990)

ACTIVITY 7: How Secure Is Your Community?

OBJECTIVES:

1. Students will identify areas of concern which they think determine the security and well-being of their own local community.

2. Students will work in teams to investigate each concern. Each student will gather quantitative data that addresses one specific question that emerges from their area of concern. Each team will present their data and discuss their conclusions with the rest of the class.

3. The class will decide on three areas of concern that they think require the community's immediate attention. Students will generate recommendations and prepare a final presentation for key community leaders.

4. Students will then present their data and recommendations to key community leaders.

5. Through writing and discussion students will assess what they learned from this project.

LEARNING STRATEGIES: Brainstorming, group discussion, investigative research and interviewing, interpretation of data, documentation and presentation skills.

TIME: Eight class periods and out-of-class research and presentation preparation time.

MATERIALS: Handouts 1:7A and 1:7B, general classroom supplies, phone books, census data about your community, government and service agency directories, and any other reports about your community that will help students in their research (Optional: access to computers for final presentation documents)

SUGGESTED INSTRUCTIONS:

Period One
1. You might want to begin this activity by placing quotes about your local community (both positive and negative) around your classroom. Ask students whether they agree or disagree with the opinions expressed in the quotes.

2. Ask students to work in small groups and brainstorm the "best things" that make their community a secure and healthy place for families and kids to live and five "worst things" that make your community a less secure and desirable place to live. Ask someone in each group to record their lists on two separate pieces of paper. As students read their lists to the rest of the class, ask two students to record the "best" and "worst" lists on newsprint. Put a check by any item which is repeated.

Period Two

3. Using the "best" and "worst" summary lists as a starting point, brainstorm and agree on eight areas of concern that your class wants to investigate. You may want to refer back to **Handout 1:2B Aspects of Personal Security** to review key aspects of security. **Handout 1:7A** is a sample list of security concerns and quantitative questions that could be used to assess the security of your community.

4. Select one security concern on the list to examine with the whole class. Let the class know this is the one the class itself will investigate. Generate specific questions with the whole class that can lead you to **quantitative data (numbers and statistics) that will help you find out how well or poorly your community is doing in this category!**

5. Divide class into groups of three or four. Each investigation team will choose one of the other seven areas of concern to research. Give each group about fifteen minutes to brainstorm at least five specific questions that will help them generate the quantitative data they need. Ask each group to identify a question editor who will review their questions with you. When you check in with each "question editor", separate out those questions that you think can be answered fairly easily and those that are a "long shots." Be sure question editors have at least one researchable question for each student on their teams.

Period Three:

6. Give each student **Handout 1:7B Community Investigation File**. Select one of the questions the class has generated earlier for your area of concern and discuss questions **3.** and **4.** on **Handout 1:7B** using that particular question. Review the rest of the handout with students so they know the process they will be using to complete their individual research to get the information they need. Post on newsprint the following list of project steps:

> **Student Teams:**
> 1. Each team chooses one security factor to investigate.
> 2. Each team generates quantitative questions that will help you get the data you need.
> 3. Each team member selects one question to research.
>
> **Individual Team Members:**
> 4. Each student will contact people and organizations that can help her or him get the data needed.

5. Each student will collect data from the most recent three years on record.
6. Each student will determine whether data shows improvement or decline in security of the community.
7. Each student will decide how to present data to the whole class.

Student Teams:
8. Each team will prepare their presentation to the class including data, conclusions, and recommendations.

Whole Class:
9. Class will listen to each team's presentation.
10. Class will prioritize three areas of concern that they think require the community's attention and agree on recommendations for action in those three areas.
11. Class will decide how to present their data, conclusions and recommendations to key community leaders.
12. Class will meet with key community leaders to discuss their research and recommendations.

Be sure to discuss what students can do and use to begin their search. For example, the "blue pages" in the phone book will identify government offices that may be good first contacts. Reassure students that they will probably not find out everything they need to know on the first phone call. Encourage students to ask people to mail them information. Give students several days to gather their data outside of class time. Check in with students to see if they're on track. You may need to walk through the process with some of your students; agree on a time during the day or after school when you can sit with them when they telephone.

Period Four (several days later):
7. Have teams meet to share their data with each other. Give each team the rest of the period to decide how they will present their data, conclusions, and recommendations to the whole class. Set the time for presentations.

Periods Five and Six:
8. Each team makes its presentation to the class. Discuss their work on two levels:

Level One: The Content and Meaning of the Data
* Were there any surprises in your findings? What were they?
* Are things better or worse than you originally assumed? How do you know?
* What else did you learn from the people you contacted?
* Do you think your community is aware of the data you collected? Would community priorities and policies change if this data were "public knowledge"?

* What do you want to know more about after your initial research? Is there anyone you contacted whom you would like to invite to speak to the whole class?

Level Two: The Project Process
* What "tools" did you use to get the data you needed?
* What was hard, challenging? What was easy?
* Did some people in your group have more trouble getting data than others? Why do you think that happened?
* Would you do anything differently next time?

Period Seven:
9. Work through **Steps 10 and 11 of the Project Process** with the whole class. Arrange for a time to meet with key community leaders in a separate session or find out how to get on the agenda of an official civic meeting. Work with a small group of students outside of class to finalize public presentation. Scheduling and transportation constraints may limit the number of students who actually make the final presentation. Try to take photographs so that you can have a permanent record of your meeting. Be sure to record the names of key public officials and community leaders who are present.

Period Eight:
10. After the public presentation, debrief what happened with rest of class. Brainstorm what follow-up steps students might want to take to keep their concerns on the public agenda. Encourage students to write thank-you notes to people who helped them get their data and listened to their concerns. You may want to maintain connections with good sources who can help you and your students with future projects.

✐ **Assessment:** As a final assignment ask each student to write a personal reflection of their project experience - what students learned, what "tools" they used, what new insights they have about their own community. You may also want to use some of the questions from #8. to help frame writing guidelines for student reflections.

Security In Your Community

Key Security Concerns	Quantitative Questions
1. Physical Safety - - - - ->	How many handguns in your community? How many handguns per 100 or 1000 people? What kinds of crimes against persons occur most frequently? How many violent crimes are there per hundred or thousand people? How many incidents of police brutality? How many crimes per year involve a gun? How many shootings per year? How many murders per year with a gun?
2. Job Opportunities - - ->	What is the unemployment rate? What kinds of jobs has the community lost or gained in the last five years? Do new jobs pay the same, more, or less? Are there any particular groups who are having a hard time getting jobs?
3. Healthy Children and Teens - - - - - - - - - - - - - - - ->	What is the infant mortality rate? What percentage of children have been fully vaccinated? What % of children have health insurance? What % of teens have experienced substance abuse?
4. Quality Educational Opportunities for All Students - - - - - - - - - ->	What is the high school drop-out rate? How many students (%) continue their education after high school (college, technical school, etc.)? What % students have "B" or better average?
5. Housing - - - - - - - - ->	What are the # & % of public housing, rental and owned properties available? How many people are waiting for public housing? How many people are homeless or live in sub-standard housing?
6. Stable Households - - >	What is the % of two parent families? How many families live on $10,000 or less? How many (%) teenage mothers? How many households have lived in the same place for more than five years?
7. Public Services, Beautification, and Property Maintenance - - - - - - >	What is the number of vacant buildings? How often are streets repaired? How much is spent on public parks? Summer youth programs? Plantings?
8. Racism/Discrimination>	Are there differences between whites and minorities regarding average household income, employment, college attendance & graduation, % of homeowners, etc?

Community Investigation File

Name _____

1. Security Concern my team is investigating_____

2. My specific question _____

_____

3. What resources/contacts will help me find the information I need?

_____

4. What agencies, organizations, or government offices might have the data I need? _____

_____

5. Record of my investigation:

Institution and Contact Person:	Phone Number (📄) Sending Info	What I Found Out / Who I Call Next

6. Data that answers my question (most recent three years on record):

19____	
19____	
19____	

7. Are conditions getting better or worse? _____

8. Recommendations _____

9. How can I present my data? (graph, chart, table, coded map, photos, etc.)

ACTIVITY 8: Imagining a Secure Future

OBJECTIVE:

1. Students will imagine a personal picture of security and then write down their visualizations.
2. Students will identify what security issues will be of most concern to them at different points in their future.

LEARNING STRATEGIES: Individual writing and drawing, small and large group sharing

TIME: One to two class periods

MATERIALS: Lined and blank white paper (optional - felt tip markers, colored pencils, pastels, and/or crayons)

SUGGESTED INSTRUCTIONS:

1. Take students through a brief pre-writing visualization where they close their eyes and imagine a place and time in which they feel completely safe and secure. After students have imagined themselves in this specific place, ask questions which will help them complete the mental picture they are imagining. "Who is with you? What do you see and hear that tells you it's safe here? Someone has just arrived with a special gift that will help keep you safe and secure the rest of your life. This gift could be something you can see or it might be something invisible that becomes part of you. What is it? Who brought it? How will this gift change your life?"

2. Have students write down their visualizations. Suggest that students try to paint word pictures that capture what they see, hear, and feel in concrete language — lots of verbs and nouns. Ask them to write in present tense to convey immediacy in their writing.

3. Ask students if they would like to share their word pictures either with a partner (reading each other's writing) or with the whole class.

72

꙳ Going Further: Drawing Your Visualizations

An alternative way of doing this activity is to give students a choice of whether they would like to draw or write their visualization. Sometimes students are more eager to explain their drawings than to read their writing. Students also find it interesting to compare their images.

꙳ Going Further: Making a Security Time Line of the Future.

1. Explain that students will be designing personal security time lines of the future. The nature of security changes as needs, conditions, and relationships change. Invite students to think about the aspects of security that will be the most important to them at the ages of 20, 30, 45, 65, 85. Students can use **Handout 1:2** as a guideline for their considerations. Are there any aspects of security that will remain important to them throughout their lifetimes? Are there changing responsibilities and commitments that will change what they need to feel secure at different ages?

2. Students may want to make a time line that is sequential

AGE 20   30   45   65   85

or choose another way to map their future security using drawings, symbols, cartoons, pictures, etc.

3. After students have completed their time lines, you may want to divide the class into small groups of three or four in which students can to talk about their time lines and identify similarities and differences in their predictions and expectations.

Chapter 2: Dealing With Differences

Activity 1:   Discovering Our Differences

Activity 2:   Talking and Writing About Us!

Activity 3:   Letting Go of Labels

Activity 4:   We All Belong to Groups

Activity 5:   Exploring Human Adaptation and Variation

Activity 6:   We All Do the Same Things—Only Differently

Activity 7:   Different Strokes for Different Folks

Activity 8:   Checking Out Assumptions

Activity 9:   We Each See the World a Little Differently

Activity 10: How Do We See Others? How Do They See Us?

Activity 11: When Differences Become Our Enemy

Activity 12: Turning Differences into Resources

ACTIVITY 1: Discovering Our Differences

OBJECTIVE: Students will explore their differences by interviewing each other during a Bingo game.

LEARNING STRATEGIES: Peer interviews

TIME: 15 - 20 minutes

MATERIALS: Handout 2:1, stickers

SUGGESTED INSTRUCTIONS:

1. Pass out **Handout 2:1: "Discovering Our Differences Bingo"** to each student. Explain that they will have 15 minutes to complete as many Bingo's as they can—across, down, and diagonally. The two rules are as follows:
   - Students need to interview each other to find their opposite or contrasting "matches." Students will be seeking to **identify differences —not similarities**. When they find a contrasting match with another person, they write their own names in the boxes on each other's sheets.

   - Students cannot use the same person's name more than once on their sheets.

2. Ask if there are any questions about the meaning of the categories in the boxes. Choose one category and ask students to generate some questions that they would ask each other to determine whether there is a "match for differences."

3. When students have a Bingo, they can call out, "Bingo," and the teacher or student facilitators will check it and place a sticker on their papers. Let students know that they can keep playing until time is up. You may want to give a prize to the students who completed the most Bingo's.

4. When time is up, you may want to call out a few categories and see who fits the various descriptions. You may also want to explore these questions with students:
   - What did you find out about your classmates that you didn't know before?
   - Were there any surprises that you discovered about your classmates?
   - Were there some boxes for which it was easier or harder to find a contrasting match?

77

DISCOVERING OUR DIFFERENCES

Make a BINGO (5 across, 5 down, or 5 diagonally) by interviewing and discovering people who are contrasting matches to you for each category. When you find a contrasting match, have that person write his or her name in the box. You may not use anyone's name twice.

Handedness	Ethnic / racial heritage	Most important family gathering during the year	Country you would **most** like to visit	Morning---> Late night energy
Most typical meal that your family eats	Eye color	Typical family or summer vacation	Country you would **least** like to visit	Neighborhood you grew up in (ethnicity; urban/ rural/ suburban; economic status)
Household chore you hate to do the most	Favorite place to visit in the U.S.	Month in which you were born	Number of generations in your family who live in community where you live	An ethnic group you know very little about
Like to figure things out on my own<--->Like to talk things over with someone	Favorite relaxing weekend activity	City and state of birth	Favorite music	Your mom works/doesn't work outside the home
Most admired foreign leader, writer, artist, musician	Only child<---> Other brother(s) and sister(s)	Low-key and take things as they come<---> Goal oriented & driven	You live in an Apartment<---> Condo<---> House	Favorite T.V. program

78

ACTIVITY 2: Talking and Writing About Us!

OBJECTIVE: Students will reflect on their own personal experiences and find out more about each other through paired interviews and circle dialogues. You may want to do this activity several times in the beginning of the school year as a way to build community and connection among students in each of your classes.

LEARNING STRATEGIES: Reflective writing, pair-share and circle dialogues

TIME: 10 to 30 minutes

MATERIALS: None

SUGGESTED INSTRUCTIONS:

The questions and topics suggested can help students become more self-aware and help them move beyond surface impressions of their peers as they find out more about each other. You may want to use some of the topics for journal writing and then have students share their ideas in small groups. You might also try these two ways of facilitating peer dialogues.

1. **Ask students to pair up with each other at random or ask students to silently choose a person to interview that they do not know very well.**
   OR
2. **Divide students in half and have students form inner and outer circles, so that each student from one circle is face-to-face with a partner from the other circle. Each time you ask a new question, ask students in the outer circle to move to the right. This way students will get to dialogue with many of their classmates.**

Topics:
   1. **Personal Likes and Dislikes**—Ask pairs to discover 1) two things they both like; 2) two things they both dislike; and 3) two things about which they have different preferences and opinions.

   2. **Talking About My Family**—Ask students to bring in something from home (a photograph, object or memento passed down in the family) that tells about their family history and traditions. If students don't bring something to school, they can talk about a family tradition or ritual which is very important in their home or a treasured possession which has been passed on to them or their family.

   3. **First Memories**—1) Your first-ever memory. 2) Something you remember a family member teaching you how to do. 3) One of the first family gatherings you remember—who was there? where was it? what did you do?; 4) Your very first friend. 5) The first house and neighborhood you remember living in.

4. **The Best!**—1) The best present you ever received. 2) The best meal you ever ate. 3) The best surprise you ever experienced. 4) The best trip or vacation. 5) The best adventure you've ever had (that was maybe a little bit scary or risky). 6) The best, goofiest, most embarrassing, or weirdest family story.

5. **Kids and Grown-ups** — 1) Two things in your family that everyone is supposed to do and two things in your family that no one is ever supposed to do. 2) Three "rules of the house" in your family, 3) Three things that kids do that make your parents really "aggravated!" 4) Three things that parents do that made kids "aggravated!" 5) The most interesting and likable grown-up you know who is not a member of your immediate family.

6. **Where I Live** — 1) One thing you like and one thing you don't like about the neighborhood where you live. 2) Compare a neighborhood you have lived in and the neighborhood you live in now. What's the same / different?

7. **School Stuff** — 1) What kinds of schools have you attended? Is there one you like better than others? What would you change about the school you attend now? 2) Describe a learning experience that was very negative for you. What were you doing? What made it negative? How did this feel for you? What do you wish you could have done? 3) Describe a learning experience that was very positive for you. What were you doing? What did you learn? Why did this experience work for you? 4) Describe a teacher who helped or inspired you to truly put forth your best effort. How did s/he treat you? Why did you learn better with this teacher than others? Why do you value this experience even now? 5) Describe an experience where you learned something that you will never forget. Why won't your forget it?

8. **More Topics to Write and Talk About**—*The Kids' Book of Questions*, by Dr. Gregory Stock, is a great resource for interesting questions that students enjoy talking about.

After students have interviewed each other ask them to share some of their discoveries with the whole class. Open up a broader discussion with any of these questions:

- Would any of you like to live in a community where everyone acts the same and thinks the same? Why or why not?
- How do differences make life more interesting?
- How do differences make life more difficult?
- What might be the advantages and disadvantages of going to school with students or living in a neighborhood with people who share a similar cultural identity? What might be the advantages and disadvantages of attending a school or living in a neighborhood that is more reflective of the cultural diversity of the American population?

ACTIVITY 3: Letting Go of Labels

OBJECTIVES: Through an interactive exercise students will become more aware of their "comfort and discomfort zones" in social situations and experience what it feels like to be labeled by others.

LEARNING STRATEGIES: Interactive exercise, class discussion

TIME: One class period

MATERIALS: Handout 2:3 (labels for headbands), masking tape

SUGGESTED INSTRUCTIONS:

1. Introduce this activity by asking students to brainstorm a list of some of the labels students and teachers use to describe people at school. Then ask whether any of these labels have positive or negative overtones. Are some labels perceived positively by some students and negatively by others? You might explore the connection between the teenage compulsion to label everyone, the need to belong, and the need to differentiate between the "innies" and the "outies."

2. Explore with students the "social comfort zone" that we experience with people whom we think are "like us" and the "discomfort zone" we experience with people whom we don't know or mistrust. Reassure students that the discomfort we feel with those whom we see as different is natural. Ask students to jot down three groups that they would be most uncomfortable being around (for their eyes only!). Without naming groups ask students why it feels more awkward to be with some groups than others. They will likely say things like, "I don't know what to say or do," or "I don't want to say the wrong thing or offend anyone," or "I don't think they like me." Discuss the kinds of "social barriers" that may become obstacles to getting to know people who are different from you.

3. Cut headband labels on Handout 2:3 into strips and attach a loop of masking tape to the backside of each strip. The headband strips included are most appropriate for older adolescents. For younger students you may want to add some and eliminate others. Explain to students that they will each receive a headband that labels them as a member of a specific group or as an individual with a specific behavior or personality trait. <u>They will not know what their headbands say!</u>

Tell students that after everyone has a headband on their foreheads, they will have about ten minutes to socialize with each other. Encourage students to "mingle" — to interact with lots of different people. They must, however, follow three rules:

- Respond to everyone as if the headband that each person is wearing is true for that person.

- Do not tell anyone what is on their headbands.

- Talk to people whose headbands identify them as people who are in your social comfort zone! When you encounter someone who would not be in your comfort zone you might want to ask them some questions, give them some advice , or simply walk away. You decide!

You may want to ask three or four students to help stick headbands on the students. When everyone has on a headband remind students about the rules for interaction. There will probably be a lot of awkward laughter and confusion as students read each other's headbands. This is okay.

4. When about ten minutes are up, say "Freeze!" and ask everyone to stay right where they are. Then ask students to think about how people reacted to them:—did they feel that they got friendly, hostile, or confused responses from their peers? Ask all students who think their headbands have labels that people perceived as positive to stand on one side of the room. Ask all those who think their headbands have labels that people perceived as negative to stand on the other side of the room. Ask students who were totally confused by other people's responses to them to stand in the middle.

5. Ask several students from all three groups to explain what students said or did that made them feel that their labels were positive, negative, or a little of both. It's especially important to discuss how students reacted to each other physically (facial expressions and physical gestures). Remind students that 70% of communication is nonverbal. We often give away what we really think without ever saying a word! Ask these students if anyone told them to hang out with particular people. What comments or questions gave them clues about their labels? Ask if any of these students thinks they know what their headbands say. Then let them take off their headbands and read the labels. Finally let everyone else take their headbands off and read them before returning to their seats.

6. **Debriefing:** This is not an activity to debrief in detail. Rather, the purpose here is to have students share the feelings they experienced and think about what happens when we label people <u>one way</u> to the exclusion of everything else about them. Some observations and questions you may want to include in your discussion:

- Although some of you may be embarrassed or angry about the label you received, there are students here at school, probably even in this class, who fit every label.

- What labels do you think hurt people the most or make people the angriest? Why?

- All of us wear labels we want everyone to know about' and we keep other labels hidden. What kinds of labels do we want to hide? Why do we want to hide them? The bottom line is that when we label, attack, or make fun of groups and individuals within the listening distance of others, we never know who might be hurt by what we say.

- Think about the people you interacted with and those you didn't —those who are not in your social comfort zone. How did people who perceived themselves as "positive" interact with people who perceived themselves as "negative"? Did people with negative headbands hang out together? How did this happen? Why do you think it happened?

* Discuss this observation: "Perhaps the best kind of shedding is to know how to cast off the comfortable and the known to make way for an idea or set of thoughts whose time has come." Alf McCreary

* What can you do personally or through organizations at school that could help students stretch beyond their own personal comfort zones and get to know others who are different? Think about: Where and with whom do you sit in class? Who gets invited to participate in special projects at school? Are there unspoken codes about who does what at school? Are there many opportunities to talk with students who are not part of your group?

HEADBAND LABELS

I'm an SAT "1400."

I'm white and I have black friends.

I'm a computer nerd.

I'm gay but I haven't told anyone.

84

I'm an atheist.

I'm very religious.

My family is very wealthy.

My family is poor.

I'm a "no-brainer" football jock.

I'm a virgin.

I belong to a church youth group.

I'm African-American and just hang with my group.

I've been hospitalized for depression.

I am black and have white friends.

I'm sexually promiscuous.

I'm dyslexic and have trouble reading.

I'm school phobic.

I'm a preppie.

I'm a burn-out.

My Mom gets welfare.

I'm a school leader and really have things together.

I've had an abortion.

I drink a lot.

At school, I move from group to group easily.

I pressure girls to have sex with me.

I'm a good student, and I "go with the flow."

I'm the head cheerleader.

I'm a basketball player, and I know I'm cute.

I've been abused at home.

I'm pretty, smart, and well-liked.

I'm a recent immigrant, and I don't speak English well.

I make fun of everything and everyone so people won't know I'm kind of confused and scared.

I try to be the perfect kid at school – good grades, activities, a peer mediator.

I don't wear a smile all the time – you have to try and get to know me before I respond.

I'm white and don't really want to know anyone who isn't like me.

I'm really liberal and am constantly challenging everyone's beliefs about the world.

I'm really conservative and don't want anything to change here or anywhere else.

I'm a recent immigrant from Mexico, and I don't speak English very well.

I don't like people who think interracial dating is okay.

I think abortion is murder.

92

ACTIVITY 4: We All Belong to Groups

OBJECTIVES:

1. Students will identify the groups to which they belong by birth, by culture, and by choice and write down their thoughts and feelings about belonging to these groups.
2. They will share their reflections with two other partners.

LEARNING STRATEGIES: Self-reflection, three person dialogues, group discussion or written reflections, independent investigation (optional)

TIME: One class period

MATERIALS: Handouts 2:4 A and B

SUGGESTED INSTRUCTIONS:

1. Introduce the activity by asking students to identify some of the groups (formal and informal) which are a significant part of life at your school. Explain that everyone belongs to many more groups than just the ones that are present at school. The sense of belonging that comes from group identity and affiliation is a powerful human need.

   We are **born into** some groups (i.e., we may be female, Chinese, deaf). Other groups reflect the **culture** in which we grow up (we may come from a large family, go to a Catholic church, live in the Southwest in a Mexican-American neighborhood, have parents who attended college). We belong to other groups that we **choose** (We may join a soccer team, work part-time, play in a band, write for the school newspaper, or volunteer at the local food pantry).

2. Pass out **Handouts 2:4A** and **2:4B**: "Groups I Belong To" to each student and review the examples given on **Handout 2:4A**. Then ask students to identify some of the groups that they belong to by birth, by culture, and by choice on **Handout 2:4B**. You may want to fill out one for yourself ahead of time that you can share as an example.

   Point out to students that all of us have mixed feelings about some groups we belong to. There are some things we really like that make us proud of our group affiliation; there are other things that make us uncomfortable or angry about belonging to certain groups.

Sometimes we might even like our group identity to disappear so that people could see us as we really are regardless of group identities. Give students about ten minutes to fill out the sheet.

3. Divide students into diverse groups of three to share their responses with each other. Remind students that they can choose what they want to share and what they don't. Encourage to students to ask open-ended questions to each other that help them learn more about groups that are unfamiliar to them. Give groups fifteen or twenty minutes to dialogue.

4. **Debriefing:** Use any of the following questions for discussion or reflective writing:

   • How did this experience change your understanding of some groups? One way to respond to this question: "Before this conversation I didn't know that_____."

   • Think about one of the groups to which you belong. When were you first aware that you were a member of a group that was different from other groups?

   • Think about a group that is culturally different from one that is part of your own identity - a cultural group to which you do not belong. When were you first aware of this group? What do you remember hearing from others about this group? What was your first personal experience with someone from this group? How did your "first thoughts" about this group change after coming to know individuals who were members of this group?

   • Sometimes we're uncomfortable with the assumptions and stereotypes associated with groups to which we belong. What stereotypes and assumptions do you wish would disappear? Consider this observation:

      It is utterly exhausting being black in America....While many minority groups and women feel similar stress, there is no respite or escape from your badge of color... The constant burden to "prove" that you are as smart, as honest, as interesting, as wide-gauging and motivated as any other individual tires you out...
      Marian Wright Edelman

   Share an experience when you felt you had to defend against a stereotype of a group to which you belong.

- Consider this observation about the generation gap. What kinds of experiences and attitudes would help generations understand each other better?

  Can a stranger from one generation say much that is helpful to members of another generation standing on a different doorstep in time? Just as a life is a particular life, so a generation lives in its own unique time."

  Bill Moyers

- Sometimes our loyalty to a group conflicts with the feelings, values, and desires that we experience as unique individuals. Does this observation ring true for you?

  To have one's individuality completely ignored is like being pushed quite out of life. Like being blown out as one blows out a light.

  Evelyn Scott

  Discuss or write about an experience where you had to make a choice between following the "party line" of the group or following your own conscience or beliefs.

☞ Going Further:

Making It Safe to Ask Questions and Openly Discuss Group Differences:

1. Give each student a notecard and invite students to write down the "burning questions" that they would like to ask about groups that are culturally different from their own. Encourage students to frame questions will elicit information and greater understanding.

2. Ask for three or four student volunteers to read through questions and select out the ones that they think will be most compelling to discuss.

3. Use a "fishbowl" process for discussion. Choose a diverse group of six or seven students to be part of the fishbowl in a center circle. Ask the rest of the students to form a circle around the fishbowl. Begin with one of the questions and do a "go-around" in which each fishbowl participant speaks to the question without being interrupted. After each student in the fishbowl has spoken, students can make comments and ask questions to each other. Students in the outer circle can tap someone in the fishbowl and take his or her place. Continue the dialogue introducing other questions that students have selected.

Groups We Belong To:

Groups By Birth:
Gender - Male / female
Racial group - African, Amerindian, Asian, European, South Pacific ancestry
Age and Population Cohort -The time period/decade of your birth
Nationality - The nation of your birth; you citizenship status by birth
Groups which share a similar inherited trait - For example: tallness, deafness, nearsightedness, diabetes, Down syndrome, dyslexia, etc.
Sexual Orientation - Heterosexual, homosexual, bisexual

Groups Which Reflect Your Cultural Identity Growing Up:
Ethnicity - The group with which you share similar values, traditions, and living habits and a common language, history, literature. For example - Italian, African-American, Anglo, Japanese, Mexican-American, Palestinian, Polish, German, Vietnamese, Indian, etc.
Family Structure - Who are the significant family members in your life? For example: a small family of you, Mom, and a sister or a large extended family of Mom, Dad, two brothers, aunts, uncles, cousins, and grandparents
Religion - Catholic, Islamic, Atheist, Protestant (Methodist, Baptist, A.M.E., Presbyterian, etc.), Jewish, Greek Orthodox, Ethical Humanist, etc.
Geographical Region - Midwestern, Southern, Eastern, Californian, etc.
Community Where You Live - Urban (within boundaries of a city), suburban (towns and neighborhoods surrounding a city), small town (distant from a large urban area), or rural (in the country)
Educational Background - Parents completed grade school, high school, two year college, four year college, graduate school / Type of school you attend
Social / Economic Background of Your Family - Lower, middle, upper-middle class / Jobs and careers of your parents / Things your family does in the community
Unusual Circumstances / Family Crises That Have Affected Your Growing Up - For example: the loss or absence of a parent, divorce, living overseas, living with an alcoholic parent, etc.

Groups You Choose to Belong To or Identify With:
These are groups that you choose to do something with on a regular basis or groups with whom you share common interests. **Examples:** Sports teams, computer hacker, youth groups, community volunteer, rap music fan, school clubs and organizations, church groups, part-time job, summer job, MTV fan, professional sports fan, cheerleader, college-prep classes, band member, Jr. ROTC, Scouts, amateur music group, Star "Trekkie", etc.

Groups I Belong To:

1. Identify two groups that you belong to by **birth** (Physical differences, gender, race/ethnicity):

   _____

2. Identify four groups that reflect your **cultural identity** (Nationality and cultural heritage, family history and status, geographical region and neighborhood, religious beliefs, social & economic status, educational background, work experience):

   _____

   _____

   _____

   _____

3. Think about two **values or beliefs that are really important** in your family that are also very important to you:

   _____

   _____

4. Identify three groups that you belong to by **choice** (Sports, clubs, youth / political / service groups, job, informal affiliations or interests, etc.):

   _____

   _____

   _____

5. Describe **one way you feel different** from everyone else:

   _____

   _____

6. Choose to focus on **gender** or **racial/ethnic identity** for this question. Write down three things you like about belonging to this group and three things you don't like about belonging to this group:

   What You Like: **What You Don't Like:**

   _____   _____

   _____   _____

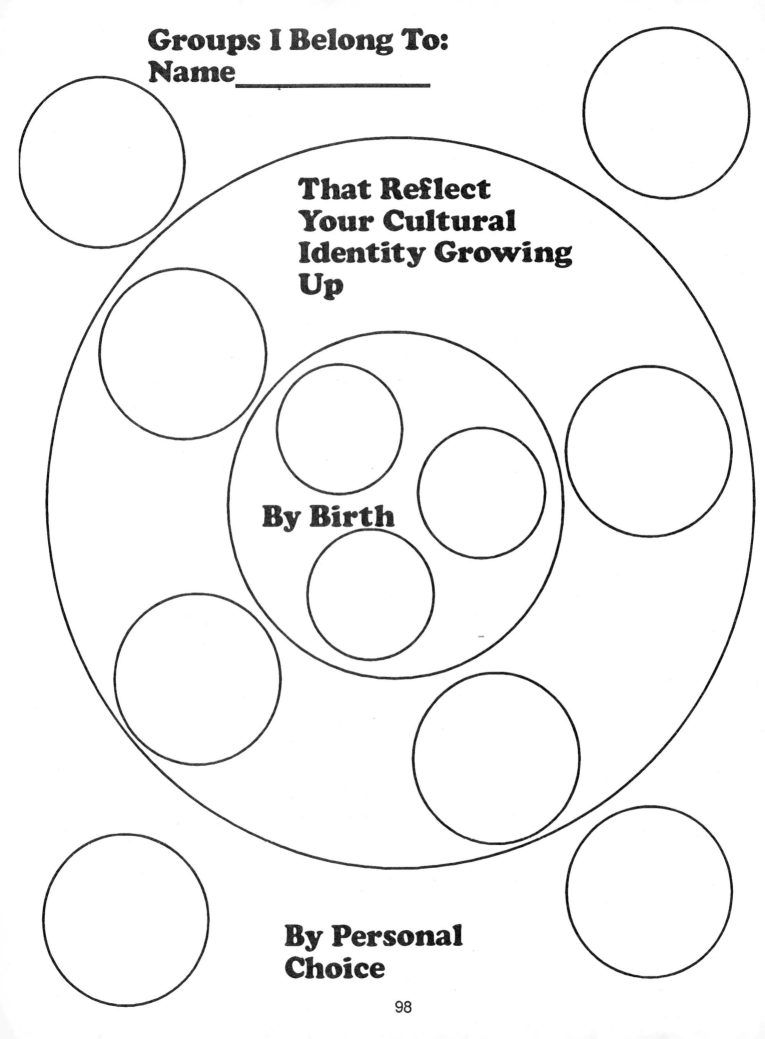

Groups I Belong To:
Name_____

That Reflect Your Cultural Identity Growing Up

By Birth

By Personal Choice

ACTIVITY 5: Exploring Human Adaptation and Variation

OBJECTIVES:

1. Students will investigate questions they have about early humans and explore the concepts of human adaptation and variation.
2. Students will be able to distinguish between physical, cultural and individual differences in human beings.
3. Students will create their own self-portraits by describing their own physical, cultural, and individual characteristics.

LEARNING STRATEGIES: Brainstorming, investigation, reading for understanding, observation, and cooperative learning

TIME: Three class periods

MATERIALS: Map of the world, reference materials, photographs of people from around the world who reflect physical differences among human beings, newsprint, markers, Handout 2:5

SUGGESTED INSTRUCTIONS:
FIRST CLASS PERIOD

1. Before you begin this activity, gather resources from the school or local library about early humans.

2. Divide students into groups to brainstorm what they know about any of the following topics: The First Humans, The Origins of Early Man, Human Adaptation, Culture, Human Migration, Natural and Social Selection, Human Evolution, etc. Ask for a volunteer in each group to record their group's responses to these questions on newsprint:
    What do you know about this topic?
    What do you think you know but are not sure of?
    What questions do you have? What do you want to find out?

3. Discuss the small group brainstorms, identifying information students want to verify and questions that interest them the most.

4. Ask students to pair up with a partner to find out what they can about one question that interests them. Have maps and resources available for students to use for their investigation.

SECOND CLASS PERIOD
5. Have students present what they found out to the rest of the class. Use maps to point out the regions of East Africa and South Africa where the remains of the earliest humans have been discovered. Review the original brainstorms and summarize what you've learned that you didn't know before. In your discussion, be sure to include these two points:

A. We are all part of the same human species (*Homo sapiens sapiens*) and we can all trace our origins back to Africa;

B. Human beings have had a two-million year history of migration—moving from Africa to the Middle East, Asia, Europe, and finally to Australia, the Pacific, and North and South America.

6. Then either post a collage of people pictures which illustrate physical human differences or distribute packets of people pictures to groups of three or four students. In small groups, ask students to make observations about themselves and the people in the photographs as they generate a quick list of physical differences (features that we all have but appear different from one person to another, i.e. hair, eye, and skin color; shape of nose, eye, and mouth, shape of head and body,etc.). Take no more than ten minutes to do group brainstorming.

7. Write students' responses on the board or newsprint. Be sure to separate out responses that describe cultural and individual differences—save these separate lists to use with instruction #9. Ask students if they have ideas about why humans look differently if we are all members of the same species. In your discussion, try to include the following information:

A. We all look differently from each other because human beings have been able to adapt to more places and climates on earth than any other species.

B. Thousands of combinations of inherited traits are possible.

C. Long ago, when human groups migrated to other regions, certain inherited traits were more suited to some climates than others - these favorable traits helped people to survive better in a particular location. This evolutionary process is called ADAPTATION. There are hundreds of human groups (not just four or five) with distinct combinations of inherited physical traits. This is one reason why scholars are increasingly reluctant to identify people by racial type and prefer to identify people by ethnic group.

D. If people with these favorable traits marry each other and reproduce, more and more people in that cultural group will have similar traits. The process of "social selection" is an important factor that influences the unique qualities of various ethnic groups.

E. The chart on the next page illustrates to two common physical adaptations which evolved thousands of years ago.

TWO EXAMPLES OF HUMAN ADAPTATION:

BODY TYPE—ESKIMO	BODY TYPE—WATUSI
For Eskimo natives who lived near the Arctic Circle, the most desirable mates would be short and round because people with less skin surface will retain more body heat against the cold. An extra layer of fat will also protect them. Think about what parts of you get the coldest - your feet, hands, and top of your head. The more compact your body is the warmer you will be.	To a Watusi woman who lived in East Africa, the most beautiful partner would be a very tall, very thin, long-legged man. Because he lived on an equatorial plain with few trees and heat over 100 degrees, his long body would be a great advantage. The taller and thinner he is, the more body surface he has, so that he has a greater capacity to sweat and release the heat.

SKIN COLOR—LIGHT	SKIN COLOR—DARK
People with light skins live or have ancestors who lived in cold, northern climates where there are fewer, shorter sunny days and less direct sunlight. All humans need vitamin D, which the skin produces by absorbing the ultraviolet rays of the sun. If people don't have enough vitamin D, they get rickets, a bone-weakening disease. The pigment Melanin, which makes skin darker, blocks ultraviolet rays. So in the north, those with the least melanin in their skin would be able to absorb more sunlight and have a better chance of survival.	People who have dark skins live or have ancestors who lived near the equator where there are long days of direct sunlight. Thousands of years ago, those with the darkest skins would have a better chance of surviving because they could hunt and work longer in the sun without discomfort or getting burned. Lots of melanin would protect the body against skin cancer, while the skin could still absorb enough ultraviolet rays to produce needed Vitamin D.

THIRD CLASS PERIOD

8. Ask students if they can identify other broad categories of human differences other than physical ones. They will probably mention cultural and individual differences. Refer back to the separate list you made in #6. When students point out differences in clothing, hairstyles, and human activities, explain that these differences emerge from differences in our cultures (The simplest definition of culture? CULTURE IS ALL LEARNED BEHAVIOR). Explain that while most physical differences are those that we inherit (are born with), cultural differences include all the customs, activities and behaviors that we learn from our families and communities.

INDIVIDUAL DIFFERENCES (personality traits, unique talents and abilities, and personal preferences) are shaped by both our genetic heritage and the culture in which we live. Generate some examples of cultural and individual differences. Remind students that *all personality types and all types of physical and mental abilities are represented within all cultural groups. No one racial, ethnic, religious, or gender group is the exclusive province of great cooks or athletes, humanitarians or hate-mongers, professors or entrepreneurs.*

9. Divide students into groups of three or four and pass out one **Handout 2:5: "Human Differences, Adaptations, And Variations"** to each group. Together, review the categories of human differences across the top of the handout. From the list at the bottom of the page, identify one difference that would match each of the five categories. Do these examples together as a class.

Then ask each group to match the other twenty characteristics to the five categories. Ask one student in each group to record the group's answers. Remind students that the group must all agree to the match before the recorder writes it down. Review answers with the whole class and take time to discuss examples which elicited differences of opinion within and among groups. The answers below are subject to interpretation. This is one way of categorizing responses:

Answers: Physical Inherited Traits—3, 11, 15, 22, 24; **Physical Changes and Adaptations**—1, 4, 12, 21, 25; **Cultural Differences**—7, 9, 13, 16, 20; **Personality Characteristics**—6, 8, 14, 17, 19; **Individual Preferences, Talents, and Abilities**—2, 5, 10, 18, 23.

☞ **Going Further:**

1. Ask students to write brief self-portraits (beginning "I am....," "I have....," "I can....") identifying six or seven physical, cultural, and individual characteristics which accurately describe who they are. Ask for volunteers who feel comfortable having their self-portraits placed in a pile from which you select some to read out loud. Then ask students to guess whose self-portrait it is. Another way to do this activity is to have partners write each other's self-portraits.

2. Present Howard Gardner's work on "multiple intelligences" to your students (Sources: *Frames of Mind* by Howard Gardner and many current articles in weekly news magazines and educational journals). This is a powerful framework to get students to think about their own capacities, strengths, and individual differences.

HUMAN DIFFERENCES, ADAPTATIONS, AND VARIATIONS

PHYSICAL DIFFERENCES		CULTURAL DIFFERENCES	INDIVIDUAL DIFFERENCES	
Inherited Traits passed through the genes you inherit from your parents	*Changes and Adaptations* which occur during an individual's lifetime	*Learned Behaviors* shaped by your family, ethnic/national heritage, physical environment, gender, religion, etc.	*Personality Characteristics* shaped by heredity and culture/environment	*Personal Preferences, Talents and Abilities* shaped by heredity and culture/environment
1.	1.	1.	1.	1.
2.	2.	2.	2.	2.
3.	3.	3.	3.	3.
4.	4.	4.	4.	4.
5.	5.	5.	5.	5.

1. You're a math whiz
2. You have green eyes
3. You cut your hair short
4. You're a "morning person"
5. You are very rebellious
6. You eat mostly rice and fish and eat with chopsticks

8. You celebrate Hanukkah
9. You love to write stories
10. You are very short
11. Your legs are strong from cycling and running
12. You get to vote in elections
13. You are cheerful /optimistic

15. You live in a house on stilts
16. You are shy around people
17. You like to baby-sit
18. You're ambitious and goal-oriented
19. You don't know how to read
20. You've had heart surgery

22. You're a great athlete
23. You have Down's syndrome so your growth and development are slow and delayed
24. Your growth is stunted from malnutrition

ACTIVITY 6: We All Do the Same Things - Only Differently

OBJECTIVES:

1. Students will brainstorm a list of activities that are common to all human groups (cultural universals).
2. Students will work in small groups and choose a project to do which demonstrates their understanding of cultural universals.

LEARNING STRATEGIES: Brainstorming, collaborative projects, group sharing, and discussion

TIME: Two class periods

MATERIALS: Handout 2:6, large poster board or paper, magazines (especially *National Geographic*), scissors, glue

SUGGESTED INSTRUCTIONS:

1. Ask students to quickly jot down a list of 15 to 20 activities that they and their families do every week. Give them ten minutes to do their "brainwriting." Ask students to identify the activities on their lists that they think people do everywhere. In other words, make a list of universal cultural activties that cross time and space.

2. Give each student a copy of **Handout 2:6: "Cultural Universals."** Explain to students that this is a list of cultural activities that most anthropologists agree are present in all human groups. Review the list and generate examples as needed. Ask students to refer back to their own lists and match their activities to the corresponding cultural universals.

3. Ask students to pair up and share their activity lists with each other. The goal here is to discover if students have described different ways of doing the same activity.

4. Discuss how these activities are carried out differently from culture to culture. Is one way of doing these activities necessarily better than another? What factors (i.e. location, climate, local resources) might shape how these activities are expressed in different societies? Working independently, in pairs, or in threes, ask students to choose one of the following activities to complete using the cultural universals as a guide.

a. Make a picture collage that includes examples of all twelve universals as they are expressed in different cultures.

b. Pick one cultural universal and make a poster or collage that shows how this cultural universal is expressed differently in five or six different cultures.

c. Choose one culture you know very little about and make a chart or poster which shows how six of these universals are expressed in that culture.

d. Compare and contrast how four of the universals are commonly expressed in the U.S. and a non-Western nation.

e. Survey your class about a particular cultural activity to see how students carry out that activity in their families. For example:
   - The meal most frequently cooked in your home
   - The most typical recreational/fun activity that your family does
   - Curfew and "going out" rules for teens
   - The people you identify as part of your immediate family
   - The two or three most important family gatherings/celebrations during the year.

5. Have students share their work in small groups or with the whole class.

✎ **Going Further:** Have students generate a list of physical gestures and communication signals that they think have universal meaning for people and cultures throughout the U.S. and the world. Some examples: smiling, frowning, nodding, shaking head sideways, etc. Then bring in resources that focus on nonverbal communication so that students can check out the accuracy of their predictions.

Sources: *Do's and Taboos Around the World, Gestures: The Do's and Taboos of Body Language Around the World, Valuing Diversity and Similarity: Bridging the Gap through Interpersonal Communication*

CULTURAL UNIVERSALS

1. Production, preparation, and distribution of food

2. Construction and maintenance of shelter

3. Manufacture and distribution of clothing and ornamentation

4. Use of tools, technology, and transportation

5. An economic system for production and distribution of goods and services

6. Values, spiritual beliefs, rituals, and ceremonies

7. Development of language, counting systems, and use of symbols

8. Recreation and play

9. Creative expression the use of arts, music, dance, drama, stories

10. Organization of families, sex roles, and social classes

11. Childrearing practices, rites of passage, education, and passing of a people's history from one generation to the next

12. Development of ethics, laws, and leadership

ACTIVITY 7: Different Strokes for Different Folks

OBJECTIVES:

1. Students will explore the implications of "right/wrong" versus "it's just different" thinking when making judgments about other people's cultural habits and behaviors.
2. Students will examine distinctions between private behavior and public norms and generate public norms for situations familiar to most young people.

LEARNING STRATEGIES: Whole group discussion, cooperative learning

TIME: One class period

MATERIALS: Newsprint, markers, **Handout 2:7**

SUGGESTED INSTRUCTIONS:

1. On the board or newsprint write the title, **BURPING RULES** Then ask students what the "burping rules" are in their families. Jot down their responses. You will probably get a ridiculous variety of rules, which is the point of this exercise!

2. When you've completed the list discuss whether students think one of the rules is better than all the others. Is one rule right and all the others wrong? (They will most likely say "NO!" because every family is different with its own customs, habits, and history.)

   Then ask students if they can agree on one official burping rule that every family in the community must follow at home. (Again, students will most likely say "NO!" because families have the right to privacy within their own households.) Point out that there are many cultural customs and habits which vary greatly from family to family, group to group, culture to culture—ways of doing things which are not really right or wrong, simply different. Generate other examples of habits which vary from family to family and group to group.

3. Write the words **PUBLIC** and **PRIVATE** on the board. Check out what students think these words mean. Try to come up with a collective definition for each word. Ask students if they've ever heard their parents begin a sentence with, "When you go out in public,

remember to...." For some students this will sound all too familiar; for others this may be a phrase they've never heard. Explore with students why the distinction between private and public behavior might be important.

4. Ask students to think again about the burping rules that they listed earlier. Are all the rules on the list okay to use in public? Why or why not? Ask students how they would go about deciding on what's okay to do in public and what's not.

5. Introduce the concept of "public norms"—behavioral expectations that we would ideally like everyone to observe and practice in public places. **Norms are behaviors that are widely accepted among most community members and are least likely to hurt, upset or offend significant groups in the community.**

   Norms in local communities operate similarly to rules of diplomacy in the international community. Discuss potential problems if *all behaviors are acceptable in public—if the norm is, "Anything goes!"* How might this make communication among strangers difficult? Point out to students that in public places we are likely to encounter a far more diverse group of people than we are likely to find among our own families and friends.

   Norms form a common code that we can use with everyone in public, whether they are strangers, acquaintances, or people we've known all our lives. Not knowing the difference between private behavior and public norms can lead to confusion, miscommunication, and misunderstandings, especially in a multicultural society.

6. Do a quick brainstorm of public spaces that people use to do things or to get from one place to another and public places that serve the general public. (For example: sidewalks, streets, schools, movie theaters, malls, workplaces, libraries, restaurants, parks, etc.)

7. Divide students into groups of three and give each group of three one copy of **Handout 2:7. Private Behaviors and Public Norms.** On the board, write the following:

   Choose One Responsibility to Carry Out in Your Group:
   - Record your group's responses on the chart on **Handout 2:7.**
   - Help your group brainstorm **private behaviors** for each activity.

108

- Help your group come to agreement on a **public norm** for each activity.

Ask each group member to choose a responsibility from the list above. Explain that for each activity listed, groups are to generate a range of behaviors that might be acceptable at home and with friends and then suggest a "norm" that would be the best option for everyone to practice in public spaces and places.

8. When students finish, discuss their responses as a whole class. One focus might be to discuss norms that groups found easy to reach agreement about and those norms that were more difficult to reach agreement about.

☞ Going Further:

1. Begin a discussion with this question: "How does your behavior and communication style change when you're with different groups of people?" Ask students to share experiences in which they have been conscious of acting differently when they are with certain groups.

2. Explore the topic of **group norms** (widely accepted behaviors within a specific group in which age, gender, ethnicity, religion, class, etc. becomes the defining characteristic of that group's identity and behavior). All of us cross cultures and groups everyday. The more we are aware of what's okay and what's not okay within a particular group, the more comfortable we can be when we cross cultures. Discuss what attitudes and behaviors might be helpful to someone who is a "guest" in someone else's cultural group. If positive and productive intercultural communication is a goal, what might be an outsider's responsibilities? What might be an insider's responsibilities?

3. Identify some communication responses that you think are expressed differently within specific groups. Examples: eye contact, physical distance between two people talking, form of address used when speaking to someone, touching, expression of feelings, the role of silence, criticism, praise, ways to save face, etc.

Private Behavior and Public Norms - What's the Difference?

ACTIVITY	PRIVATE BEHAVIORS	PUBLIC NORMS Do's and Don't's
How you watch a movie	with friends at home	in a movie theater
How you eat dinner	with just family at home	in a restaurant
How you do homework	in your room at home	in the public library
How you take care of property and physical environment	in your bedroom	in your classroom
	in your living room	on a downtown street
How you dress	hanging out at your friend's house	to a job interview
How you disagree	with your brother or sister at home	at work with your boss
		at school with a friend
When you arrive	at a friend's party	at work
How you play music	in the basement at home	in a public park
Talk - What you say and how you say it	with friends at home	in a class
	with your parents	at a shopping mall

110

ACTIVITY 8: Checking Out Assumptions

OBJECTIVE: Students will answer questions about each other based on assumptions, reasons we make assumptions, and positive and negative consequences of making assumptions.

LEARNING STRATEGIES: Peer interviews, class discussion

TIME: 30 minutes

MATERIALS: Handout 2:8, pencils

SUGGESTED INSTRUCTIONS:

1. Pass out a copy of **Handout 2:8: "Checking It Out!"** to every student. Explain to students that they will try to guess how their partners would answer the questions on the handout. Students will need to pair up with someone they do not know well. After students have paired up, ask students to spell their full names for each other so that they can write their partner's correct name on the top of their handout. At this point, let students know that they will have **five minutes of complete silence** to guess how their partners would answer each question. Students need to write down what they think their partners would say.

2. After five minutes (or the time it takes for students to finish), ask students to interview each other as they check out their assumptions and compare them with their partner's actual responses to see how accurate or off-base their predictions were.

3. **Debriefing:**
   - Ask students how it felt to do this exercise. Many will say it was uncomfortable to make assumptions without knowing if they were correct.
   - Ask the class to define the word *assumption*. One practical definition: **Assumptions are the quick predictions and automatic judgments we make based on what we believe to be true rather than what we actually observe.**
   - If assumptions so often lead to inaccuracies, why do we make so many of them every day?

111

- Make this chart on the board:

ASSUMPTIONS	
+'s	—'s
1.	1.
2.	2.
3.	3.
4.	4.

- With the class brainstorm a list of positive reasons for making assumptions. For example:
    1. They make life more predictable.
    2. There's enough uncertainty already; if we didn't make them it would be as if we started out each day knowing nothing.
    3. They can help us frame goals and expectations for others.
    4. If we make positive assumptions, they can help people do their best.

    Then brainstorm a list of negative consequences of making assumptions. How can they hurt us and hurt our relationships with others? For example:
    1. They can lead to misunderstandings ranging from the embarrassing to the disastrous,
    2. Assumptions can quickly lead to stereotypes where we make generalizations about a whole group based on one experience or encounter,
    3. They can prevent us from "doing our homework" and checking out the facts,
    4. They can diminish our sense of curiosity to know more.

- Are there optimal situations in which making assumptions is okay? (For example, with friends or in repeat situations)

- Are there circumstances in which making assumptions is a lousy idea? (For example, in interactions with people you've never met before or in a situation that is completely new or different)

- Ask students to share personal experiences when assumptions led to confusion, miscommunication, and misunderstandings.

You might want to develop some rules of thumb about making assumptions and post them in your classroom.

CHECKING IT OUT!

Your partner's complete name _____

Family ancestry (ethnic groups that are part of your family history)

_____

A place you'd like to travel that you've never visited _____

Favorite food_____

Favorite color _____

Favorite relaxing activity_____

Favorite holiday _____

Favorite music or musical group_____

When people describe you, what would be the first two or three words
they would use? _____

One thing you'd like to own now that you don't have _____

One thing you'd like to do that you've never done.

_____

Your desk at home (a complete clutter........everything in its place)

ACTIVITY 9: We Each See the World A Little Differently

OBJECTIVE: Students will play a perception game that reveals how individuals perceive and interpret words and ideas differently.

LEARNING STRATEGIES: Small group dialogues

TIME: One class period

MATERIALS: Handout 2:9, scissors, scrap paper, pencils

SUGGESTED INSTRUCTIONS:

1. Write the word **OCEAN** on the board. Ask students to close their eyes for a minute and let their senses take over as they imagine **OCEAN**—see it, hear it, feel it, smell it. Then ask students to share their thoughts and word pictures of **OCEAN**. Write down the words and phrases you hear. How are the images different? Some students probably have very detailed pictures of ocean while others may have never seen an ocean except on a map. Some images may be dark and stormy while others may convey a stillness filled with white heat. Discuss how personal experiences filter what we see, hear, and imagine—all of us have slightly different filters which help us to make meaning of the world. Our perceptions are never exactly like anyone else's.

   One example: Jamake Highwater, a Native American, who is now an art historian and writer in New York City, recalls his confusion when he first encountered the English idea of *"wilderness"— an untamed land, a wild and unpredictable place beyond the reach of "civilization."* As a Blackfoot Indian, he understood "wilderness" to be ordered and balanced, a natural state of the world as the seasons moved predictably from one cycle of life to another. For Mr. Highwater's mother, her first visit to New York City seemed to match the English definition of the idea of "wilderness"!

2. Divide students into groups of five. Each student will need a pencil and a sheet of scrap paper. Make enough copies of **Handout 2:9: "Perception Cards"** so that each group of five students receives five or six different cards. Cut the cards apart beforehand.

   Explain that groups will select a card and students will write down what the word on the card means to them. Then each student in the group will read their definitions in a "go-round" (no interruptions or questions during this phase). Remind students that the purpose here is to see how perceptions vary, not to determine a correct definition. This is also an opportunity to monitor for active listening skills. Each group will choose only three words to use in the exercise. Take about ten minutes for each round.

Round #1
1) The group picks the first word they want to define(for example, **Family**).
2) Each student in the group takes a minute or so to jot down a few words and phrases which give the word meaning.
3) When everyone is finished writing down their ideas, the group does a "go-around," each student taking turns sharing what they wrote.
4) If there is time left in Round #1, students can ask each other clarifying questions to further explore the meanings each person shared.
5) After about 10 minutes, tell students to move to Round #2, choosing the next word.

4. In closing the exercise, check out whether students' understanding of these words changed after they were discussed in their groups.

Adapted from the work of Marian O'Malley, *North Carolina Center for Peace Education*

PERCEPTION CARDS

tolerance	prejudice	morality
community	sexism	injustice
friend	family	freedom
democracy	police	racism
human rights	sex	success

ACTIVITY 10: How Do We See Others? How Do They See Us?

OBJECTIVE:

1. Students will be asked to consider how people who are not American citizens perceive Americans.
2. Students will compare their own perceptions of Americans with those of foreign citizens.
3. Students will role play dialogues between U.S. and foreign citizens to explore differences in perceptions.
4. Students will explore how "enemy imaging" (love/hate and us/them relationships) escalates tensions between and among individuals, cultural groups, and nations.

LEARNING STRATEGIES: Small and large group discussion, reading for understanding, role-playing, pair-sharing, reflective writing

TIME: Two class periods

MATERIALS: Chalkboard, newsprint, markers, **Handout 2:10**

SUGGESTED INSTRUCTIONS:

1. Explain that the class is going to make some predictions concerning how people from other nations and regions perceive America and Americans. The following questions can be used for class discussion or written journal reflections.

   • How might foreign citizens describe Americans?
   • How might citizens from other nations perceive the U.S.'s role in the world?
   • What do you think they would most admire and most dislike about America?
   • What might they cite as Americans' best traits? Worst traits?

2. If it's possible, have students interview foreign nationals who attend their school or live in the community. Use the same questions in #1, and have students compare their own predictions with the responses of foreign nationals. Are there any surprises? Do students' perceptions generally agree with the comments and observations of foreign nationals? Why or why not?

117

3. Distribute quotations on **Handout 2:10: "How People From Other Cultures View America and Americans."** Discuss some or all of the quotations with the whole class. Again, have students compare their predictions with comments of foreign observers. Are there areas where there seem to be real gaps in understanding? What role does the media play in these misperceptions?

4. **Follow-up Activities:**

   - Students may want to role-play dialogues, taking on the perspectives of Americans and foreign nationals as they attempt to explain and communicate their perceptions of each other. This type of exercise encourages active listening skills—paraphrasing, clarifying questions, listening for agreement; remind students to keep the "Yes, but's" out of their role-plays.

   The purpose here is to listen for deeper understanding of the other person's point of view.

   - Even better, try to sponsor roundtable dialogues of U.S. and foreign citizens at your school.

   - Collect political cartoons, ads, and quotes that underscore these differences in perceptions.

How People From Other Cultures View the United States and Its Citizens

1. In 1945 we were the children. We did what our American parents told us what to do. Now we have grown up.

2. Americans think they are a race above everyone else — that they can do no wrong.

3. It's true, of course, that people do envy America for its prosperity, its convenience, its appliances. But that's where it stops. The dollar controls the values, and in my opinion that is the negative factor in America.

4. I would like to live in America for a while because you can study freely there and get the chance to specialize and excel in certain fields. But drugs, sexual diseases, and the weakening of social ties would work against my wanting to live in America for good.

5. I like the American people a lot. They're very easygoing, very straightforward. I admire the American can-do spirit. But I think Americans should realize that the more No. 1 mentality they harbor, the quicker their No. 1 position will slip away. We used to be No. 1 hundreds of years ago. We thought we were the greatest, the Middle Kingdom. Then we lost it because we became complacent and self-centered.

6. Europe is a great sort of ferment, with rivalries and cross-fertilization, but America has a sort of sameness about it. There's no intellectual challenge at all. The only challenge is making more money.

7. There is a widely perceived disparity between American preachment and practice: preach free markets and practice trade restraint, however selective; preach equality and let the poor sleep in the gutters. I don't think the social system in the U.S. is the best we can hope for mankind. There are some very serious problems that need to be addressed.

8. The quintessentially American characteristics are cheerfulness, optimism, and generosity; a general buoyancy of spirit; a belief that tomorrow will dawn a better day. So it may, but suddenly many Americans seem not so sure. They assumed the American Century, born in 1941, would endure a hundred years; now, after fewer than 50, they fear it is on the wane.

9. America combines qualities among its national traits that you don't find elsewhere -- a lack of pettiness, a breadth of vision, a readiness to learn and to be optimistic, and to believe in a capacity for change.

10. The American empire is a true historical phenomenon. The fact that Americans don't speak other peoples' languages or don't know about other peoples' cultures shouldn't surprise anyone. Empires don't have to speak other languages or know about other cultures. They are simply the *empire*, everything they do or don't do reflects that reality.

11. To Americans, geography consists of the fifty states of the United States of America. To my mind, this is a result of their materialism. They are busy thinking about a house, a car, money in the bank. This keeps them narrowly focused on their immediate physical goals to the degree that the rest of the world is a blurred fog of ignorance.

12. Americans don't have a national experience of suffering in the Twentieth century, which is what makes a nation a nation. It's very bad that America has become such a powerful nation without really understanding how other nations may ache.

13. We are always reminded and even lectured when we complain about United States foreign policy, that the United States is an isolated country, that most Americans are not aware of what happens in the rest of the world. We see a country that is obsessed about its role in the world, but at the same time it is a country that is very little inclined to learn anything about the rest of the world.

14. We are skeptical of creeping Cola-Colonization. When we say the culture of the West, we think of Europe. Deep in our hearts, we say Americans aren't as civilized as Europeans. We think America is too young, too rich, and sometimes it's vulgar.

15. If you look at Japan or West Germany or France, you see increasing interest in democratic capitalism, in tax cuts and deregulation. Whatever they may say about American economic policy, they're following at least some parts of it. The interest in both capitalism and democracy that is spreading throughout the world is a sign that America is still in the ascendancy.

Statements (quoted in *Time* magazine) by:
1. Betate Lindemann, **Germany**
2. Carlos Tunnermann, **Nicaragua**
3. Galia Golan, **Israel**
4. Nasser Seliim, **Jordan**
5. Zhang Yi, **China**
6. Ian Grant, **United Kingdom**
7. Zhou Lifang, **China**
8. *The Economist,* **United Kingdom**
9. Sir Nicholas Henderson, **United Kingdom**
10. Hugo Tolentino Dipp, **Dominican Republic**
11. Mohammed Al-Barwani, **Oman**
12. Yuri Borlav, **Russia**
13. Adolfo Aguilar Zinser, **Mexico**
14. C.C. Tung, **Hong Kong**
15. Adam Myerson, **USA**

ACTIVITY 11: When Differences Become Our Enemy

OBJECTIVE:

Students will discuss the reasons we image those who are different as "enemies" and examine the consequences of "enemy thinking."

LEARNING STRATEGIES: Discussion and/or reflective writing

TIME: One class period

MATERIALS: None

SUGGESTED QUESTIONS FOR WRITING AND DISCUSSION:

1. Explore the love/hate relationships between the U.S. and other nations. For example, many Americans criticize the Japanese but grudgingly admire the very traits we would like to see more visible in the United States. Are nations and people naturally distrustful and threatened of other nations who share power with them? Does it matter that nations and people are resentful of the U.S.? What are the costs of being perceived as #1 in power, influence, and wealth? How can governments and citizens reduce these tensions?

2. With students, generate lists of us/them relationships (within your school, in your community, in the U.S. at large, and between the United States and other nations). What makes these groups adversaries?

Sam Keen writes in *Faces of the Enemy*,

> We are a hostile species, *Homo hostilis,* the enemy-making animal. We are driven to fabricate an enemy as a scapegoat to bear the burden of our denied enmity. From the unconscious residues of our hostility, we create a target; from our private demons we conjure a public enemy. The majority of tribes and nations create a sense of social solidarity and membership in part by systematically creating enemies.

121

The identity of most peoples depends on dividing the world into:

US	versus	THEM
INSIDERS	versus	OUTSIDERS
THE TRIBE	versus	THE ENEMY

It is both normal and admirable, the essence of tribal loyalty and patriotism, to direct vitriolic hatred toward strangers we hardly know, and to reserve love for those familiar to us. Before the weapon comes the image. We *think* others to death and then invent the battle-ax or the ballistic missiles with which to actually kill them. Propaganda precedes technology.

3. Do groups and nations need enemies to protect their own identity and heritage? How do the images of the "*other*" shape U.S foreign policy and international relations?

4. Do we create enemies or find them? Do we need enemies? If we didn't have them, would we have to invent them to satisfy some psychological or sociological need within us?

5. Do we need to see life as a struggle between good and evil, heroes and villains? Can we have heroes without villains?

6. Why do we automatically suspect and mistrust people who are different than we are? Do we always perceive the unknown as evil, dangerous, foreign, and fearful? Are there any circumstances where the unknown is perceived as positive, hopeful, exciting?

7. What kinds of words, images, and metaphors do we use to describe those we fear and hate? By contrast, how do we describe those we love and cherish?

8. How do we stereotype different human groups? (Arabs, Israelis, Russians, Hispanics, African-Americans, white Europeans, etc.) Do editorial cartoons and comic strips reinforce certain stereotypes? How do popular action films reinforce stereotypes?

9. Are competition, conquest, and one-upsmanship the driving forces in American culture? Is success in America defined by these forces? Are all people motivated primarily by a quest for power, by first looking out for "Number One"?

ACTIVITY 12: Turning Differences into Resources

OBJECTIVE: Each student will identify specific skills and knowledge that s/he can contribute to a classroom resource file.

LEARNING STRATEGIES: Personal reflection and individual brainstorming

TIME: One class period

MATERIALS: Newsprint, markers

SUGGESTED INSTRUCTIONS:

1. This is an opportunity for students to recognize the richness of the resources they bring to school with them everyday. Label ten to fifteen pieces of newsprint with any of the suggested topics or choose other topics more appropriate to your students.

FIXING THINGS	BOOKS, TV, FILM	ART, MUSIC, DANCE, DRAMA
RELIGION	COOKING SPECIALTIES	
PEOPLE, PLACES, AND CULTURES I KNOW ABOUT	BABY-SITTING/CHILDCARE	JOBS I'VE DONE / TIPS ABOUT WORKING
	TUTORING SPECIALTIES	SPORTS STUFF
SPECIAL INTERESTS OR HOBBIES	ORGANIZATIONS AND GROUPS I BELONG TO	WHERE TO BUY
CLOTHING, JEWELRY, HAIR		HOLIDAY TRADITIONS
	RESOURCES I'M WILLING TO SHARE	CARS

2. Post newsprint sheets around the classroom and place several markers by each sheet. Explain to students that these sheets will become a resource file for the class. Review the topics that you've included and invite students to take a few minutes to jot down specific things that they know about and specific things that they can do (however weird!). Ask students to share a couple of examples and record them under the most appropriate topics.

3. Tell students that they will have 15 minutes to record their names and contributions on the sheets. This activity can be a bit manic, but the end result is always amazing!

4. When time is up, invite students to take a good look at the scope of the class's resources. Are there any unusual entries that the class would want to know more about? Discuss how you might compile and use this "resource file" inside of class and outside of class.

5. For closure, here are two quotations to chew on:

> If we cannot end our differences, at least we can help make the world safe for diversity. For, in the final analysis, our most basic common link is that we all inhabit this small planet. We all breathe the same air—we all cherish our children's future.
>
> John F. Kennedy

> What sets worlds in motions is the interplay of differences, their attractions, and repulsions. Life is plurality, death is uniformity. By suppressing differences and peculiarities, by eliminating different civilizations and cultures, progress weakens life and favors death. The idea of a single civilization for everyone, implicit in the cult of progress and technique, impoverishes and mutilates us. Every view of the world that becomes extinct, every culture that disappears, diminishes a possibility of life.
>
> Octavio Paz (1967)

Chapter 3: Exploring the Nature of Conflict

Activity 1: What Is Conflict?

Activity 2: Conflict, Violence, and Peacemaking: What's Your Opinion?

Activity 3: Conflict: You Know It When You See It

Activity 4: Writing and Performing Conflict Dialogues

Activity 5: Getting the Message About Conflict

Activity 6: Five Dimensions of Conflict: An Overview

Activity 7: Dimensions of Conflict: A Closer Look

Activity 8: Responding to Conflict: What Do You Do?

Activity 9: A Closer Look at Conflict Styles

Activity 10: Using Your Conflict Toolbox

Activity 11: Writing Conflict Stories With Solutions that Work

Activity 1: What Is Conflict?

PURPOSE: Drawing on familiar experiences and personal perceptions students will develop a working definition of conflict and consider what makes some conflicts worse than others. Students will also complete an initial assessment survey about interpersonal conflict.

LEARNING STRATEGIES: Whole group discussion, brainstorming, and written reflection

TIME: One class period

MATERIALS: Newsprint, markers, **Handouts 3:1A** and **3:1B**, and pencils

SUGGESTED INSTRUCTIONS:

1. Write the word **CONFLICT** again on the board or on newsprint. Ask the class what they think of when they hear the word "conflict". Brainstorm all the words and phrases that come to mind and make a **WEB CHART** of responses around the word **CONFLICT**. You may want to use different colored markers to write words and phrases or circle categories of words in different colors when brainstorming is finished (black = wars and violent responses to conflict; red = feelings; green = sources of conflict; orange = negative words which describe conflict; blue = neutral or positive words describing conflict or words that imply nonviolent means of resolving conflict).

2. Ask students how they would differentiate the word groupings you have circled or written in different colored markers. Discuss some of the aspects of conflict noted in #1 above. Explain to students that we often see conflict as a negative or destructive experience, rarely seeing disagreements and differences as constructive opportunities to learn, change, and grow. You may want to make another web in which you generate words that describe ideas, feelings, and actions associated with resolving conflict and problem solving.

Suggested discussion questions:

- Is a fight different than an argument? How? Why do conflicts become violent?
- How do you feel when a conflict isn't worked out?
- Are conflicts always bad? Can conflicts ever be positive - have good endings?
- How do you feel when you've successfully resolved a problem?
- Can you think of a conflict that helped you learn something about yourself or other people?
- Can you think of conflicts you've experienced that actually improved the situation in the long run?
- Could there be a world without conflict? Why not? If conflict is a fact of life, if we can't make it go away, what do we do with it?

3. Ask students to work in pairs and compose a working definition of conflict. See if the class can agree on a definition that incorporates various responses. Pass out **Handout 3:1A: "What Is Conflict?"** or write all or part of the definition on the board to discuss.

4. As a class, discuss the conflict continuum on **Handout 3:1A** or draw it on the board or newsprint. Ask students to share experiences and examples that would match the meaning and intensity of each word or phrase. What changes as you move to the right on the continuum?

Remind students that in this exploration of conflict we will be looking at conflict as an opportunity, that our goal is to explore the choices we can make when we experience conflict. As we work with conflict we will be learning systematic ways to think about conflict and building skills to deal with conflict more effectively.

✐ **Assessment:** Give each student a copy of **Handout 3:1B A Survey About Me and Conflict** to fill out. Remind students to be as honest as they can as the respond to the questions. Assure them that other students will not see their responses. You may want to keep these so that you and your students can compare their original responses with their responses at the completion of your unit on conflict. The survey also provides you with a good data base for creating role-plays, conflict situations, and verbal responses that you can use in conjunction with other exercises.

What is Conflict?

Conflict is often defined as a strong disagreement or collision of values, needs, interests, or intentions among individuals, groups, organizations, communities, and nations. Conflict occurs when basic needs are not met, or when an individual or group is interfering with or obstructing an individual's or group's attainment of certain goals. Conflicts often involve struggles over the allocation and use of resources and power.

When people are competing to win or coerce an "adversary" into submission, conflicts are often intense and protracted. People in conflict bring deeply felt emotions to the situation even though these emotions may not be expressed out loud. Conflicts within a diverse population are more frequent when people are unable to tolerate and live with value and cultural differences.

A Conflict Continuum

Confusion or lack of information--->
  Misunderstanding--->
    Difference of opinion--->
      Disagreement / Argument--->
        Dispute--->
          Verbal threats, intimidation, and abuse--->
            Physical threats and intimidation--->
              Physical acts of aggression and abuse

Survey About Me and Conflict:

Name_____

1. Most people **fight or argue when** they _____

2. Most people **fight or argue over**_____

3. One **good thing** people get from arguing or fighting: _____

    _____

4. One **bad thing** about arguing or fighting: _____

    _____

5. People generally **respond to conflicts by:**

    _____or by_____

6. **I fight or argue** when _____

7. **I get upset or angry** when other students _____

    _____

8. **When I am really angry or upset** with someone, the most

    important thing for me to do is _____

9. **When I'm upset at, mad at, or bothered by another student I can:**

    *   _____

    *   _____

10. **I make others angry** when I_____

    _____

11. When I am talking to **someone else who is really angry or**

    upset, the most important thing for me to do is _____

12. When I have a disagreement or conflict with someone, **we can**

    agree to _____

13. When we talk through a conflict, rules for how we talk together
    and treat each other can help us work it out. **Some good ground**
    rules are:

Activity 2: Conflict, Violence, and Peacemaking: What's Your Opinion?

PURPOSE: Students will discuss their own opinions about conflict, violence, and peacemaking, paraphrase the opinions of others, and explore the reasons for their opinions.

LEARNING STRATEGIES: Individual reflection, small group dialogues, whole group discussion (Written assignments are optional)

TIME: 30 minutes

MATERIALS: Newsprint, markers, **Handout 3:2A** or **3:2B**, pencils (**Handout 3:2C** is optional.)

SUGGESTED INSTRUCTIONS:

1. Begin by saying that the class is going to participate in an opinion poll. Ask students to define both *opinion* and *poll* before continuing. You may also want to ask the following questions:

   - Where do our opinions come from? How do we form them?
   - Are opinions right and wrong? Do some people's opinions matter more to you than those of others? Why?
   - What makes someone's ideas an "informed opinion"?

2. Give each student **Handout 3:2A: "What's Your Opinion?"** or **Handout 3:2B: "Conflict, Violence, and Peacemaking: What's Your Opinion?"** (2:3A is more personal; 2:3B is more global) Ask students to read each statement and check off whether they agree or disagree with each statement. If they are undecided or have mixed feelings and thoughts about any statement, they can put a question mark or a check in the middle. Give students a few minutes to fill out the opinion poll.

3. Then ask each student to star three statements that they want to discuss in a small group. Remind students to pick statements that they have strong reactions to because they will be discussing the reasons why they strongly agree or disagree with the statement they choose.

131

4. Explain that students will form discussion groups of five and participate in a "go-around" in which one student in the group will give her or his opinion about a particular statement and the student to her or his right will try to restate or paraphrase what was said as accurately as possible.

5. Ask a student to volunteer to do a demonstration with you. Ask the student to talk about one statement. You might write this "Opinion Starter" on the board to help students begin: **"I agree that/with........because........."** Then paraphrase what the student said. You might want to post a list of "Paraphrase Starters" on the board that can help students begin their paraphrasing: **"I heard you say...."; "You said that...."; "I understood you to say ...."; "You're saying that...."**

6. When students are divided into groups, explain that they will do three "go-arounds" taking turns paraphrasing and giving their opinions. Ask each group to answer the following questions when they report during the whole class discussion:

   • Identify two or three statements where the group seemed to share the same opinion.
   • Identify two or three statements where opinions seemed to differ the most.
   • Identify a statement that most people in your group had never really thought about before.

⌂ **Going Further:** Ask students to select two or three of the statements they want to explore further in discussion. Because many or these statements are contradictory and imply very different perceptions of human beings and the world, discussion about these statements is particularly suited to practicing effective communication skills with a focus on learning how to listen to a point of view different from your own. Some suggestions:

   • Encourage students to ask questions that help them better understand another person's point of view.
   • You might want to ask students to say one thing that they agree with in the previous student's comment before they give their own opinions.
   • Encourage students to think of examples from history, recent events, the media, or personal experience that support their points of view.

- Encourage students to define abstract words and compare their understanding of the words with definitions from reference books and current writing.

🖎 **Assessment:** Begin by asking students what changes their opinion about an issue and what tools they would use to convince someone that their idea is right. Chart students' responses. Offer students any of the options below using **Handout 3:2C: "Developing An Informed Opinion"** as a possible framework. (Also see page 14 for more ideas for working with controversial issues and opinions.)

1. Pair up with someone who holds a different opinion from yours about one of the statements. Present your contrasting opinions to the class. Encourage the class to ask questions, and give students feedback about their presentations.

2. Write an editorial for your local or school newspaper which supports the ideas contained in one of the statements and examines how young people are affected by these ideas.

3. Consider implications for U.S. domestic and foreign policy if there were genuine regard and public agreement about one of the following statements in **Handout 3:2B** - #11, #12, #14, #15, #16, #17, or #18. If citizens truly accepted this statement as true, how would public policy (laws, regulations, public programs, citizen campaigns) change? How might local, state, and federal governments allocate human and material resources differently?

WHAT'S YOUR OPINION?	AGREE	DISAGREE
1. It's possible to live in a world without conflict.		
2. You can have conflicts without fighting or resorting to violence.		
3. All conflicts can be worked out.		
4. People should never fight.		
5. People turn to violence when they refuse to listen to each other.		
6. You can still be a strong person and choose not to fight.		
7. The world would be a boring place without conflict and differences.		
8. Fighting may be the only way some kids know how to deal with their anger.		
9. "Put-downs" and "fighting words" can be as violent and hurtful as physical fighting.		

CONFLICT, VIOLENCE, AND PEACEMAKING: WHAT'S YOUR OPINION?

	AGREE	DISAGREE
1. The world would be a better place without conflict.		
2. All conflicts are solvable.		
3. All conflicts are avoidable.		
4. All conflicts are struggles.		
5. Conflicts are never really resolved unless all parties involved get something that they need.		
6. The best way to avoid conflict is to be stronger and more powerful than all of your potential enemies.		
7. A peaceful world can never really exist.		
8. The world would be dull and boring without conflict.		
9. Peace is the absence of violence.		
10. Peace is the absence of conflict.		
11. The first step toward violence is the refusal to listen.		
12. Peace is a way to deal with change and conflict nonviolently.		
13. Conflict is not good or bad - it's how we deal with conflict that has positive or negative consequences.		
14. Peace is not the absence of war but the presence of justice.		
15. Violence is an attempt to eliminate differentness, competition opposition, and diversity. Violence is often a way to eliminate "the other."		
16. Fighting and violence are learned at home before these acts are taken to the streets.		
17. We can create peace only if we turn our will and energy **toward** efforts which preserve life and help meet people's most basic human needs instead of expending huge resources to prepare for war.		
18. We think that things will always be the way they are. Nobody really teaches us how to live with change.		

Developing An Informed Opinion

1. Write down an opinion about how conflict, violence, and/or efforts to make peace affect individuals, groups, and/or society.

   ## I think that _____

   _____

   _____

   For example, "I think that violent teens and adults learned as children at home that violence was an acceptable solution to problems and conflicts." or "People fight to get some power and control they don't have in other areas of their lives."

2. State three reasons for your opinion
   .

3. Cite evidence from experts, personal experience, research, specific facts and data, concrete examples and events that supports your reasons on the left.

1.	1.
2.	2.
3.	3.

4. Why would you want people to agree with your opinion?

    _____

    _____

    _____

5. Identify two arguments that people would use who disagree with your opinion.

6. What would you say in response to these arguments?

1.	1.
2.	2.

7. If everyone believed this opinion to be true how might it change people's behavior or the world we live in?

    _____

    _____

8. Create some questions which would help someone do more thinking about this issue:

    What would happen if_____?

    If everyone _____?

    What would you do if _____?

ACTIVITY 3: CONFLICT - YOU KNOW IT WHEN YOU SEE IT!

PURPOSE: Student volunteers will act out role-plays and the audience will describe what they observed. Afterwards students will write about a conflict they have observed or experienced.

LEARNING STRATEGIES: Role-plays, whole group discussion, paired dialogues, independent writing

TIME: One class period

MATERIALS: Handout 3:3A and 3:3B, pencils

SUGGESTED INSTRUCTIONS:

1. Invite six students to act out any of the role plays on **Handout 3:3A: "Conflict Role-Plays."** Read over the conflict scenarios with them, and discuss what they will say and do. Remind students that they are to role-play how a conflict worsens by name-calling, yelling, arguing, interrupting each other, etc. Have them act out the scenarios in front of class.

   Let the class audience know that their job is to describe the conflict after the students finish. Write each question on the board or newsprint and read it to the audience.
   - What is the conflict about? What are people arguing or fighting over?
   - What does each person want?
   - How do you know that there was a conflict?
   - What were the obstacles which prevented students from working out the conflict?

   Students involved in the role-plays need to let the audience know when they are ready to begin by saying, "Curtain." They let the audience know when they are finished by saying "Curtain" at the end.

2. When each pair finishes their role-play, read the questions and write student responses to questions on the board. Summarize their responses to each question.

3. Ask students to form pairs and talk about a conflict they've experienced that didn't get resolved or worked out the way they wanted it to. This is an active listening exercise, so remind students to give their partner full attention without interrupting while s/he is talking. Let students know they will each have about two minutes to talk.

✐ **Assessment:** Use **Handout 3:3B: "Observing a Conflict"** to help students practice describing interpersonal conflicts clearly.

Conflict Role-Plays

1A. You've heard that your friend has been talking about your boy/girl friend saying she/he's a loser and she/he cheats on you. You're ready to fight over this gossip whether it's true or not!

1B. You did say to one of your other friends that you didn't like her/his boy/girl friend very much. But you didn't start talking bad about her/him.

2A. You put your new jacket over your chair in class and left your desk to get a book. The student next to your seat tries on your jacket. You think he's/she's stealing it - you don't like anyone messing with your stuff!

2B. You've never seen a jacket like this before and you really like it. You want to try it on to see how it fits. You might even want to buy one just like it.

3A. You are walking four across down the hallway with your friends and someone bumps into you. You don't like this person. It's a good excuse to pick a fight.

3B. You're talking to your friend as you walk down the hall. You don't see this big group of kids coming the other way and you brush shoulders with a student you've had trouble with before.

4A. You are sure your sister has borrowed your headset again. You can't find it anywhere in the house.

4B. You borrowed your brother's headset. He wasn't home and you went next door to listen to a new tape with your friend. You come back to the house and your brother is ready to eat you alive.

5A. Your mom has set an 11:30 curfew for you on weekends. You want to be able to stay out later when there is something special that you are doing.

5B. You have reluctantly agreed to 11:30 curfew, but you are always worried when your son/daughter is out after dark. You don't even want to talk about curfews, and when the subject comes up, you start yelling and walk away.

139

OBSERVING A CONFLICT

1. HOW DO YOU KNOW THAT WHAT YOU SAW AND HEARD WAS A CONFLICT? _____

_____

2. BRIEFLY DESCRIBE WHAT HAPPENED (**THE FACTS**)_____

_____

_____

_____

3. WHO IS IT BETWEEN? _____

4. WHAT IS IT OVER? _____

5. WHAT IS THE PROBLEM FOR **A**? _____

_____

A FEELS_____**A** NEEDS _____

6. WHAT IS THE PROBLEM FOR **B**? _____

_____

B FEELS_____**B** NEEDS _____

7. HOW DID THE CONFLICT END? _____

_____

8. HOW COULD THIS CONFLICT HAVE ENDED DIFFERENTLY? _____

_____

_____

ACTIVITY 4: WRITING AND PERFORMING CONFLICT DIALOGUES

PURPOSE: Students will write conflict dialogues to perform and debrief with the whole class. These dialogues can also be use in conjunction with other activities in Chapters 3, 4, and 5.

LEARNING STRATEGIES: Independent writing, whole group discussion

TIME: One class period

MATERIALS: Handouts 3:4A and 3:4B

SUGGESTED INSTRUCTIONS:

1. Explain to students that the class will create a data bank of role-plays to use in problem-solving practice.

2. Use **Handout 3:4A** as a guide for writing role-plays in which the conflict escalates and worsens as the dialogue continues. Use **Handout 3:4B** as a guide for rewriting role-plays in which the characters resolve their conflict in a peaceful way that works for both characters.

✐ **Assessment:** Invite students to read their dialogues to the class. Ask students to choose a partner who will read dialogue with them. Give students a few minutes to rehearse. When students read their dialogues, let the audience know that their goal is to describe the conflict in 60 seconds or less after the dialogue has ended. This is good way to do a quick check to assess if students are able to get at the heart of a conflict and identify what's happening. Use these questions:

- What is the conflict about? What are people arguing or fighting over?
- What does each person want?
- What were the obstacles which prevented students from working out the conflict?

Conflict Dialogues (Part 1)

Write about a conflict you have observed or experienced (or make one up!). You will be writing a dialogue in which the characters say and do things that make the conflict worse. Before you write your dialogue, think about these questions.

Two people are fighting over/about _____

_____

Setting (time and place) _____

Character **A** (first name, age) _____

Character **B** (first name, age) _____

Which character is most upset? Why? _____

_____

What do the characters do and say that make each of them more

angry and ready to argue or fight? _____

_____

_____A: _____

_____B: _____

_____A: _____

_____B: _____

_____A: _____

_____B: _____

_____A: _____

_____B: _____

_____A: _____

_____B: _____

Conflict Dialogues (Part 2)

Rewrite your conflict dialogue. Only this time, your goal is to have the characters talk it through and work out the problem. Make sure they agree to a solution that is realistic and works for both of them!

Setting (time and place) _____

Character A (first name, age) _____

Character B (first name, age) _____

Which character takes the first step to try and solve the problem?

_____What does s/he say? _____

_____

The "Win-Win" Dialogue:

_____A: _____

_____B: _____

_____A: _____

_____B: _____

_____A: _____

_____B: _____

_____A: _____

_____B: _____

_____A: _____

_____B: _____

ACTIVITY 5: GETTING THE MESSAGE ABOUT CONFLICT

PURPOSE: Students will explore the messages they receive from families, school, and the larger culture about conflict and how to handle it.

LEARNING STRATEGIES: Paired dialogues, whole group discussion

TIME: 20 minutes

MATERIALS: None

SUGGESTED INSTRUCTIONS:

1. Explain to students that conflicts usually generate strong feelings within ourselves — even if the conflicts are different we often feel the same feelings. How we deal with conflict is linked to our perceptions of conflict and the messages we've received about conflict since we were young children.

   Ask students to think about the messages they have received about conflict from home, school, and the culture at large. What beliefs and attitudes do they have about conflict? For example, "Is conflict good or bad at home? How do people handle conflicts at home? Are there different rules for kids and grown-ups?" Ask students to share their reflections with a partner. Give each student one to two minutes to talk.

2. Then invite students to share messages, attitudes, and beliefs with the whole class.

   Teacher's Note: Some common messages and attitudes that we learn about conflict: In some families conflict is ignored — it's not polite to even bring it up. In other families, conflict is visible and chaotic all the time, with everyone fighting for her/himself. In still other families, conflict is accepted as part of everyday experience, and family members are encouraged to work things out openly and fairly.

Some people grow up thinking all conflict is bad, that conflict should be avoided at all costs. Others believe that conflicts provide the only way to "get your way," that using power over someone else is the way to win respect and get what you want. We have all experienced situations that quickly become "tests of wills" or contests of who's right and who's wrong. Our beliefs and attitudes about conflict will vary.

3. Continue the discussion by asking students to talk about some of the more common messages we receive about conflict from adults, the news, movies, music, and T.V. Students might bring up that T.V. provides endless examples of conflicts that are settled through violence.

They might also mention that many children are taught to hit and fight back if they feel they are wronged. Remind students that conflicts in themselves aren't necessarily negative — **it's how we choose to respond to a conflict that will have positive or negative consequences.**

You might also want to point out that not only do individuals receive different conflict messages, but cultural groups do too. In some Asian cultures, conflict is rarely dealt with directly or quickly. This contrasts sharply with an American conflict style which is often direct, confrontive, and expedient. Each style in its own culture can be effective; however, if groups don't understand that different styles are operating, misperception and miscommunication can make negotiations and problem solving much more difficult.

Activity 6 : Five Dimensions Of Conflict - An Overview

PURPOSE: Students are introduced to a framework for conflict analysis which describes five dimensions present in all conflict situations:

1. Conflicting Parties or Groups
2. Sources of Conflict
3. Relationships Among Conflicting Parities
4. History of the Conflict
5. Processes We Use to Deal With Conflict

Students will practice describing and analyzing conflicts using this framework.

Note: You may want to introduce the conflict analysis framework as a whole to your students as presented in this activity or choose to introduce various dimensions of conflict separately as they are presented in Activity 7.

LEARNING STRATEGIES: Reading for understanding, cooperative learning, small group brainstorming and critical thinking, whole class discussion, written analysis

TIME: Two class periods

MATERIALS: Handouts **3:6A** and **3:6B,** newsprint, markers, newspaper and magazine articles illustrating recent conflicts

SUGGESTED INSTRUCTIONS:

1. Cut out and make copies of brief articles from magazines and newspapers that illustrate a variety of conflicts among individuals and groups, within and between local communities, and conflicts in the national, international, and global arenas. Divide students into groups of three. Each group needs at least three articles, some markers, and a sheet of newsprint.

2. Explain to students that there are many dimensions or elements that are present in all conflicts. The goal of this activity is to make a "conflict map" that illustrates the common dimensions that are present in all of your conflict stories. Each group will use this process to complete the activity:
   - Read your conflict articles silently.
   - Jot down notes so that you can summarize your conflict to your group.
   - Do a "go-around" in which each group member summarizes the conflict.
   - Brainstorm the dimensions that were present in all three conflicts.
   - Draw your conflict map.

3. Post students' conflict maps on the board and compare and contrast their maps. Look for dimensions that all groups included.

4. Give each student a copy of **Handout 3:6A: "Five Dimensions of Conflict."** Review the handout by using examples from the conflicts that students read about. Highlight appropriate discussion points from the description which follows:

Five Dimensions of Conflict:

1. Conflicting Parties - Who / How Many Are Involved?

Internal — a conflict within oneself

Interpersonal — a conflict among two or more people

Intragroup — a conflict within a group (Groups can be institutions, organizations, any groups of people who share a specific role or identity)

Intergroup — a conflict among two or more groups

International — a conflict among two or more nations

Global — a conflict that directly or indirectly affects all people and nations in the world

2. Sources of Conflict - What's it Over?

Resources (human resources, things and capital, natural resources, land and territory) — People, groups, and nations competing for the same resources may want to take someone else's resources or prevent someone from getting needed resources.

Values and Beliefs (beliefs and values, choices and preferences)— People, groups, and nations may have relations with each other but have **different deeply held beliefs** about family, culture, politics, and religion. Conflicts over "what's most important" are the most difficult conflicts to resolve.

Psychological Needs (power and control, emotional needs) — All individuals and groups want respect, love, affirmation, approval, friendship, power over their own fates, a way to belong, and an opportunity to develop and achieve. When these needs aren't fulfilled, there's a conflict between individuals and the people and institutions which present obstacles to individuals getting what they need.

3. Relationships Among Conflicting Parties

The type of relationships among conflicting parties will often determine the intensity of the conflict and its outcome.

1. What kind of **climate** is present among conflicting parties?
   Trusting<--->Suspicious
   Friendly<--->Hostile
   Open<--->Resistant
   Calm<--->Emotionally Tense
   How can climate change the outcome?

2. Do parties come to the conflict with **equal power or a power imbalance**? Does any one party control the resources and decision-making process?

3. What is the **degree of interdependence** among the conflicting parties? (In other words, do the actions of one person or group seriously impact the others involved in the conflict?) Do the parties see each other every day or once a year? Is a positive relationship valued equally by both parties? Does each party need the cooperation of the other to achieve some important goals?

4. **How well do the parties know each other?** Does it matter? Does it matter if conflicting parties come from different cultures and neither knows much about the other?

4. History of the Conflict

Usually the longer a conflict exists, the more intense and complex it becomes -- and that much more difficult to resolve. Yet, there is also a point when parties can become so battle weary that they finally see some kind of resolution as the best strategy.

Factors which complicate conflict:

The **duration** of the conflict - How long has the conflict continued?

The **frequency** of the conflict - How often has the conflict reemerged? Are there periods when the conflict escalated to severe levels? Did this conflict develop in stages?

The **intensity** of the conflict - How life-threatening is the conflict? Is the conflict emotionally or ideologically charged? How does this affect possible solutions or resolution of the conflict?

The **perception** of the conflict - How do parties directly involved perceive the conflict? How do those who witness it but don't feel directly affected by it perceive the conflict? Do people "see" the conflict as one that impacts their lives, or is the conflict perceived as irrelevant to their well-being?

Conflicts can remain unresolved when there is little or no pressure to address them. If no one -- "inside" or "outside" the conflict -- perceives it to be compelling enough to resolve, the situation is not likely to change.

5. The Process: How Do We Choose to Deal With The Conflict?

In every conflict, all the parties involved **make choices to take some action** that they think will help them get what they want and need. These choices may be spontaneous or calculated, constructive or destructive. Conflicts can develop in stages and consequently may involve many different processes as the conflict proceeds. **When we experience conflict, we first make a choice to AVOID (withdraw, deny) or ENGAGE in the conflict situation.**

If we choose to engage we can:
1. CONFRONT or COMPETE;
2. ACCOMMODATE;
3. COMPROMISE;
4. Use COLLABORATIVE PROBLEM-SOLVING.
See Handout 3:9A: "Conflict Styles" for a more detailed description of each process.

✐ **Assessment:** Use Handout 3:6B: "Describing a Conflict" as a framework for exploring historical or current political/social conflicts or for analyzing key conflicts in a story, play, or novel.

FIVE DIMENSIONS OF CONFLICT

Every conflict has at least five dimensions. The more specifically you can identify and describe a conflict, the more effectively you can use your skills to manage or resolve it.

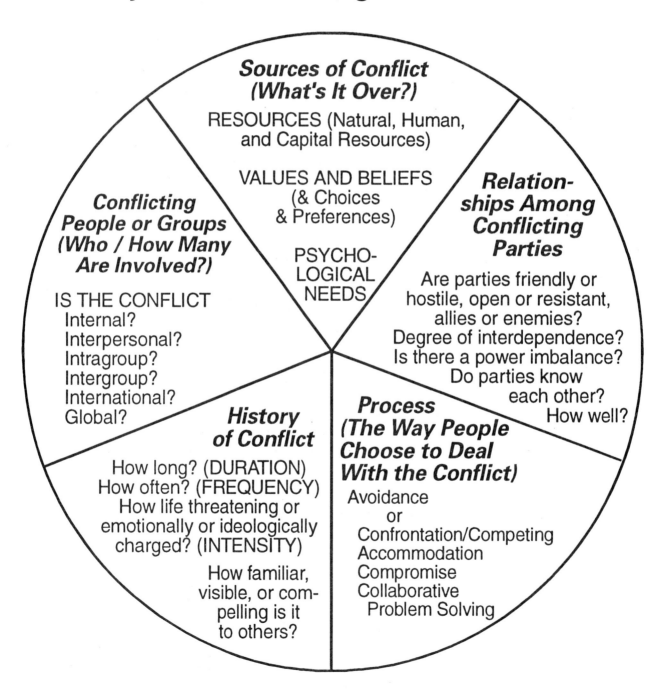

Sources of Conflict (What's It Over?)
RESOURCES (Natural, Human, and Capital Resources)
VALUES AND BELIEFS (& Choices & Preferences)
PSYCHOLOGICAL NEEDS

Relationships Among Conflicting Parties
Are parties friendly or hostile, open or resistant, allies or enemies?
Degree of interdependence?
Is there a power imbalance?
Do parties know each other?
How well?

Conflicting People or Groups (Who / How Many Are Involved?)
IS THE CONFLICT
Internal?
Interpersonal?
Intragroup?
Intergroup?
International?
Global?

History of Conflict
How long? (DURATION)
How often? (FREQUENCY)
How life threatening or emotionally or ideologically charged? (INTENSITY)
How familiar, visible, or compelling is it to others?

Process (The Way People Choose to Deal With the Conflict)
Avoidance
or
Confrontation/Competing
Accommodation
Compromise
Collaborative Problem Solving

DESCRIBING A CONFLICT

1. Describe the conflict in a phrase of five words or less----->	
2. How do you know that this is a conflict?------------------------>	
3. What type of conflict is it? (Internal <---> Global) -------->	
4. How many different parties / disputants are involved? -------->	
5. List the disputing parties ----->	
6. Describe their relationship Friendly<---> Hostile -------> Open <---> Resistant ------> Power Balance ----------------> Degree of Interdependence-> Knowledge of Each Other ->	
7. Identify the source(s) of the conflict (specific resources, values, needs?) ----->	

8. History of Conflict
 	
Duration (how long?)---------->
 	
Frequency (how often?)----->
 	
Intensity (how hot?)---------->
Visibility; significance to
    others not directly
    involved----------------->	

9. Process used (presently) to deal with conflict------------------>	
10. Source(s) for information--->	

1. What specific problem/issue seems most difficult to resolve?
2. What seems to be the major obstacle to resolution?
3. What would you suggest as a next step towards resolution of this conflict?

Activity 7: Dimensions of Conflict: A Closer Look

PURPOSE: Students are introduced to a framework for conflict analysis which describes five dimensions present in all conflict situations:
1. Conflicting Parties or Groups
2. Sources of Conflict
3. Relationships Among Conflicting Parities
4. History of the Conflict
5. Processes We Use to Deal With Conflict

Students will practice identifying, describing, and analyzing conflicts using this framework.

TEACHER'S NOTE: **Time, Materials,** and **Suggested Instructions** are listed separately for each lesson that highlights one dimension of conflict. Please refer back to **ACTIVITY 6** for detailed descriptions of each dimension of conflict. These lessons can easily be used for review or homework.

1. Conflicting Parties - Who / How Many Are Involved?

TIME: 30 minutes

MATERIALS: Handout 3:7A

SUGGESTED INSTRUCTIONS:

1. Generate a quick list of situations that produce conflict and disagreement. Ask students to think about conflicts at home, at school, in the neighborhood, on the news. Record the list on the board or newsprint.

2. Look at the list of conflicts, and identify the parties (disputants) involved in some of the conflicts. Ask students to categorize conflicts according to the parties involved. Write the six types of conflicts on the board (**Internal, Interpersonal, Intragroup, Intergroup, International, Global**). Refer back to the list that students generated, and identify types of conflicts using these categories.

3. Divide students into small groups and give each group one copy of **Handout 3:7A.** Have students take turns reading the paragraphs on handout. When the whole group has agreed on the category, the student who read the paragraph writes in the category on the blank line next to the letter. Check for agreement among different groups in a review discussion when students are finished. **Answers: A - Internal, B - Intragroup, C - Intergroup, D - Global, E - International, F - Interpersonal**

   ☞ **Going Further:** You might want to show slides, cartoons, or photographs that depict various conflicts and ask students to identify the type of conflict depicted.

2. Sources of Conflict - What's It Over?

TIME: 20 - 30 minutes for two class periods

MATERIALS: Handout 3:7B, pictures depicting conflict, tape, and staplers

SUGGESTED INSTRUCTIONS:

1. Go back to your original conflict list and ask students to identify sources of the conflicts listed. What is each conflict over? Typical responses might include RELIGION, LAND, MONEY, GIRLFRIENDS, WANTING THINGS YOU DON'T HAVE, CURFEWS, POLITICS, WHERE TO GO ON FRIDAY NIGHT. Ask students if they can group their responses into a few categories.

2. Write **Conflicts Over Resources**, **Conflicts Over Values and Beliefs**, and **Conflicts Over Psychological Needs** on the board. Review the meaning of these terms and solicit examples that match these categories (from students' list of conflicts, from their own experiences, from the media, etc.)

3. For homework, ask students to bring in pictures of conflicts or pictures in which they could imagine a conflict taking place.

4. Before the next class period, make copies of **Handout 3:6D Types and Sources of Conflict.** Cut apart symbols so that you have enough sets for each group of three or four students. Also, have extra magazines and conflict pictures available for students to use. Each group of students needs pictures and a pile of symbols. The class can share tape and/or staplers.

5. Write out the following directions on the board.
   A. Each student in the group needs to have one picture that shows a conflict.

   B. When your group agrees on what's happening in the picture, write a title and a brief description of the conflict the "Conflict Card" and attach it to the picture.

   C. Then find the symbols that identify the TYPE OF CONFLICT and the SOURCE OF CONFLICT in your picture. Attach these symbols to your picture.

   D. Use the same process with the other pictures.

6. Have students put their pictures on a board in the room and share their interpretations with the group. This is good exercise for working on the differences between observations, facts, assumptions, and opinions. Most of what students will say will be interpretations based on their assumptions and perceptions.

Ask students to distinguish between what they **observe** in the picture and what they **imagine** is happening in the picture. You might also explore what information would help students know more accurately what actually occurred in the picture.

☞Going Further: Use photographs and copies of book illustrations that depict conflicts as "Writing Starters." Laminate a set of photos and pictures to keep in your classroom for creative writing assignments.

3. Relationships Among Conflicting Parties
TIME: 20 minutes

MATERIALS: Handout 3:7C

SUGGESTED INSTRUCTIONS:

1. The kind of relationship among conflicting parties often shapes the outcome of the conflict. It matters whether people are friends or strangers, open- or close-minded. The goal of this activity is to think about how the qualities of a relationship affect the outcome of the conflict. Pass out **Handout 3:6E: "How Do Relationships Affect the Conflict?"**

2. Divide students into pairs and ask students to read the first two scenarios silently (or you can invite student volunteers to act out each scenario). Ask each pair to compare and contrast the relationships in both scenarios. Here are some guiding questions to consider for paired dialogues and whole class discussion:

   - How were both scenarios similar? different?

   - Which situation has a better chance for a positive outcome for both parties? Why?

   - What's the climate like in each scenario? Trusting<--->Suspicious, Friendly<--->Hostile, Open<--->Resistant, Calm<--->Emotionally Tense. How can climate change the outcome?
   - Do parties come to the conflict with equal power or a power imbalance? How might this affect what happens?

   - What is the degree of interdependence between the conflicting parties? (In other words, do the actions of one person or group impact on the other?) Do the parties see each other every day or once a year? Is a positive relationship valued equally by both parties? Does each party need the cooperation of the other to achieve some goals?

- Do parties know each other well, or not at all? Does it matter? Does it matter if conflicting parties come from different cultures and neither knows much about the other?

4. History of Conflict

TIME: One class period

MATERIALS: Markers, newsprint (optional: videotape of a recent or historical conflict)

SUGGESTED INSTRUCTIONS:

1. Show a videotape of a recent or historical conflict or choose to summarize a conflict familiar to students (a community, national, or international conflict).

2. As a class, **map a conflict history** that examines:
    The **duration** of the conflict

    The **frequency** of the conflict

    The **intensity** of the conflict

    The **perception** of the conflict

Put your **conflict history** on newsprint so that you can use it as a guide to examine other conflicts.

☞ **Going Further:** You might want to use photographs or mention examples that illustrate "invisible" conflicts — an adolescent sitting alone away from everyone else / children in a refugee camp in the Horn of Africa / a family that values politeness so much that no family members will bring up what's bothering them / gas- guzzling cars backed up on the highway. Conflicts are hard to identify when all parties are not present or when one party has ignored or withdrawn from the conflict. In these situations, the conflict remains even though it's hidden from view. Ask students to think about conflicts that at one time were not visible, familiar, or compelling to them. What raised their awareness?

5. The Processes We Use to Deal With Conflict (See Activity 8: "Responding to Conflict - What Do You Do?")

155

IDENTIFYING CONFLICTS: FROM INTERNAL TO GLOBAL

A._____

Anita was going to spend next Saturday with a friend just hanging around the house and then going to the mall. Another friend has just invited Anita to go to Six Flags for the day, and Anita doesn't have to pay for it. Anita wants to go to Six Flags, but she already made a promise to her other friend.

B._____

In your homeroom, there are a couple of kids who give the new immigrants from Mexico and Asia a hard time. They mimic their difficulty with English and begin teasing them when they walk in the door. The teacher has insisted that the whole class deal openly with their prejudices and deal with their differences.

C._____

A group of residents in the neighborhood does not want a new shopping center across the street from where they live. It will bring too much traffic into the neighborhood and put some local shops out of business. The developers insist that the new shopping area will be good for the community and increase the property values of their homes.

D._____

Every nation has different laws about fishing. Some countries use big drift nets to catch tuna, but these nets also trap a lot of birds and dolphins. Fishing practices affect life in the oceans and trade between countries. Many nations want all nations to agree to the same laws about what can be caught and where and how people can fish.

E._____

The U.S. wants Japan to stop dumping cars in the U.S. market at prices that are lower than comparable U.S. cars. Japan insists that they are practicing the "free trade" policies of the global market. U.S. workers think this practice is very unfair and want Japan to sell fewer cars or have the U.S. charge higher tariffs.

F._____

Chris's employer has a policy that three "lates" in a month and you're out. Chris had to stay late at school one day, had to take a friend to get his car last Tuesday, and today he had to take his brother to the dentist. He thought he'd be on time, but he's late for work again.

TYPES AND SOURCES OF CONFLICT

Title _____

Description of Conflict _____

Types of Conflict:

- INTERPERSONAL [BETWEEN 2 OR MORE PEOPLE]
- INTERNAL [WITHIN A PERSON]
- INTRAGROUP [WITHIN A GROUP]
- INTERPERSONAL [BETWEEN 2 OR MORE PEOPLE]
- INTERGROUP [BETWEEN 2 OR MORE GROUPS]
- INTERGROUP [BETWEEN 2 OR MORE GROUPS]
- INTERNATIONAL [BETWEEN 2 OR MORE NATIONS]
- INTERNATIONAL [BETWEEN 2 OR MORE NATIONS]
- GLOBAL [THE WHOLE WORLD IS AFFECTED]
- GLOBAL [THE WHOLE WORLD IS AFFECTED]
- HUMAN RESOURCES
- HUMAN RESOURCES

Sources of Conflict:

- THINGS AND CAPITAL — $$$
- NATURAL RESOURCES
- LAND AND TERRITORY
- BELIEFS AND VALUES — You're wrong!! / I'm right!!
- CHOICES AND PREFERENCES — I want to go........ / I like......... / I would rather... / I hate to...... / We don't like........
- POWER AND CONTROL — I'm ordering you to........
- EMOTIONAL NEEDS — RESPECT, LOVE, Friendship, We're #1!, SECURITY, A Feeling Of Belonging, I'm Okay

How Do relationships Among Conflicting Parties Affect The Conflict?

SCENARIO 1A

Roles: Mom and Perry, her 15-year-old son

Situation: Perry is asking for his allowance from Mom; he's already late for school. He needs his allowance right now because he already borrowed money from his best friend last week, and he promised to pay it back today. His friend will be very upset if he doesn't get the money.

Mom refuses to give Perry his allowance now because he had promised to clean up the yard, and he hasn't done it. She is furious with him for borrowing money.

SCENARIO 1B

Roles: Mom and Richard, her 15-year-old son

Situation: After Richard did the dinner dishes, he asked Mom if he could have his allowance two days early this week. He explained that he was making a down payment on a used set of drums from a friend. He didn't have quite enough money saved up to pay his friend half of the total cost. They had agreed that he would pay the rest at $3.00 a week. Other people are interested in drum set.

Richard plans ahead, so Mom is usually willing to work things out.

SCENARIO 2A

Roles: The chairperson of a school board and an angry citizen attending an open board meeting

Situation: The chairperson is trying to persuade citizens in the district to support a tax increase to support the schools. The citizen is very angry because a school board member was just indicted for embezzling funds and accepting bribes from a building contractor. The chairperson refuses to discuss the situation.

SCENARIO 2B

Roles: The school board chairperson, a parent who recently moved here from Korea, and a citizen (at a school board meeting) who wants to know why she needs to pay more taxes

Situation: Although the school district passed a tax increase two years ago, it cannot cover the costs of educating newly arrived students who are not fluent in English. The chairperson has invited "old" and "new" parents to speak in support of the tax increase.

SCENARIO 3A

Roles: Two trade representatives from the U.S. and Saudi Arabia, an important ally in the Gulf War and a major oil exporter to the U.S. They're friends.

Situation: Saudi Arabia wants to increase the amount of oil it exports to the U.S. ; the U.S. wants to reduce Saudi oil imports. However, the Saudis are willing to buy more defense weapons in return.

SCENARIO 3B

Roles: The Prime Minister of Gambia, a tiny, poor nation in Africa, and a U.S. trade representative. They're strangers.

Situation: The Prime Minister wants to sell more Gambia peanuts at a better price to the U.S. He wants the U.S. to lower their subsidies to American peanut farmers, which make U.S. peanuts much cheaper than Gambia's. (Peanuts are a major Gambia export.)

Activity 8: Responding To Conflict : What Do You Do?

PURPOSE: Students are first given an opportunity to identify and discuss how they respond to various conflict situations. Then students are introduced to the three most common responses to conflict - fight, flight, or problem-solving - through role-play presentations and whole group discussion.

LEARNING STRATEGIES: Independent reflection, small group dialogues, role-plays, and whole group discussion

TIME: One class period

MATERIALS: Handouts 3:8A and 3:8B, pencils

SUGGESTED INSTRUCTIONS:

1. Pass out a copy of **Handout 3:8A: "Responding To Conflict: What Do You Do?"** to each student. Read over the responses across the top of the page, and explain that students are to read each situation and check the response that they would most likely choose.

2. When students have finished filling out the sheet, divide into small groups of four or five. In a "go-around", ask each person to discuss one situation and explain why they chose a particular response.

3. Then, with the whole class, discuss the reasons why they are more likely to use different responses depending on the people and the situation.

4. Write **CONFRONTATION, AVOIDANCE,** and **PROBLEM SOLVING** on the board. Explain to students that the two most common responses to conflict are to **fight** (Confrontation) or **flight** (Avoidance). When we experience feelings of anger, fear, and anxiety, our bodies send us a message to either defend ourselves or run away to protect ourselves. Our preference for using one response more than the other is usually related to our attitudes about conflict and power. Give students time to write or talk about why people choose fight or flight responses.

   Explore the consequences of fighting or fleeing - the outcome usually brings an additional layer of feelings of tension, frustration, stress, hostility, anger, and resentment. Ask students why it's so tough to work through conflicts and reach solutions that satisfy all parties involved. Students will typically respond that it's too hard; it takes too much time; people don't know another way to work things out. Reliance on confronting and avoiding are hard habits to break.

159

Point out to students that the choice to resolve conflicts — through compromise and problem solving — are processes that all of us can learn.

5. Prepare three role-plays with another student or volunteer beforehand. On the board write Role-play #1_____, Role-play #2_____, and Role-play #3_____. Explain to students that you and your partner are going to play out the same conflict three times, using a different style of response each time. Pass out **Handout 3:8B: "Three Role-Plays."** Ask students to jot down their thoughts as they watch. Leave two or three minutes between each role-play so that students can write down their ideas. Don't discuss the role-plays until all three have been presented.

> **Read this role-play scenario to the class:**
>
> Alex is a pretty good student. Alex agreed to be partners for a social studies project with a friend, Jamie. Jamie is a popular kid but isn't always dependable. Even so, Alex was flattered that Jamie asked to work together. They have had two weeks to put together a presentation on the early civil rights movement of the 1960s.
>
> They had decided to play songs from the era while they would read selections from the writings of leaders of the movement. Each of them had selected three individuals to research. It's two days before the presentation, and Jamie is at Alex's house so they can get everything together. Alex has his/her stuff together. Jamie has forgotten the music s/he promised to bring and brought over only one book of writings of Martin Luther King, who wasn't even on Jamie's list of civil rights leaders. However, Jamie's Mom is getting some tapes and books tonight from a friend that they can use for the presentation.
>
> **Before class, rehearse the three role-plays on Handout 3:8A with a student who will act them out with you:**

6. **Debriefing with whole class:**
   In the debriefing, identify which type of response was used in each role-play, and discuss the questions on the handout. Some points to consider:

   - **Role-play #1:** Both people become so angry and defensive that there is no way to address the problem at hand and the work doesn't get done.

160

- **Role-play #2:** Alex never says how s/he feels, so that Jamie really doesn't know how frustrated s/he is. When Alex walks away, s/he gives up any control over the final outcome of the project but will probably be ready to blame Jamie if anything goes wrong.

- **Role-play #3:** Alex listens and doesn't discount Jamie's last-minute efforts. Alex's primary concern is finding the time to finish up project details so that they are completely prepared for class. Alex remained focused on this goal even when Jamie didn't hear his/her concerns at first. Alex also gave Jamie a way to "save face" and help participate in finding a solution that would work for both of them.

More Discussion Questions:

In each role-play, how is the perception and use of power different for each person?

Do people talk and listen differently depending on the conflict style they are using?

How does avoidance often lead to both parties losing?

If you really want to resolve a problem, choosing not to just get mad or get even, what are the key points that will help you get there?

RESPONDING TO CONFLICT: CHOOSING WHAT TO DO!

Check The Response That You Would Most Likely Choose In Each Situation	Argue to Get Your Own Way or Prove that You're Right	Deny There's A Problem or Walk Away If You Disagree	Do What Others Want or Quickly Compromise	Make a Trade-off or Talk It Through, Find a New Solution	Check It Out, Another Response?
1. Your mother insists that you go out with your family on Sunday night. You already have plans with a friend.					
2. Your best friend is always borrowing your tapes and never returns them.					
3. Your ride home from a party is too drunk to drive. This is the third time this has happened.					
4. You think your teacher has been unfair in grading an essay. Your grades are always lower than you expect.					
5. The same kid wants to start an argument with you again! You know you will both end up screaming.					
6. You and two friends have spent twenty minutes arguing about what movie to see. You've had enough.					
7. A friend wants to copy your math homework. It took you an hour and a half to do.					
8. Your friend, whose birthday is today, wants you to skip school and celebrate.					
9. As you pass by in the hall you know that two students who have class with you have just been talking about you.					
10. As you are talking to friends, someone passes by and stops. S/he thinks you just insulted her/him.					
11. Your boss at the store where you work is always criticizing you. Your work never seems to be good enough.					
12. Your Mom's really mad. Your were supposed to put the laundry in this morning and you forgot!					
13. Someone is making fun of your girlfriend/boyfriend. You're angry because this kid does this stuff all the time.					

Three Role Plays

Role-Play #1 Confronting/competing
Alex is angry when Jamie arrives empty-handed.

Alex: I knew this would happen! You never get stuff in on time. I should have known I couldn't count on you...

Jamie: Hey, I'm really sorry. But, look, tonight...

Alex: Tonight? Tonight is too late! You can't wait until the last minute if you want to do something right.

Jamie: Alex, just listen for a minute. My mom has got some tapes and stuff, and we can...

Alex: You don't have any idea how to do a project like this. I'll have to do it all myself, I can see that now.

Jamie: Come on, Alex. We can still work together.

Alex: What a loser! Why did I ever say I would work with you?

Jamie: If this how you're going to act, I wish I'd never asked you. You have to do it all your way, don't you?

Alex: Yeah, that's the only way it'll get done if I'm stuck with somebody who can't even...

Jamie: Quit saying...

Alex: Why can't you get yourself together?

Jamie: Shut Up!

Role Play #2 Avoidance/denial
Jamie: I forgot the music. I did bring this book. It's on Martin Luther King --well, he's not one of the people on my list, but my Mom says she can get some tapes and some other books from a friend and we can use them.

163

Alex: Well, that just leaves tomorrow, and I have to go to work at 4 o'clock. I guess we could work late tonight. When will your mother get the tapes and stuff?

Jamie: Oh, I can't do it tonight. But I'll get it together tomorrow. It'll work out okay.

Alex: Look, you take the outline and do whatever you want with it. I guess we'll see each other in class. I'm going upstairs now to work on something else.

Alex leaves.

Role Play #3 Collaborative problem solving

Jamie: I forgot the music. I did bring this book on Martin Luther King; I guess he's not on my list -- but my Mom says tonight she can get some tapes and some other books from a friend, and we can use them.

Alex: I'm glad your mom can get the stuff. I've got a problem, though. I changed my work hours to tomorrow so we could do this tonight. I'm really frustrated because now we don't have what we need to work now.

Jamie: Yeah, I should have asked my mom about this sooner. But I promise I'll get it all together for tomorrow.

Alex: This last-minute stuff may be okay with you, but it's not okay with me. I don't want to walk into class without having everything together, and this is my only time to work on it. I'm wondering what we could do...

Jamie: Yeah, I see what you're saying. Look, what if we go over the outline together now, and then when I get home I'll call you and we can fill in the details? Then maybe we could go over it quickly after school tomorrow.

Alex: Well, that sounds okay, but I'd need to get a ride to work...

Jamie: I'll take you and that will save some time. Would that work?

Alex: Yeah, thanks. Okay, let's get to it.

164

THREE ROLE-PLAYS

	ROLE-PLAY #1	ROLE-PLAY #2	ROLE-PLAY #3
What conflict style does Alex use?			
What did you *see* and hear that helped you decide the conflict style?			
What did Alex or Jamie say that: made the conflict worse?			
What did Alex or Jamie say that helped them work it out?			
How do you think Alex felt at the end of the role play?			
How do you think Jamie felt at the end of the role play?			
What were the consequences for each person at the end of the role play?			

ACTIVITY 9: A CLOSER LOOK AT CONFLICT STYLES

PURPOSE: Students will review five basic conflict styles and practice identifying conflict styles in various situations.

LEARNING STRATEGIES: Cooperative learning, whole group discussion

TIME: 30 minutes

MATERIALS: Handouts 3:9A and 3:9B, pencils

SUGGESTED INSTRUCTIONS:

Give each student copies of **Handout 3:9A: "Conflict Styles"** and Summarize the characteristics of each conflict style encouraging students to generate examples of each style. The first two rows in the handout are the most important to review. Be sure to encourage students to consider the value of each conflict style and explore when confrontation/competing and avoidance may be the best "tool" to use. Reassure students that there is never just one way to handle a conflict. The more comfortable they are using all styles, the more success they will experience getting what they need.

✐ **Assessment:** Pass out **Handout 3:9B: "What's Going On?"** to each pair of students. Have students work in pairs to identify which conflict style is used in each scenario. Remind pairs not to write in their responses until they both agree on the answer.

Answers: 1. Confronting 2. Compromise 3. Accommodation 4. Problem solving 5. Avoidance 6. Accommodation and avoidance 7. Problem solving 8. Problem solving. Discuss answers as a whole group.

↪Going Further: Ask students to create impromptu skits or write quick scripts of scenarios in which conflicting parties use various conflict styles. Present them to the class and have the audience guess the conflict style that they are using. Then ask for volunteers to replay the scene using a different conflict style. When each scene is finished, ask students how they felt at the conclusion of the scene. Did the outcome work equally well for both parties in each scene? Why or why not?

CONFLICT STYLES — HOW DO YOU RESPOND IN DIFFERENT SITUATIONS WITH DIFFERENT PEOPLE?

CONFLICT STYLE	TYPICAL BEHAVIORS	POTENTIAL USES	LIMITATIONS	SITUATIONS
AVOIDING Denying there's a problem Leaving well enough alone — Not addressing the conflict—Pretending nothing is wrong	*Withdrawing from the situation; leaving *Postponing dealing with the issue *Withholding feelings, opinions, information *The silent treatment *"I don't want to hear it"	*When confronting is too dangerous or damaging *When an issue is unimportant *When a situation needs to be cooled down *When you need more time to prepare a plan	The problem might never be addressed — Emotions may be "stuffed in" and explode later — An undercurrent of anger and resentment may simmer or spill over into other situations	
COMPETING AND CONFRONTING Hard bargaining — Might makes right — Getting what you want at another's expense — Using power to threaten — Win/Lose approach — Taking non-violent action to raise awareness or change power-balance	*Interrupting / Taking over *Dominating conversation *Discounting other people's ideas and feelings *Stereotyping others *Loud, judgmental, argumentative tone of voice *Concealing feelings and information/ keeping secrets *Verbal intimidation or physical violence	*When immediate action is needed for reasons of safety *When you believe in the absolute "rightness" of your action and can identify no other alternative	This style is intimidating — People become defensive quickly — It becomes hard for people to be open and straight — Emotions often heat up and conflict escalates	
ACCOMMODATING Soft bargaining — Yielding to another's point of view — Paying attention to other's concerns while neglecting your own	*Apologizing / Just say yes *Allowing yourself to be interrupted, stereotyped, discounted, used *Communicating feelings of defeat and resignation *Sounding indecisive	*When you think you've made a mistake or perceived the situation inaccurately *When "smoothing over" or future "credits" are more important	You may work hard to please everyone else and never get your own concerns addressed or your own needs met — Being "nice" or soft doesn't necessarily solve a problem	
COMPROMISING Splitting the difference — Each person wins some and loses some — My turn/Your turn	*Willing to talk about it *Interest in solving the problem and "getting it over with" *Willing to make trade-offs and deals	*When all else fails *For fast decision-making on minor issues *When strong parties are committed to mutually exclusive goals	You might "fix" the surface conflict but not deal with the underlying conflict — Larger issues, values, and feelings may be ignored — Parties may not be satisfied	
COLLABORATIVE PROBLEM-SOLVING Exploring sources of conflict — Generating alternatives — Finding a mutually satisfactory solution — Win/Win	*Taking initiative to solve problem *Directly stating feelings, needs, and wants *Exchange of information *Skillful communication	*Can enable resistant party to move towards solving problem *When long-term decisions must meet both parties' concerns and needs	Collaborative problem-solving requires time, some "good faith", mutual respect, and effective communication skills —It's hard work	

167

WHAT'S GOING ON?

With your partner, decide which conflict style is being used in each situation:

Confrontation   Avoidance   Accommodation

Compromise   Collaborative Problem Solving

1. _____ You start screaming at your sister who's been on the phone for an hour and a half. You slam the phone down in her face.

2. _____ Your committee is having a hard time deciding on the band for a dance. You decide to have a D.J. instead who will play a variety of music. Most people wanted a band.

3. _____ You always know the answers and the questions in your history class. Some of your friends hate that, so you've decided to play dumb every other day.

4. _____ Your Mom is upset because you stayed out after your midnight curfew. You don't get mad; instead, you ask if you can talk about this tomorrow when she's not so tired. You Mom agrees to do this.

5. _____ Two students are talking in the bathroom about someone you know but don't know well. You know what they are saying is untrue. You go about your business and leave.

6. _____ Your parents are concerned about your grade in math. You really don't understand what's going on in class, but they think the problem is you're not spending enough time doing your homework. You agree and go upstairs to doodle around math problems that you can't solve.

7. _____ You are Mexican-American. You notice that there is not one piece of Latino literature in your American Literature book. Your write a note to your teacher and ask to discuss this with her.

8. _____ A guy keeps harassing you in the halls. You tell him how angry you are when he calls you a babe and leers when you don't even know him. You tell him you want to go to mediation about this.

Activity 10: Using Your Conflict Toolbox

PURPOSE: This activity helps students to become more familiar with a large repertoire of "tools" and choices they can make when they experience interpersonal conflict. Students work in pairs as they practice talking through the choices they would make in various conflict situations.

LEARNING STRATEGIES: Cooperative learning, whole group discussion, personal reflection, role-play demonstrations

TIME: One class period

MATERIALS: Handouts 3:10A, 3:10B, 3:10C, and 3:10 D, pencils

SUGGESTED INSTRUCTIONS:

1. Ask students to brainstorm 10 to 15 responses (in two minutes) that they can use to work out a conflict or solve a problem peacefully without fighting or hurting someone's feelings.

2. Pass out **Handout 3:10A: "The Conflict Toolbox"** as a reminder of all the "tools" we have available to use when we experience conflict. You might want to enlarge this to poster size to hang in the classroom or have students create another version of this to display.

3. Divide students into pairs. Describe a conflict situation, and give pairs 60 seconds to agree on one "tool" they would use to work out the conflict constructively. Ask students to share their reasons for choosing one response over another. Use conflict situations on **Handout 3:10B: "What Would You Do and Say When_____?"** and make up your own using conflict situations that are typical among your students.

   Choose to discuss the situations that you think will have the most varied responses. Encourage students to consider how context easily alters choices. It matters whether something has happened for the first time or the fifth time. It makes a difference if a "someone" is a friend or a stranger.

4. Use **Handout 3:10C: "In What Situation Would You....?"** for more practice. Have students work in pairs to brainstorm situations in which they would use various responses on the handout. Then form groups of two pairs to discuss their responses. Ask students to check if pairs chose similar situations. Encourage students to ask each other questions which help them better understand their responses.

✐**Assessment:** Use **Handout 3:10D: "Choosing the Best Conflict Tool"** to assess students' thinking about choices they can make when they experience conflict. Use **Handout 3:10A: "The Conflict Toolbox"** with this activity. Ask each pair or small group to choose five situations they want to think about. Students need to read each situation and talk it through so that the group agrees on the conflict tool that they want to use. Discuss students' responses as a whole class afterward. You may want to extend this activity by exploring solutions for each situation.

As an alternative, students can complete this activity on their own and choose one conflict situation to discuss in detail, responding to these questions:

1. What are the consequences of doing nothing?
2. What are the consequences of arguing or fighting it out?
3. What are the reasons for the choice you made? How will it help you solve the problem?
4. What are two solutions or agreements that might work with this problem?
5. How do you think the other people involved will feel about this solution?

↻**Going Further:** Extend the activity by inviting students to role-play some of the conflict situations using different tools.

Handling conflict skillfully means choosing the best tool for the situation you're in. You always have choices!

THE CONFLICT TOOLBOX

SHARE

TAKE TURNS

SAY, "I'M SORRY"

LISTEN, PARAPHRASE, REFLECT

IGNORE IT AND WALK AWAY

ASK QUESTIONS

MAKE A REQUEST

ASK FOR HELP

COMPROMISE

CHECK IT OUT

OFFER HELP

SAY HOW YOU FEEL AND WHAT YOU NEED

TALK IT OUT AND PROBLEM SOLVE

TAKE RESPONSIBILITY AND FIX IT

AGREE TO DISAGREE

WHAT WOULD YOU SAY AND DO WHEN_____?

_____ 1.   The kid behind you in class keeps rapping his pencil on your chair.

_____ 2.   Your Mom is yelling at you because you haven't done your job of cleaning up the living room. Some of the mess is your sister's.

_____ 3.   Your teacher is aggravated that your homework isn't done for the third straight day. She's given up and says, "Forget it. You probably can't do it anyway."

_____ 4.   Someone has taken your textbook off your desk. Class is about to begin.

_____ 5.   Your locker partner has used the entire floor of the locker for her clothes, coats, and stuff that she never takes home.

_____ 6.   Your friend's family is violent and abusive. She's crying in the bathroom.

_____ 7.   Someone you don't like calls you a "retard."
            A friend who wants you to hurry up calls you a "retard."

_____ 8.   Your friend who picks you up every morning has been late twice this week. Yesterday, you got to class five minutes late and missed a test.

_____ 9.   A boy is hurling a sexual insult your way.
            A girl is openly flirting with you in front of your friends.

_____ 10. Someone is pushing her/his way down the hall. He/she bumps into you, and you accidentally push someone into the wall.

_____ 11. Your sister has worn your favorite sweater again without asking.

_____ 12. You don't know how to do the algebra problems, and you got a D on the last test.

_____ 13. A rumor about you is going around. It's not true, and you are now facing one of the kids who started the rumor.

_____ 14. Someone asks you to come to a party. You know there will be plenty of drugs and alcohol and no adults. Your parents trust you to be safe.

_____ 15. One of your friends uses racial and ethnic slurs in her conversation all the time. Other kids, including students of other races, have overheard her.

_____ 16. You're worried that this bully in class will make fun of you because you like school and get good grades.

_____ 17. You're grounded the same week you have tickets for a favorite music group.

IN WHAT SITUATION WOULD YOU ____ ?

1.	*Ignore it and move on.* *Make an excuse and move on.*	
2.	*Make the quick apology.* "Sorry, didn't mean to do that." "Sorry, it won't happen again. I guess we got in each other's way."	
3.	*Just say no.* "No. I don't do that." "No. I'm not interested." "I don't like it when you_____. I want you to stop_____now."	
4.	*Use surprise or humor.* "Really! I didn't know that about myself." "You're right. It's a tough world out there." "No kidding! I'm going to have to check this out."	
5.	*State your feelings and let the other person think about it.* "I feel _____when you_____ because _____."	
6.	*Ask a focus question.* "What do you need?" "What can you do about it right now?" "What would you like to change?"	
7.	*Ask for help.* "Can you help me out with this? I need_____." "I can't find my _____. Can you help me look for it?" "This is a mess. Can you help me clean it up?"	
8.	*Problem solve.* "Can we talk about this so we can work it out?" "Can we figure out a way to solve this together?" "Do you want to try to talk this through?" "Let's negotiate a plan that we can both agree with."	
9.	*Agree to disagree.* "We don't agree about this. Let's drop it and talk about it later." "I'm too mad to talk about it now. Let's talk later."	

Choosing the Best ``Conflict Tool``

I can solve this on my own.	I need to work this out with others.	The CONFLICT TOOL I would choose to use is_____	Here's the situation:
			1. The kid behind you in class keeps banging his foot on your chair.
			2. Your Mom is yelling at you because you haven't done your job of cleaning up the living room. Some of the mess is your sister's.
			3. I have only three hours to do my homework, cook dinner, and get all my laundry together, and I still want to watch my favorite TV show.
			4. Someone has taken your textbook off your desk. Class is about to begin.
			5. It's 9 p.m. Saturday night. I suddenly remember that tomorrow is Mother's Day. I haven't gotten my mom a present yet.
			6. Your locker partner has used the entire floor of the locker for her clothes, coats, and stuff that she never takes home.
			7. I'm baby-sitting for my sister until 4 p.m. My friend calls and asks me to go to the movies, but I would need to leave at 3:30 p.m.
			8. Your teacher is angry that your homework isn't done for the third straight day. She's given up and says, "Forget it. You probably can't do it anyway."
			9. You need to have your part in a play memorized in two days. You just found the script that you lost. How are you going to practice your lines?
			10. You don't know how to do the math problems, and you got a D on the last test.
			11. Someone asks you to come to a party. You know there will be plenty of drugs and alcohol and no adults. Your parents trust you to be safe.
			12. You want to buy a new sweat suit for $25, but you only have $18.

Activity 11: Writing Conflict Stories With Solutions That Work

PURPOSE: Students will write stories after choosing conflict response cards which describe various ways that the characters will work out their conflict.

LEARNING STRATEGIES: Independent writing

TIME: 30 minutes to one class period

MATERIALS: Handouts 3:11A and 3:11B, pencils

SUGGESTED INSTRUCTIONS:]

1. Cut out the cards on **Handout 3:11A** and put them in a basket. Let each student pick a card.

2. Then pass out copies of **Handout 3:11B: "Writing Conflict Stories With Solutions That Work"** to each student. Students use their cards as a guide for how characters in their story will work out their conflict. You may want to give students the option of trading cards with each other.

3. Invite students to read their stories to the class. This might also serve as a quick check to see if the audience is able to 1) describe the conflict, 2) identify the conflict tool that the characters used, and 3) identify the solution the characters chose.

Listen to the other person who is really upset. S/he feels much better after talking it through.

Take turns.

The two characters brainstorm solutions to a problem until they reach a WIN/WIN solution they both feel good about.

One of your characters really goofed and made a mistake. This character accepts responsibility for the mess and fixes things up.

One character shares what she has with the others even though it means less for everyone, including the one who is willing to share.

The character who has the problem goes off by himself, thinks over the problem, and solves it on his own.

After a heated conversation both characters agree to disagree.

The character who is really upset tells the other person how he feels and what he needs.

The character with a problem decides that it's too big to handle by herself. So she gets help from a grown-up to solve it.

The characters flip a coin to decide what they're going to do.

These characters are involved in a conflict with group of kids. They all decide to talk it through until they reach a decision that everyone agrees with.

These characters are members of the same family. They all have "family meeting" to decide what to do.

One of your characters is so upset that he needs to cool off his anger first and then try to work it out.

You're in the middle of something you didn't start and you don't feel very safe. You walk away before anything bad happens.

One of your characters says, "I'm sorry, I didn't mean it." The other character accepts the apology.

Both of your characters decide that what they are arguing about is not that big a deal, so they "let it go".

Your characters have a misunderstanding. One of them is willing to "check it out" and ask questions so they can clear up the confusion.

Your characters agree to compromise or make a trade-off.

One of your characters decides to just come out and ask for what she needs. And it turns out okay.

Your characters agree to solve the problem and together they come up with a new solution they hadn't thought of before.

One of your characters is a great listener. He helps his friend just by listening, paraphrasing, and reflecting feelings.

One of your characters makes a choice to say, "No!" because he is being asked to do something that he knows is wrong.

One character helps to "cool down" two of his friends who are ready to fight.

One character admits what she said was a lie and offers to "put things right".

Writing Conflict Stories With Solutions That Work

Name _____

How do people work out this conflict? (Look at your card) _____

_____

_____

Who are your characters? (Name, age, description)

1._____

2._____

What incident or issue sparked the conflict? What are people disagreeing

about or fighting over? _____

_____

What does each character need?_____

_____

What solution do your characters agree to? _____

_____

Begin writing your story here:

Continue your story on the back.......

Chapter 4: Resolving Interpersonal Conflict

Activity 1:   Does Conflict Have to Be a Contest?

Activity 2:   Obstacles to Resolving Conflict

Activity 3:   What's the Big Deal About Communication?

Activity 4:   The Power of Listening

Activity 5:   What is Active Listening?

Activity 6:   Someone Knows You're Listening When

Activity 7:   Giving and Receiving Feedback

Activity 8:   From the Other Person's Perspective

Activity 9:   Practicing the Art of "I-Speak"

Activity 10: The Problem Solving Process

Activity 11: Learning How to Negotiate

ACTIVITY 1: Does Conflict Have to Be a Contest?

PURPOSE:

1. Students will explore the advantages and disadvantages of competitive and cooperative strategies for solving problems.
2. Students will distinguish differences between Win-Lose, Lose-Lose, and Win-Win outcomes when faced with a conflict situation.

LEARNING STRATEGIES: Interactive exercise, group discussion, cooperative learning

TIME: 30 minutes

MATERIALS: Bag of Hershey Kisses, **Handout 4:1**

SUGGESTED INSTRUCTIONS:

1. Students will play the game called **"Kisses"** to explore the ideas of competition and cooperation. Have two students of approximately the same strength and size sit across each other at a desk. Explain that each student will be representing half the class in this game. Position students so that their right or left elbows are on the desk and they are clasping each other's hands. (This is an arm wrestling position but *don't use this term*; if kids use the term, explain that it's similar, but the rules are different.

2. The object of the game is for both students to get as many chocolate kisses as possible for their teams in the time allowed.
   The rules are as follows:

   - Once the game has begun, the two players may not talk.
   - Every time the back of one player's hand touches the desk, the other player will receive a chocolate kiss for his/her team.
   - Someone from each team needs to keep track of the number of kisses the team receives.

   Say "Begin," and allow thirty seconds for students to play.

3. Students will automatically compete against each other and will probably only get a few kisses. Discuss what happened.
   - What did you see?
   - How many kisses did each team receive?
   - Why didn't you get a lot of kisses?
   - What was the goal of the game? Did you succeed?

4. Ask students if they can think of another way to play the game so that each team can get enough kisses for everyone. Have students whisper to

you how they might play it differently. When you find a student who suggests that each person take turns without resisting, have that person explain the idea—still whispering—to a person on the other team.

5. Let them try again, allowing thirty seconds. This time, each team will probably receive enough kisses for everyone. Discuss what happened.
   - What was different this time?
   - Did you achieve the goal of the game?

6. Ask students to compare the two strategies that students used. Students will often interpret what they saw the first time as *a struggle against* each other. Explain that this was a competitive Win-Lose strategy. They will use words and phrases like *cooperation* and *working together* to describe the second approach. Explain that this was a cooperative Win-Win strategy. Explore the differences between competition and cooperation. Think about other situations in which we compete without thinking whether it will get us what we want or need.

7. Explain that the two strategies, Win-Lose and Win-Win, are the same strategies we often use when faced with conflicts or problems.

   - Think of situations in which the result was Win-Lose. How did it feel when you were the winner? the loser? (If situations are framed as Win-Lose, are there usually more winners or losers?)

   - Are there some situations that seem to be Win-Lose but turn out to be Lose-Lose? (Fights and screaming matches are the most common examples).

   - Win-Win outcomes are possible when both parties agree to work out the problem in a way that they both get something important that they need and both feel good about the solution that they've chosen. Generate examples of Win-Win outcomes that students have experienced. How was this experience different than a Win-Lose experience? How did you and the other person feel afterwards?

Going Further:

1. Divide students into pairs and give each pair **Handout 4:1: "Win or Lose-It's Your Choice."** Explain that each pair should choose three situations and write down three possible outcomes for each situation they have chosen - a Win-Win, Win-Lose, and Lose-Lose outcome. Do an example before students work on their own.

2. Share responses with the whole class.

Assessment:
Invite students to write about two situations where competition works best and two situations where cooperation works best.

"KISSES" adapted from *Day of Dialogue*, Educators For Social Responsibility
"WIN OR LOSE: IT'S YOUR CHOICE" adapted from *Elementary Perspectives*, William J. Kreidler

184

Win or Lose - It's Your Choice!

1. Tonya wants to use the phone. Her sister, Lisa, has been on the phone for over an hour.
2. Juan calls Cho Min a name in the hall. Cho Min is hurt and mad.
3. You don't know how to do a very important homework assignment. If you don't get it in you know your teacher will call home.
4. A friend who drove you to a party is now drunk.
5. Mom wants Scott to unload the dishwasher. He'd rather do anything but that!
6. Your parents want you to go visit Grandma. You've already made plans to go to the movies with two of your friends.
7. Kim got mad at Ceil for not inviting her to a party, but Kim didn't say anything to Ceil. Ceil doesn't know why Kim is giving her the silent treatment.

Situation #_____

WIN -LOSE
LOSE-LOSE
WIN-WIN

Situation #_____

WIN -LOSE
LOSE-LOSE
WIN-WIN

Situation #_____

WIN -LOSE
LOSE-LOSE
WIN-WIN

Activity 2: Obstacles to Resolving Conflict

PURPOSE: Students will identify the most common obstacles to resolving conflicts in ways that promote Win-Win solutions. They will generate ideas for overcoming these obstacles.

LEARNING STRATEGIES: Paired and group brainstorming, group discussion

TIME: 30 minutes

MATERIALS: Newsprint, markers

SUGGESTED INSTRUCTIONS:

1. Begin by asking students to pair up and brainstorm a list of attitudes, behaviors, and other factors that make it difficult to deal constructively with conflict and block the possibility of Win-Win solutions.

2. Make a chart on the board or on newsprint as illustrated below. Write a list of obstacles that students discussed in pairs. Then, next to each obstacle write in students' suggestions for first steps which could help parties overcome the obstacles which make it difficult to handle conflict effectively. Some examples:

OBSTACLES	FIRST STEPS TO OVERCOME OBSTACLES
Refusal to acknowledge that there's a problem	Be willing to talk it over and agree on what the problem is
Determination not to compromise; goal is "I win; you lose!"	Agree that both parties need to get something from the agreement
Impatience	Set aside enough time to talk it out
Failure to consider how other party feels	Let each party say how they feel
Suspicion of other party's motives	Take time to get to know other party
Lack of information; assumptions	Exchange information; ask questions
Refusal to listen; interrupting	Practice active listening skills

3. Remind students that the most frequent obstacles that people mention are :
   a. Inability to express feelings appropriately or manage anger
   b. Poor communication skills
   c. Lack of problem-solving tools and systematic processes for working out conflicts.

ACTIVITY 3: What's the Big Deal About Communication?

PURPOSE: Communication is *the* critical foundation for managing conflict and solving problems. Students will participate in several quick exercises which illuminate the importance of effective communication.

LEARNING STRATEGIES: Demonstrations, interactive exercises, group discussion

TIME: One class period

MATERIALS: Chalk board and flip chart stand, markers, paper, pencils

SUGGESTED INSTRUCTIONS:

1. Begin by making a web chart with this question in the center of the chart: "Why Do We Listen?" Generate responses from the group. Extend the discussion by raising these questions:
   - When is it hard for you to listen? What makes it hard to listen?
   - When is it easy for you to listen? What makes it easier to listen?
   - How do you listen differently in different situations?

2. Do a demonstration of "Mirroring (With a Glitch!)." Ask a student to be your partner in a mirroring exercise. First, you make slow movements and motions which your partner follows as closely as possible to make a mirror image. Do this for about a minute. Then, let the student know that it's their turn to go first and your turn to follow the student's movements and motions. But, *you don't follow the motions exactly* as your partner would expect you to do. Instead you make up your own motions; you look like you are intending to follow the person, but you're doing something else! This is very disconcerting for your partner.

   When a minute is up, ask your partner how s/he felt when you did not follow. Point out that this is similar to what we experience in conversations when one person is not following what the other says. Ask students to brainstorm what they can say and do that would help them follow the other person in conversation. Following means being able to read facial expressions and body language as well as practicing effective verbal communication skills.

3. Have several pairs of students practice "Mirror Drawing." Have the first two students stand at chalk boards or chart stands where they cannot see each other. Ask one person to make a very simple drawing using geometric shapes like those on the next page:

187

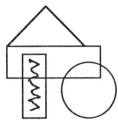

The objective of the exercise is for the student who is the **messenger** to give the student who is the **receiver** verbal directions so that s/he can make an identical copy of the original drawing without seeing the original. As the first student draws, ask her or him to give directions step by step. The one rule is that the **receiver** cannot ask questions or talk back. When the first person has finished the original drawing, check out how the copy compares with the original.

Ask students what made it hard or easy to copy the drawing. Most students will say that directions weren't specific enough. Ask the audience what directions they might have changed along the way. Students will also suggest that it would have been much easier if the **receiver** could have asked questions and both people could have talked to slow down the directions, check for understanding, repeat, etc.

Students can all practice **"Mirror Drawing"** in pairs at desks sitting back to back; or students can face each other across a desk or table and use cardboard barriers to prevent partners from seeing each other's drawings. When students finish their drawings, remind them to give each other feedback about directions and clarifying questions.

Ask students how this exercise demonstrates some basic principles of communication. The following description is one way to explain the communication process.

> **Communication is always a two-way process, but it can get muddled at four points along the way:**
>
> 1. **The messenger forms an idea of what s/he wants to say.** If the message is confusing from the beginning it will be hard for the receiver to understand it.
>
> 2. **The messenger puts the idea into words and sends the message (verbally and nonverbally) to the receiver.** The messenger may have trouble finding the right words to convey the message. What the messenger really means may not clearly expressed in what the messenger actually says.
>
> 3. **The receiver receives and interprets the message.** The receiver may interpret the words s/he hears differently from what the messenger intended.

4. The receiver gives verbal feedback to let the messenger know that s/he has understood the message. The receiver may have trouble finding the right words that show that s/he understood the message or not know how to show that s/he understood in a way that makes sense to the messenger.

✐ **Assessment:** Invite students to recall or write about experiences where the message got muddled during the communications process, and ask them to identify at what point communication broke down.

Or, watch a sit-com video clip and identify communication breakdowns.

ACTIVITY 4: The Power of Listening

PURPOSE: Students will listen to a story which illuminates the power of listening and then discuss and write their reactions to the story.

LEARNING STRATEGIES: Listening, written reflection

TIME: One class period

MATERIALS: Handout 4:4

SUGGESTED INSTRUCTIONS:

1. Read **Handout 4:4: "A Story About the Power of Listening."** to the class. It is much more effective for students to hear this story than to read it themselves. The story is about an encounter among people on a subway in Japan in which one passenger diffuses the dangerous anger of a man by listening and responding with an open heart and unconditional regard for a person in trouble.

2. When you have finished reading the story, have students write their reactions before you discuss the story with them. You might suggest these questions:
   * What is your personal reaction to the story?
   * Did anything surprise you about the outcome? What made the story unusual or powerful?
   * How are you like the young Aikido student? How are you like the old man? How are you like the angry laborer?
   * What do you think is the lesson or message of the story?
   * Why is it harder to listen than to physically react?
   * Did the story remind you of any experiences you have had?

3. Discuss students' reactions to the story and their reflections about listening.

A Story About The Power Of Listening

The train clanked and rattled through the suburbs of Tokyo on a drowsy spring afternoon. Our car was comparatively empty--a few housewives with their kids in tow, some old folks going shopping. I gazed absently at the drab houses and dusty hedge groves.

At one station the doors opened, and suddenly the afternoon quiet was shattered by a man bellowing violent, incomprehensible curses. The man staggered into our car. He wore laborer's clothing, and he was big, drunk, and dirty. Screaming, he swung at a woman holding a baby. The blow sent her spinning into the laps of an elderly couple. It was a miracle that the baby was unharmed.

Terrified, the couple jumped up and scrambled toward the other end of the car. The laborer aimed a kick at the retreating back of the old woman but missed as she scuttled to safety. This so enraged the drunk that he grabbed the metal pole in the center of the car and tried to wrench it out of its stanchion. I could see that one of his hands was cut and bleeding. The train lurched ahead, the passengers frozen with fear. I stood up.

I was young then, some twenty years ago, and in pretty good shape. I'd been putting in a solid eight hours of Aikido training nearly every day for the past three years. I liked to throw and grapple. I thought I was tough. The trouble was, my martial skill was untested in actual combat. As students of Aikido, we were not allowed to fight.

"Aikido," my teacher had said again and again, "is the art of reconciliation. Whoever has the mind to fight has broken his connection with the universe. If you try to dominate people, you are already defeated. We study how to resolve conflict, not how to start it."

I listened to his words. I tried hard. I even went so far as to cross the street to avoid the *chimpira*, the pinball punks who lounged around the train stations. My forbearance exalted me. I felt both tough and holy. In my heart, however, I wanted an absolutely legitimate opportunity whereby I might save the innocent by destroying the guilty.

"This is it!" I said to myself as I got to my feet. "People are in danger. If I don't do something fast, somebody will probably get hurt."

191

Seeing me stand up, the drunk recognized a chance to focus his rage. "Aha!" he roared. "A foreigner! You need a lesson in Japanese manners!"

I held on lightly to the commuter strap overhead and gave him a slow look of disgust and dismissal. I planned to take this turkey apart, but <u>he</u> had to make the first move. I wanted him mad, so I pursed my lips and blew him an innocent kiss.

"All right!" he hollered. "You're gonna get a lesson." He gathered himself for a rush at me.

A fraction of a second before he could move, someone shouted "Hey!" It was earsplitting. I remember the strangely joyous, lilting quality of it--as though you and a friend had been searching diligently for something, and he had suddenly stumbled upon it. "Hey!"

I wheeled to my left; the drunk spun to his right. We both stared down at a little, old Japanese man. He must have been well into his seventies, this tiny gentleman, sitting there immaculate in his kimono. He took no notice of me, but beamed delightedly at the laborer, as though he had a most important, most welcome secret to share.

"C'mere," the old man said in an easy vernacular, beckoning to the drunk. "C'mere and talk with me." He waved his hand lightly.

The big man followed, as if on a string. He planted his feet belligerently in front of the old gentleman, and roared above the clacking wheels, "Why the hell should I talk to you?" The drunk now had his back to me. If his elbow moved so much as a millimeter, I'd drop him in his socks.

The old man continued to beam at the laborer. "What'cha been drinkin'?" he asked, his eyes sparkling with interest.

"I been drinkin' sake," the laborer bellowed back, "and it's none of your business!" Flecks of spittle spattered the old man.

"Oh, that's wonderful," the old man said, "absolutely wonderful!" "You see, I love sake too. Every night, me and my wife (she's seventy-six, you know), we warm up a little bottle of sake and take it out into the garden, and we sit on an old wooden bench. We watch the sun go down, and we look to see how our persimmon tree is doing.

My great grandfather planted that tree, and we worry about whether it will recover from those ice storms we had last winter. Our tree has done better than I expected, though, especially when you consider the poor quality of the soil. It is gratifying to watch when we take our sake and go out to enjoy the evening--even when it rains!" He looked up at the laborer, eyes twinkling.

As he struggled to follow the old man's conversation, the drunk's face began to soften. His fists slowly unclenched. "Yeah," he said. "I love persimmons, too. . . . " His voice trailed off.

"Yes," said the old man, smiling, and I'm sure you have a wonderful wife."

"No," replied the laborer. "My wife died." Very gently, swaying with the motion of the train, the big man began to sob. "I don't got no *wife*, I don't got no *home*, I don't got no *job*. I'm so *ashamed* of myself." Tears rolled down his cheeks; a spasm of despair rippled through his body.

Now it was my turn. Standing there in my well-scrubbed youthful innocence, my make-this-world-safe-for-democracy righteousness, I suddenly felt dirtier than he was.

Then the train arrived at my stop. As the doors opened, I heard the old man cluck sympathetically. "My, my," he said, "that is a difficult predicament, indeed. Sit down here and tell me about it."

As the train pulled away, I sat down on a bench. What I had wanted to do with muscle had been accomplished with kind words. I had just seen Aikido tried in combat. I would have to practice the art with an entirely different spirit. It would be a long time before I could truly speak about the resolution of conflict.

From *How Can I Help?* by Ram Dass

Activity 5: What Is Active Listening?

PURPOSE: Students will identify poor and good listening and responding skills and then practice "active" listening.

LEARNING STRATEGIES: Demonstration, group discussion, paired skill practice

TIME: 30 minutes

MATERIALS: Handout 4:5

SUGGESTED INSTRUCTIONS:

1. Begin by asking students to think about why we listen. Examples: We listen for instructions, to understand a person's feelings and point of view, to get information that we need, to help another person, to learn about other people and the world, to entertain ourselves, etc.

2. Do a demonstration of poor and good listening skills. Explain to students that you want them to observe you, the teacher, in a conversation with another student. Ask students to look for things you do and say that show poor or good listening skills. Ask a student who likes to talk to volunteer to have a conversation with you in front of the class.

   Ask the student to begin a conversation about something that interests him or her. You might want to suggest talking about a favorite movie or television show, a favorite place or vacation, a favorite birthday, what s/he did over the weekend, something that happened at school that really bothered her/him, the last game the _____ team played, etc.

   When the student begins to speak, you do everything imaginable that illustrates poor listening (interrupting, looking at your watch, no eye contact, looking bored and impatient, talking about yourself, putting down what the other person says, fidgeting, etc.)

   After you finish, ask the student how she or he felt during the conversation.

3. With the rest of the class, make a list of poor listening skills.

4. Explain that good listening requires active participation and write down students' suggestions for how to be an active listener. Use a *T-chart* to brainstorm active listening skills.

194

Active Listening Skills

What You See (Nonverbal Attending Skills)	What You Hear (Verbal Responding Skills)
Eye contact; focusing on the other person	Verbal encouragers like, "Uh huh"; "Tell me more"; "Yeah"
Leaning forward a little or nodding	Agreeing with something the person has said
Sitting still; no fidgeting or playing with stuff	Restating what someone says
No interrupting; letting the other person finish what he or she is saying completely	Reflecting what someone is feeling
Interested silence; giving a person time to respond	Asking open-ended questions like, "What happened? How did you feel about that?"

5. Do the demonstration again, this time asking two students to use active listening skills that they have suggested.

6. Pass out copies of **Handout 4:5** to each student to read, then have them practice active listening skills in pairs. Each person gets two minutes to talk about something that interests them. Then partners switch roles. Here are some topics that work.

   • Ask students to talk about an experience when they felt they were treated unfairly.

   • Ask students to talk about something a family member does that really bothers them.

   • Ask students to talk about a rule at school that they think is unfair.

   • Ask students to talk about an experience when they were a "star," a time when they did something that made them proud.

7. **Debriefing Questions:** How did you know that your partner was listening to you? What did it feel like to really be listened to without being interrupted? What made this a challenging exercise for you?

IT'S EASIER FOR OTHERS TO TALK AND LISTEN WHEN I. . . .

Have good eye contact

Have nonthreatening posture (not too close, not too distant)

Am relaxed and show interest in other person

Listen attentively/Don't interrupt

Paraphrase or restate what other person is saying to make sure I understand

Ask clarifying questions (Could you explain that? Can you say that in another way? Did this happen recently?)

Encourage the other person to talk (Can you say more about_____?)

Affirm and reflect the other person's feelings

Let person know I've heard what seems most important

Exchange facts and information freely

Disclose my own feelings and thoughts

Try to see the issue from the other person's perspective

Don't try to solve the problem for other person

Show respect for other person, even if I disagree

Don't raise my voice or use an angry or hostile tone

Don't give advice, lecture, preach, judge, blame, or criticize

Don't use sarcastic language or try to make a joke that might backfire.

Activity 6: Someone Knows You're Listening When.....

PURPOSE: Students will review and practice paraphrasing, reflecting feelings, saying encouragers and "door openers," and summarizing.

LEARNING STRATEGIES: Partner skill practice

TIME: 15 minutes to a full class period. You may want to practice in short doses.

MATERIALS: Handouts 4:6A and 4:6B

SUGGESTED INSTRUCTIONS:

1. Divide students into pairs and pass out **Handout 4:6A: Active Listening Partner Practice** to review and practice paraphrasing, reflecting feelings, saying encouragers, and summarizing. Follow directions for each exercise as described in the handouts. For each exercise, do a demonstration with a volunteer first.   Then have students practice in pairs.

2. Use triads to practice active listening skills. Divide students into groups of three to participate in conversations where the focus is on using a variety of active listening skills. Each person in the group will participate in two conversations and observe a third conversation. Pass out **Handout 4:6B: Listening Triads Feedback Sheet.** Review the handout so everyone knows the skills they will be practicing in each role and the skills that observers will be looking for. Quickly brainstorm a list of five or six topics about which there is likely to be heated disagreement among adolescents or issues that bring up intense feelings and opinions. The partners in each of the three conversations pick the topic they want to talk about.

   Give participants two or three minutes for each conversation round. Remind students that after the conversations are over, there will be an opportunity to share observations. When students are finished, ask students what communication skills were hardest to use consistently. Ask observers to identify the skills they saw their partners using effectively.

197

☞ Going Further: Listening Wheel Review

Divide students into two concentric circles so that students pair up with partners who are facing each other. Explain that you will call out a topic that one partner will talk about and call out a listening skill that the other partner will practice. Then the outside circle will move one person to the right so that students change partners for the next topic. Here is a sample of the process. Use any topics that are appropriate for your students.

A. **Inside Wheel** - Topic: What do you do that makes your parents really upset?
   Outside Wheel - Skill: **Paraphrasing / Restating**

Switch partners:
B. **Outside Wheel** - Topic: What makes a good friend?
   Inside Wheel - Skill: **Attending Skills** (Nonverbal ways that you show that you are listening)

Switch partners:
C. **Inside Wheel** - Topic: Your are upset about being "grounded". You think that your parents have been really unfair.
   Outside Wheel - Skill: **Reflecting Feelings** ("You feel _____because_____")

Switch partners:
D. **Outside Wheel** - Topic: Three things you want to do before you are 25 years old.
   Inside Wheel - Skill: **Summarizing**

Active Listening Partner Practice

Practice Paraphrasing (restating the other person's thoughts and ideas, showing that you understand the facts of the conversation) Person 1 reads the statement and person 2 paraphrases what person 1 said. Then switch— person 2 reads the next statement and person 1 paraphrases what person 2 said.

Example: Last night I had a great time at Denise's party. I met some kids from Metro High that I really liked.
So you had fun at Denise's party and met some kids you liked being with.

1. I can't get my locker open. I've tried to turn my lock every way possible and it still won't open.

2. My parents told me that we're going to New York this summer. I can't wait. We're going to visit my best friend from grade school.

3. I hope we get through this book by next week. It's really really boring. I'd rather spend my time reading on my own.

4. I saw the weirdest thing yesterday. I saw a car that was painted all over to look like a tropical rain forest.

5. I don't have the money to go to the movies this weekend. Maybe we can go next week.

6. Last night I heard all this noise and I saw a bunch of police cars and an ambulance. I think people were fighting in the apartment across the street.

7. I like my new job even though I spend most of the time putting stuff on the shelves. The people I work with have been nice to me.

8. I'm not sure I have all the stuff to make my mom's birthday cake. I'm going to need to go to the store and I don't have a car.

9. I think rec centers should be open all weekend so that kids have somewhere to go.

10. I wish we had more time to get to know each other at school. This is my first year here and I don't know most of the kids in my classes.

Practice Reflecting Feelings Person 1 reads the statement and person 2 tries to reflect back the spoken or unspoken feelings in the statement. Then switch—person 2 reads the next statement and person 1 reflects back. Use starting phrases like, *"You feel_____because_____." "You sound_____." "You seem_____." " I can see that you're feeling_____because_____.*

Example: "It seems like I spent the whole day waiting. I waited for the bus for 20 minutes, then waited to to get my concert tickets. Then I had to wait on my brother before he could drive me home. I am so tired of waiting!"

You're feeling impatient because you've had to wait all day long.

1. My brother is driving my crazy. He always picks up the phone when I'm talking to my boyfriend and then he pretends he needs to use it.

2. I hope I get accepted as a counselor at camp this summer. There are so many kids applying, I just don't know if I'll get the job.

3. Jeff asks to see my lab write-up every time before we have to hand them in. I'm sick and tired of Jeff depending on me to do his work.

4. When we have relatives over for dinner, my mom talks about all the stuff I've been doing at school. I get really embarrassed.

5. My dad won't let me get a license until I can pay for car insurance myself. I'll be out of high school before I can save that much money.

6. I can't believe the grade I got on my history test. I studied hard and what was the payoff? Nothing.

7. Guess what? My mom said I could stay by myself when they go visit my grandparents. I'm shocked that she trusts me to be okay.

8. I've been kind of down since my dad lost his job. My goofy jokes don't even make him smile. He just sits around staring. I wish I could do something.

9. Nothing is going right for me this week. I lost my good jacket. I can't find my project notes, and my mom needs me to baby-sit tonight. I wish this week would hurry up and get over with.

10. Can you believe it? My aunt won the lottery, and she's going to take us all on a cruise in the Caribbean.

Practice Using Encouragers that encourage the other person to keep talking. Some starting phrases you might try:
- *Tell me more about that.* or *Say a little more about that.*
- *I'm interested in what you think about_____. Tell me what you're thinking.*
- *Tell me what happened.*
- *What else?*

Practice Using Clarifying Questions that help you understand what the person is saying or help the speaker give more information or give more detail. Try these questions:
- *What happened next? How did this happen? Where? When?*
- *How did that feel for you? Tell me what you're feeling.*
- *Can you say that in another way?*
- *Can you say more about that?*
- *Is there anything else that's bothering you? Is there anything else you need right now?*
- *What was your reaction to that? How did you feel afterwards?*
- *What else should I know?*

Practice Exercise: Person 1 talks about a recent experience but gives no details. For example, *"My mom's really been on my case lately."* or *"I'm really upset with my sister."* or *"Nobody trusts me."* or *"I'm having a lot of trouble writing this paper."* or *"What a relief! I finally finished."* Person 2 practices paraphrasing, encouraging, and open-ended questioning skills with Person 1. Person 2's goal is to understand Person 1's situation more clearly.

Practice Summarizing the key ideas and facts in the conversation. Person 1 talks about the first topic for one minute and Person 2 then summarizes what Person 1 has said. Then switch roles.

1. Where would you want to go on summer vacation for two weeks?

2. What do you think about 11 p.m. weeknight curfews for teens under 18?

3. How would you change the daily schedule at school?

4. What other kinds of classes do you think should be offered in your school.

5. Talk about an experience when they felt they were treated unfairly.

6. Ask students to talk about something a family member does that really bothers them.

Listening Triads Feedback Sheet

When you are the speaker......talk about something that is really bothering you—something that you have strong feelings about—something that has upset you or something that you're really excited about. You have about 3 minutes.

After your time is up, give feedback to the listener:
What kind of "body talk" did the *listener* use that showed good non-verbal listening skills?
What did the *listener* say that showed that s/he was listening to you?
How do you know the *listener* understood what you were thinking and feeling?
How did it feel to be listened to in this way?

When you are the listener.....your task to listen in ways that let the speaker know that you understand her/his thoughts, ideas, and feelings.

Try to use the following listening skills:

☐ Restate /paraphrase thoughts and ideas.

☐ Restate /reflect the person's feelings.

☐ Give the speaker time to talk. Try using "interested silence."

☐ Encourage the speaker to say more about something, to be more specific, to give more detail or more information.

☐ Summarize what you heard at the end of the 3 minutes.

When you are the observer.......you are to note specific ways that the *listener* used and showed good listening skills:

What kind of "body talk" did the *listener* use that showed good non-verbal listening skills?
What did the *listener* say specifically that showed that s/he was really listening?

☐ How do you know the *listener* was restating/paraphrasing the *listener's* thoughts and ideas?

☐ How do you know that the *listener* was restating the speaker's feelings?

☐ How do you know that the *listener* encouraged the speaker to say more about something, to be more specific about what s/he was thinking and feeling, to give more detail or more information.

How accurate was the *listener's* summarizing at the end?

Activity 7: Giving And Receiving Feedback

PURPOSE: Students will learn the difference between praise and criticism and feedback and then practice giving concrete feedback to their peers.

LEARNING STRATEGIES: Group discussion, written observations

TIME: As needed in your classroom

MATERIALS: Handouts 4:7A and 4:7B

SUGGESTED INSTRUCTIONS:

1. Begin by performing a role-play with a student in which you play a student and the student plays a teacher. The student's goal is to openly criticize you, what you're doing, and the way you're doing it. You and the student can decide what activity you're doing. Ask the audience to discuss the following:
   a. What was the teacher's underlying goal?
   b. What approach did the teacher use to meet this goal?
   c. Was the teacher successful in meeting this goal? How do you know?
   d. How was the student affected by this exchange? How do you think the student felt? How do you know?

2. Debrief the role-play and begin a larger discussion about criticism. Ask students to think how we criticize others and why criticism doesn't work for most people. Some common forms of criticism:

   - Judgment about who you are and what you're doing, which people don't like to come from others.
   - Personal attacks, which make people immediately defensive.
   - Lecturing or moralizing that makes people feel stupid, bad, guilty, and embarrassed.

3. Read out some of the phrases below using a harsh voice:
   "Why didn't you do your homework?"
   "Who did that?"
   "Why can't you do what you're told?"
   "What's wrong with you?"
   "What did you say?"
   "Why are you doing this?"
   "What's your problem?"
   "You know better than that."
   "Why are you doing this?"
   "Why are you doing this?"

203

"I have never had a class this bad."
"Didn't anyone ever teach you to..........?"
"How many times do I have to tell you this?"
"It's obvious that you've never had any home training."
"You have no respect for yourselves."

4. Ask students how they felt as they heard these phrases. How do they react when they hear these kinds of criticisms directed at them? Talk about the ones which bother them the most.

   Ask students why we criticize others, if we hate it so much? Suggest to students that the goal of most criticism is to change someone else's behavior. The problem is that criticism usually doesn't give anyone the safety, information, or motivation to change.

5. Ask students to pair up and think of a time when someone brought a problem to their attention in a way that helped them make a positive change (personally, socially, academically). What was different about that experience? Give each student two minutes to talk about their experience.

6. Make a list of positive ways people can bring things to our attention.

7. Introduce the concept of Feedback—a process of giving us information that let's us know how we're doing and also helps us make decisions about what we want to change or improve.

8. Pass out copies of **Handouts 4:7A** and **4:7B**. Read and discuss handouts together. Explore the reasons why the positives come first in a "feedback sandwich."

9. Make a list of opportunities in class when feedback would be more helpful than either praise or criticism. Make a commitment to give students an opportunity to practice giving feedback (out loud or in writing) several times a week.

☞ **Going Further:** You may want to suggest times when students can volunteer to be feedback observers for particular activities and practice skill sessions. Before students give feedback, it is critical to involve the group in deciding what they want the "feedbacker" to look and listen for.

Giving and Receiving Feedback
(Instead of Praise and Criticism)

Criticism shuts us down. We're usually too defensive to listen, evaluate, and assess what we're hearing.

<u>Empty praise</u>, like criticism, often judges the doer, not the deed.
Praise often make us uncomfortable and anxious. It **doesn't tell us what we did** that was good or valued. We end up seeking approval of the person who's judging us, rather than focusing on our behavior and the goals we set for ourselves.
Examples of empty praise: "Good job" "You're doing great." "Excellent" "You're terrific." "You've improved since last week."

<u>Give feedback on the deed not the doer.</u> Feedback about the deed puts the focus on **what you did or said and how you did it** - not whether you are a good or bad person. Think of feedback as a way of playing back the video tape of what just happened. Feedback lets the other person know that we were paying attention. **Feedback places the "receiver" in control of the data. The "receiver" can assess what feeback rings "true" for her or him.** The receiver decide what to do with the feedback, how to use it, what to incorporate in "next time" behaviors and responses.

For the receiver: "Think of FEEDBACK as a package you receive in the mail. You can choose to:
- **Return it to the sender; it came to the wrong address.**
- **Keep the package and communicate that you've received it.**
- **Keep the package, open it, and use what's in it right away.**
- **Keep it on the shelf for now; you might want to use it in the future.**

<u>Use concrete, specific language</u> that indicates what you saw, heard, felt, or experienced. If you use **"fat words"** like *okay, great, interesting, not good enough, that's better,* the "receiver" won't get specific information that is really helpful.

Feedback statements begin in different ways:
- **Naming what you heard a person say or saw a person do:**
  Examples: "You let me take as much time as I needed." "You made everyone in the group feel welcome by inviting them to all say something in the beginning." "You spoke loud enough so that we could all hear you." "You found three different solutions to the problem."

- **Giving reactions from your perspective:** When someone gives us feedback, they're letting us know how our words and behavior affected them. For example: "I liked it when you......I noticed that.....I observed that you.....I appreciated it when you.....It would have helped me understand

FEEDBACK SANDWICH

POSITIVES →

What worked well?
What was effective?
What did you like that
(Name) said or did?
What did you like best?

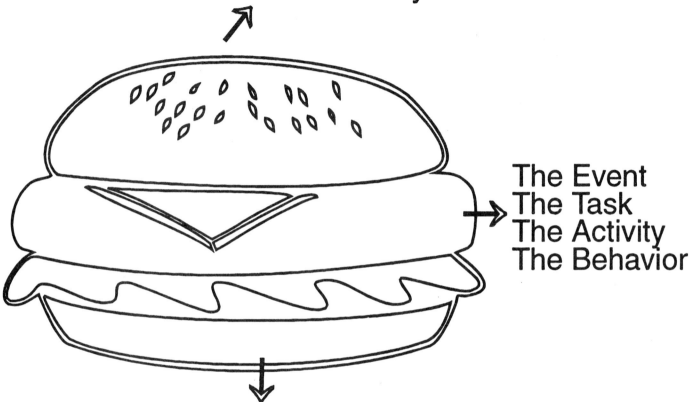

The Event
The Task
The Activity
The Behavior

What could have made it even
more effective?
What could you have done
differently?
What could have made it work
better?
What's one thing you would
change for next time?

Adapted from the work of Marion O'Malley, North Carolina Center for Peace Education

Activity 8: From The Other Person's Perspective

PURPOSE: Students will practice thinking and speaking about a conflict from another person's point of view.

LEARNING STRATEGIES: Whole group discussion, independent reflection, and interactive exercise.

TIME: One class period

MATERIALS: Handout 4:8

SUGGESTED INSTRUCTIONS:

1. Ask three students to stand in different places (perhaps at different heights as well) in the classroom and then ask them to tell the class what they see directly in front of them. Ask the rest of the class if they can identify what was different about each person's point of view. Explain that we all see the world a little differently because no one is in exactly the same place and no one thinks exactly alike. Explain that we each see conflicts differently too.

2. Make up a role play or use video clip, a snippet from a short story, a children's book, or the scenario that follows to present an interpersonal conflict to the class.

   > *Characters: Mom and Michael, her son.*
   > *Situation: Mom comes home from work and she is very tired. She's had to work late twice this week. She wants to fix a real dinner for the family tonight and discovers that the kitchen is a mess. Michael got really hungry after school and took out lots of food from the refrigerator to fix something to eat. He dropped a jar of mayonnaise and spilled the juice. He tried to clean up, but the floor is still greasy, and he left dirty dishes in the sink. He left all of his belongings strewn across the kitchen table and then went upstairs to work on his paper for English. He knows this will take him a long time. He's eaten already and has the rest of the night ahead of him to work.*

   After the conflict is presented, pass out **Handout 4:8** and have students identify the problem, needs, and feelings of each person in the conflict. Discuss students' responses. Ask students to think about these questions: "What might be important to both characters?" "Is there anything that they could both agree on?" ,

"When you don't understand or acknowledge the other person's point of view what happens? How does this make it harder to resolve a conflict or maintain a good relationship?

Ask students if they've ever said, "You just don't understand me." Discuss what's going on when students feel that way. What can the other person say that will let you know that s/he understands your point of view? This is a good opportunity to review active listening skills.

Going Further: Using literature or a current issue, read about or discuss a conflict that involves three or four individuals or groups who perceive a conflict very differently. In the middle of your classroom place three or four name cards of people involved in the conflict. Ask students to step into the shoes of these individuals and describe the conflict from that person's perspective. Then ask students to switch places and take on the perspective of one of the other individuals.

Invite students in the audience to ask questions that every individual can respond to—for example, "What do you need?", "What matters most to you in this situation?", "How is this situation affecting your life?", "What would you like to happen?", "What do you think is going to happen?" "How do you feel about_____?"

Continue switching roles as students keep asking questions and invite students from the audience to change places with students in the middle. You might want to end this exercise, by brainstorming possible solutions which would be acceptable for all of the characters.

Points of View

Problem:

Feelings:

Wants:

Needs:

Problem:

Feelings:

Wants:

Needs:

Activity 9: Practicing the Art of ``I-Speak``

PURPOSE: Students will learn and practice "I-speak", that is, taking responsibility to speak from their own experience and state their feelings, needs, preferences, and requests.

LEARNING STRATEGIES: Group discussion, partner skill practice

TIME: As needed in your classroom. You may want to focus on one or two role plays in one session and then review and practice in short doses.

MATERIALS: Handouts 4:9A and 4:9B

SUGGESTED INSTRUCTIONS:
1. Ask several students in advance to read through the role-play scripts you choose to use from **Handout 4:9A** so that they feel comfortable performing them in class.

2. Explain to the class that students will be role-playing very familiar situations. The audience's goal is to identify and jot down the communication problems that they observe in each role-play.

3. After each role-play, ask questions from the list below that are appropriate to each specific scenario:
   a. What's going on?
   b. What's the problem?
   c. What was said that "shut down" communication?
   d. How do you think _____ feels?
   e. What did _____ say that made the situation worse?
   f. What do you think _____ would have wanted _____ to say?
   g. If you were _____, how would you have responded?
   h. If you were _____, what would you have wanted _____ to say to you?
   i. What could _____ have said instead?

4. For each role-play, the chart on **Handout 4:9B** identifies: a) a key communication problem that the role-play illustrates; b) the "I-speak" response that could improve communication and improve chances of getting what you need; and c) suggestions for paired practice.

5. After students have discussed the role-play and practiced using "I-speak" responses, replay the role-play, practicing these communication strategies. Be sure to debrief the role-plays, identifying the strategies students used, asking both role-players to share how they felt and to comment on what worked. The role-players and the audience might also suggest other responses that would have helped to keep the "lines of communication open.

6. **Debriefing:** After you have practiced several of the strategies, use any of these questions to talk or write about:
    * For you, which kind of "I-speak" is easiest to do? Hardest to do?
    * Are there any strategies that you use a little? a lot? Are there some strategies that you've never really used?
    * Which strategy do you want to use more often? How will it help you?
    * Which strategy would help you the most with a problem you are facing right now?
    * Think about a difficult situation you know will come up again. What strategy would you like to try next time?
    * Write about a bad situation you don't want to repeat and rewrite how you will approach a this situation differently next time.

"I-Speak" Role-Play Scripts

Role Play #1

Student A: Lori said that she saw Cheryl talking to Michael the other day. I think they're going out together. I've heard that Michael treats his girl friends really nasty.

Student B: You know, rumor has it that he never takes "No" for an answer.

Student A: Cheryl must be wanting a boyfriend awful bad to go with that creep.

Student B: I'll bet her Mom is furious with her. They must have really had a big fight over this.

Student A: I just can't understand Cheryl. She must be more of a loser than I thought she was.

Role Play #2A

Student A: I can't believe you won't let me go. You never let me do what I want. You're always saying, "Maybe when I'm a Senior" and now I am, and you won't let me go.

Mother: You're just too young to take the car for the whole weekend. Look at what happened when Josh did some crazy thing like this. It's too much responsibility. You're just not ready.

Student A: I'm not Josh. And we planned to go to the lake for just two days. Two lousy days. You're so mean to me. You just want my life to be totally miserable. You never trust me enough.

Mother: You never should have said you could take the car. You're always jumping ahead without checking first.

Student A: But you said we could go when I'm a Senior. You're just not fair. You're not like Cindy's Mom.

Role Play #2B

Student A: Hey! Where have you been? How many times do you need to be told to be here on time? My brother is more responsible than you are.

Student B: Listen. Let me explain, will you?

Student A: No excuses! You're always late when it really matters. Don't you ever wear a watch? Can't you tell time?

Student B: Well, if that's the way you feel, forget you. Find your own ride. You're so wrapped up in your own little world you don't even care what happened to me.

Role Play #2C

Student A: (You are talking to yourself in the back of the classroom.) I just don't understand this math. Mr. Thompson made me feel really stupid today. He calls on me when I don't know the answer. He does it just to show me up. I hate that! Why should I even try? He's going to fail me anyway.

Role Play #3A

Student A: (You're slouched in a chair and looking at the floor. You're not saying anything.)

Student B: Hey, what's up? Why are you looking at me like that? What's the problem?

Student A: Just forget it. You can't do anything anyway.

Role Play #3B

Dad: Oh, come on. You'll like this, I just know it. You said you wanted a summer job. So I found you one.

Student A: I know Dad. I really need a job.

Dad: So what's the problem? Why do you look so down?

Student A: I don't know. Never mind.

Role Play #3C

Student A: (Sitting alone and muttering) I always do what Juanita wants me to do. I never get to do what I want to do. I just hate following her around like a dog on a leash.

Role Play #4A

Student A: Look, I'll get it done by tomorrow. Don't worry about it. It's no big deal.

Student B: You said you'd help me get the trip organized. We've got to present the plans tomorrow.

Student A: Okay! Okay! I'm cool, all right? I'll have my stuff together. I just have a few more phone calls to make. Get off my case about it.

The Next Day

Student B: So do you have it done?

Student A: I just didn't have the time. Find someone else to do it.

Student B: It's too late for that. I was counting on you!

213

Role Play #4B

**Older
Sibling:** Look, I forgot, okay? Why is it so important anyway? You won't die if you have to wait for another week.

**Younger
Sibling:** You promised me you would fix my bike this week. I counted on you fixing it so I could use it this weekend.

**Older
Sibling:** I said I'd do it when I had time.

Role Play #5A

Student A: I don't know about this. It's sounds a little risky.

Student B: Oh, come on. You'll have a great time. Just wait to you get there.

Student A: Well, okay. But we better not get in any trouble.

Role Play #5B

Student A: (Talking to Student B) Sure, I'll do it. Just let me know when we need to get together.

Student A: (Talking to Student C) Okay, If it's not until the weekend.

Student A: (Talking to Student D) Let me get the week over; then I can do it.

Practicing the Art of "I-Speak"

Role-Play #	Communication Problem	"I-Speak" Suggestions	Practice Suggestions
#1	Talking about other people's experiences with out the facts; guessing what others are thinking and feeling; spreading rumors and gossip.	Speak from your own experience and your own perspective - what you see, think, feel, experience.	Choose a hot topic that will bring up different reactions (i.e. drug use, the latest scandal, rap music, the latest trends in hair cuts and clothing, etc.) In small groups of four or five, do a "go-around" in which people respond to the issue beginning their responses with "I think...," "I feel...," "For me...," "In my experience...," "It seems to me...," "From my perspective...," etc.
#2 A, B, C	Using blaming, accusing, "You" Messages", hurtful criticism, statements of helplessness. For example, "You're such a slob." "You never do anything right. Now the whole project's messed up."	Give "I Messages" that let someone know what you feel and what you need without blaming or attacking the other person. For example, "I feel frustrated when you're late to pick me up because then we have to go in the office and get late slips. I don't like getting to homeroom after the bell rings." "I feel embarrassed when you tease me about my boyfriend in front of others. I want that conversation to be private between us."	Make a list of "You Messages" that attack, blame, and place responsibility for your situation outside of yourself. (i.e. "You made me...," It's your fault that I...," "Why didn't you...," "I can't believe you're such a....") . As a class, turn a few into "I Messages" using these formats. *"I feel_____ when _____ because _____ .* *"I feel_____ when you _____ . I need you to _____* *"I don't like it when you_____ . It makes me feel_____ . I'd like you to _____ .* Then practice writing "I Messages" in pairs. Share and disucss them as a group. Brainstorm a list of situations where it's hard to say what you feel and really need. Discuss why it's hard. Then talk about the consequences when you don't use an "I Message". In pairs, practice writing "I Messages" for these situations and then practice role-playing, first in a class demonstration, and then in threes, taking turns as the "I Message" sender, the receiver, & the feedbacker.

#3 A, B, C

People aren't mind readers! Unless you say up front what you like and what you need, you're unlikely to get it.

When you make a request, you're giving the other person a chance to say 'yes' or 'no' without making a demand or making the other person feel guilty or criticized. Try writing requests and preferences that fit these situations:

1. You think your semester grade in History is unfair.

2. You have three games this week and see no way that you can finish your English paper by Friday.

3. You hate it when your old friends still call you a stupid nickname that you had when you were eight years old.

4. You want to be with a friend of yours, but you don't want to go with her to a party with people you don't really like.

5. You can't stand the radio station your friend plays in the car every day on the way to school.

6. You really don't see how you can clean up the yard by yourself in one day. You want some help.

Making requests, giving suggestions, stating your preferences.

For example:
"I'd like to make a request. Is it possible for you to come over tomorrow, so I can have time to work on my paper tonight?"

"Here's a suggestion. What if we_____ "

"For me, it works better if I_____ ."

"That really doesn't interest me.   I'd rather-----------".

Just going along, withdrawing, not saying what you really think or need, suffering in silence.

#4 A, B

Generate some role plays that describe typical situations for your students and practice responding in a way in which the person accepts responsibility for what happened and offers to talk through ways to work it out.

Admitting mistakes and taking responsibility to be honest and try to work out a way to deal with the problem.

Denial, making excuses.

#5 A, B

Brainstorm situations in which you wanted to say "No" but didn't. What made it hard to say 'No'? Brainstorm ways to say 'No' without offending.   For example, *"That doesn't work for me right now. I'll get back to you later."* Practice role-playing in pairs using the situations.

Saying 'NO' when you really need to.

Say 'yes'¹' to everything without thinking it through.

Activity 10: The Problem-Solving Process

PURPOSE: Students will learn and practice a problem-solving process for resolving conflicts using a WIN-WIN approach.

LEARNING STRATEGIES: Demonstration and practice role-plays

TIME: One class period

MATERIALS: Handout 4:10A, 4:10B, 4:10C, and 4:10D

SUGGESTED INSTRUCTIONS:

Teacher's Note: Even when students have a larger toolbox of responses to conflict, there's still the problem of deciding which response best fits a particular situation. Another problem is having the words ready to use when you need them. Again, this is where practice brings more confidence and less awkwardness. It is natural for kids to feel weird when they are trying on new behaviors. Let students know that you are aware of how "canned" this sounds in the beginning, but also remind them of things they can do now, without thinking, that were awkward or tough for them to do the first few times they tried it.

1. Write on the board *EFFECTIVE PROBLEM SOLVING*. Ask students to brainstorm a list of things that make problem solving successful. Some start up questions might include:

   How are people treating each other?

   What are some of the steps that can help people come to a satisfactory solution?

   How do you want to feel at the end of the process?

   What makes a good solution?

   How do you know your solution is one that will probably work?

2. Pass out copies of **Handout 4:10A The Problem-Solving Process** or **Handout 4:10B Problem Solving Step By Step** to all students. Read and review the steps of collaborative problem-solving with them. Emphasize that WIN-WIN solutions involve a process in which:

   Both parties get some important needs met and

   Both parties feel good about the solution they have chosen to implement.

3. Ask students to choose a partner to practice the process. Use either the Baby-Sitter Problem or The Party on **Handout 4:10C** as a practice role-play (or make up a scenario that works better for your students). When students practice the first time, it is helpful to "freeze-frame" the steps, stopping to check in at different points to see how students are following the step by step process.

217

4. Have students share their solutions. Ask both partners if they are satisfied with the solution. Ask what made one choice better than another.

☞ **Going Further:** One way to do a "skill check" is to role-play with a feedbacker who listens to his or her partners and notes how partners are doing on **Handout 4:10D Feedback Check List for One to One Problem-Solving** . Use any of the other role-play scenarios elsewhere in the curriculum or have students help create their own using . When students have finished role-playing have the observer share her/his notes and suggestions.

Problem Solving Step By Step

1. **Both of you** agree to solve the problem.

2. **Both of you** agree to listen to each other and be as honest as you can.

3. **Person A:** Say what happened; how you see the problem. Say how you feel about what happened.

4. **Person B:** Restate what Person A said. Say what happened from your perspective. Say how you feel about what happened.

5. **Person A:** Restate what Person B said. Explain what you need.

6. **Person B:** Explain what you need.

8. **Both of you** talk about the consequences of various solutions. Eliminate solutions that neither of you like.

9. **Both of you** choose the best **Win-Win** solution that:
   meets some important needs for eachf of you.
   won't hurt anyone.
   both of you think will work.
   both of you feel good about.

10. **Both of you** decide what each of you will do to implement the solution. (what, when, where, how much, how often?)

11. **Both of you** agree to check in with each other so that you know the solution is working.

219

The Problem Solving Process

1. ACKNOWLEDGE THAT THERE'S A CONFLICT — AGREE TO SOLVE IT

At least one party needs to acknowledge the conflict and initiate the first conversation — the sooner the better. This calls for a certain amount of self awareness and "tuning-in". If you are already feeling emotional, acknowledge it and then try to use techniques to stay calm. If this is impossible, postpone (not put-off or avoid) dealing with the conflict until your emotions are more settled.

2. DEFINE THE PROBLEM

Each party describes her/his perception of the problem. Agree on the problem you want to work on right now. Take turns listening to each other's stories and state your feelings, wants, and needs openly and honestly. Paraphrase what the other person is saying. Try to get to underlying issues and concerns that sparked the conflict. Identify interests and clarify areas of agreement **first** (common ground). Ensure that you each are clear about the areas of disagreement.

3. BRAINSTORM SOLUTIONS

List all ideas, practical and impractical that might resolve the conflict. Do not evaluate ideas at this point. Criticism here can stop the creative flow. Reframe questions in ways that ensure that each of you is willing to make some changes and meet some of the other's needs. ("What about ____? Could we ____? What if I _____ and you____? What can we do to make sure that you can..... and I can....?") Think about trade-offs and "my turn. . . . your turn" options.

4. EVALUATE SOLUTIONS

Consider the consequences of each possible solution. Which ones are most realistic and responsible? What constraints or limitations make some solutions more impractical or less "do-able" than others. Discard ideas with a low chance of success or those that are too impractical (too costly in terms of time, money, or personal energy).

5. CHOOSE A SOLUTION

The question to keep asking is, "Does this solution satisfy both of us? Does it meet some important needs for both of us?" It is crucial that both parties agree on the chosen solution and feel good about process they used to reach it.

6. IMPLEMENT THE SOLUTION

What is the plan for making the solution work? How will you know it's working? It can be helpful to write out the plan. Decide on a time to later evaluate the implementation of the plan.

CONGRATULATE YOURSELVES ON A JOB WELL DONE!

THE BABY-SITTER PROBLEM

Roles: A girl or a boy your age
           Your mom or dad

Time: Friday, around 5:30 p.m.

Conflict: You and three friends have made plans to go to the mall for pizza and a movie tonight at 6 p.m. You've helped make all the arrangements in advance. Your dad is driving you there and another mom is going to take you all home. You've had a good week at school, your room is spotless, and you've done the laundry! And you've stayed out of fights with your siblings.

Mom has just come home from work, and the phone rings. Your great Aunt Bea just fell and is having emergency surgery. Your dad is going straight to the hospital from work and your mom is leaving for your aunt's house to take care of Uncle Henry. Neither of them will be home until after 9 p.m. You will have to baby-sit your brother and sister and fix them dinner.

The Party

Tom: He is 16 years old. He wants to have a party but is embarrassed about having his mother around at the party. The other kids will laugh at him for it. Tom especially wants to feel equal to his new friend, Bill. Bill recently had a party with no parents present, and all went well.

Mom: She is a single parent. In particular, she is concerned about alcohol/drug use and too much making out. Tom is her only child. She has a friend whose son recently died by being hit by a drunk driver who had been to a party. Tom has not shown himself to be too responsible lately, especially in the last three weeks. He has not done his chores (the lawn, the garage, and the trash) as agreed. He has stayed out past curfew twice. Can he be trusted?

FEEDBACK CHECK LIST FOR ONE TO ONE PROBLEM-SOLVING

HAVE YOUR PARTNERS:	YES	NO	KIND OF
1) Agreed to solve the problem?			
2) Defined the problem?			
heard each other's perceptions of the problem?			
paraphrased each other?			
stated and acknowledged each other's feelings?			
explained what each needs?			
3) Brainstormed solutions?			
heard solutions without putting them down?			
tried to generate more ideas?			
4) Chosen a best solution?			
asked how this solution satisfies both of them?			
summarized what each needs to do to implement solution?			
decided on a "check in" date to review progress?			
congratulated each other?			
COMMUNICATION SKILLS			
A. used encouraging phrases			
B. maintained eye contact			
C. paraphrased or restated other's thoughts/feelings			
D. asked good clarifying questions			
E. kept voice low/tone friendly			
F. acknowledged & appreciated other person's efforts.			

Activity 11: Learning How to Negotiate

PURPOSE: Students will learn key negotiation concepts and incorporate them into practice role-plays and problem-solving exercises.

LEARNING STRATEGIES: Partner and whole group skill practice

TIME: One to several class periods depending on the amount of practice

MATERIALS: Handouts 4:11A, 4:11B, 4:11C, 4:11D, 4:11E, and 4:11F.

SUGGESTED INSTRUCTIONS:

1. Ask students what they think a negotiatior does. Brainstorm a list of qualities and skills that would help someone negotiate effectively. Then brainstorm and prioritize a list of five things an effective negotiator would not do or say. Keep these lists for reference.

2. Pass out **Handout 4:11A Key Steps to Effective Negotiation** and read and review with students.

   One of the most important concepts to highlight is **position and interest.** Problem-solving and conflict resolution are more effective when disputing parties understand the differences between their positions and interests. Good agreements between people and groups may satisfy all or some of their NEEDS AND INTERESTS, but will not necessarily result in getting what each party wanted originally. When parties negotiate they need to be prepared to explore alternative solutions that satisfy some vital interests of both parties.

   Pass out one copy of **Handout 4:11B Positions and Interests** to every two students. Using the examples below, read **positions** to students. Have students pair up and take a minute to talk over what they think is the **interest** that underlies each position. It's important to note that there can be **multiple interests.**

ONE POSSIBLE POSITION	ONE PRIMARY INTEREST
"Friday curfew is 12:00. Why can't I stay out 'till 1:30?"	"I want to be trusted enough so that if there is a special night I can stay out later"
"I can't ask you to the prom."	"I embarrassed that I can't afford all the prom 'extras' like limos and stuff."

"I've had it! I will do no more carpooling this weekend"	"I'm on "driving overload". We need to schedule things so five trips aren't scheduled in the same day."
"I don't want you driving with_____ to that party."	Concern for safety above all else.
Spend more money for drug rehabilitation for American addicts.	Ensure that urban neighborhoods can reduce the risk of violent crime.
"If you're going to spend your clothes allowance on ridiculous things, we'll go back to the old system where I'm in charge of the shopping."	Concerns about prudent spending and wise choice-making.

4. Make two copies of **Handout 4:11C Sibling Dispute.** Cut off the script sections and ask two students to read the script in class. After they have read the script, return to **Handout 4:11B** and use the bottom half to identify **positions** and **interests** of Ron and Jenn. Ask students to work in pairs. Let them take a couple minutes to think through Ron's and Jenn's positions and interests and write their responses on the handout. Write students' responses on the board. You might also want to ask students to describe the **climate** and brainstorm a good **problem-solving question** that includes important concerns of both Jenn and Ron and could help them focus on solving the problem.

5. Replay the conflict, only this time each party tries to use effective negotiation skills to resolve the conflict. You might want to do a demonstration role-play in front of the class or have everyone practice at the same time. You might also want to use observers who give feedback about the process after Ron and Jenn have come to an agreement. Share solutions in class and ask students to identify what they did that helped them to come to a successful agreement.

5. Use role-plays you construct yourself for further practice. Use **Handout 4:11D and E** to practice group negotiations.

6. Try to make a commitment to incorporate negotiation into your classroom management and curriculum as much as possible. As you practice problem-solving on a day to day basis you may want to refer to **Handout 4:11F When You Are Experiencing Conflict**....as you and your students continually build and refine your skillfulness.

KEY STEPS TO EFFECTIVE NEGOTIATIONS

A. **Agree to Negotiate** Negotiations are possible when parties agree that there is a conflict, agree on what the conflict is, agree to talk about it, and try to resolve it.

B. **Be Willing to Seek an Alternative Solution** Both parties must be willing to let go of their original solutions. Negotiation is not about fighting over which original solution is better. Negotiation requires the willingness to search for alternative solutions that satisfy both parties.

C. **Identify Positions and Interests** It's important to understand the positions and interests of both parties.

A **Position** is a statement of what a party demands or wants. Often it is the solution that is immediate, short term, and appears to be the easiest way to solve problem (often at another's expense). It is <u>one way</u>, among many, to meet a party's need.

An **Interest/Need**, although sometimes short term, **is usually the long-term concern underlying a position.** Important needs do not go away and must be addressed in negotiated agreements. A need is often the **"why" behind the position**.

D. **Identify and Clarify Your Goals** What do you want to accomplish now? What is your goal for this conversation, this meeting? What are long-term goals that you would like to work on in the future?

E. **Be Respectful of Value Differences** Values are deeply held beliefs — religious, ideological, cultural. They must be understood and taken into account, but **values cannot be changed through negotiation.** Negotiations can change behavior, but not what someone believes. When there are intense value conflicts, our best tool is listening for deeper understanding.

225

F. **Create a Positive Climate** Negotiations have a better chance of success in a cooperative, friendly atmosphere than in a competitive, hostile atmosphere.

G. **Use Role Reversal** This is a technique which helps parties to put themselves in the other person's shoes. It's valuable to pause sometimes and ask, "What's the other party feeling or thinking right now? What might be the other party's greatest fear or concern?"

H. **Ask Clarifying Questions** Parties need as much information as possible in order to make good decisions. (What do you need? When do you need it? What would happen if_____? How much would it cost? How would it work? Can you tell me how_____) Open exchange of information and knowledge builds good agreements and tends to improve relationships.

I. **Frame Problem-Solving Questions in Ways that Include Important Needs of Both Parties** A good question enables parties to move beyond positions because it identifies important interests that need to be met by both parties. (What do we both want to avoid ? What goals can we both agree on? What kind of agreement can enable you to _____ and me to_____? How can we ensure that an agreement addresses [Concern A] and [Concern B]?)

J. **Look Hard for Areas of Agreement and Be Clear on Where You Disagree** This will help you develop an agreement that is "do-able", that has the best chance for success.

K. **Specific Offers** require a "yes" or "no" response. Specific offers help frame limitations and possibilities. Specific offers answer the questions "What do *you* do—What do *I* do? When? Where? How much? How often? Over what period of time?"

Positions and Interests

Interest_____

Interest_____

Interest_____

Interest_____

Interest_____

Interest_____

Interest_____

Role_____	Role_____
Position:	Position:
Interests:	Interests:

NEGOTIATION 2: SIBLING DISPUTE

TIME: Saturday, early afternoon   ROLES: RON, aged 17 and JENN, aged 14

JENN: Ron, you've got to take me to my soccer practice and pick me up in two hours. I need to leave in 15 minutes.

RON: Wait a minute! Why can't Mom take you?

JENN: She can't. I didn't tell her I needed a ride until yesterday and she'd already made plans to go to her mother's. Come on, get ready to go.

RON: Find your own ride. Look, this is my only time to relax this weekend, and the NBA play-off is on this afternoon. I've waited all week to watch this.

JENN: Listen, Ron, you know the rules. You can drive and I can't. When you're not doing any thing, and it's an emergency, Mom says you've got to help out and drive.

RON: Look, this is your fault. You're the one who messed up by not telling Mom soon enough. Just forget the practice today.

JENN: I can't miss it or I get cut! This is a big deal to me. Gimme a break, will you? I'm only asking this once. You've got the rest of the weekend to fool around.

RON: Right! I have to work tonight and I've got to study for my biology exam tomorrow. And then there's your stupid play Mom is making me go see. I just want some time for myself!

JENN: You said you wanted to come see me in the play! I can't believe this! I'm always doing things for you. Remember, the time I got you out of trouble when you missed your curfew? And the time I did your share of the housecleaning? Boy, are you a poor excuse for a human being! I'm sorry for living!

RON: Oh, shut up and stop whining!

KEY CONCEPTS	JENN	RON
POSITIONS	Jenn wants Ron drive her to and from soccer practice.	Ron doesn't want to take her.
NEEDS / INTERESTS	Not getting cut from the team Having Ron come to her play Being appreciated by Ron	Watching basketball game Relaxing; taking a "time out" Being appreciated by Jenn
CLIMATE	Stressed; antagonistic; hostile	
PROBLME-SOLVING QUESTION	How can Jenn get to and from practice and Ron get to watch the basketball game?	
ALTERNATIVES	*Ron takes Jenn to practice, but doesn't come to the play. *Jenn takes a taxi to practice and calls Ron to pick her up if she can't get a ride home. *Ron takes Jenn and videotapes the game. *Ron takes Jenn, but she has to find another way home. *Ron listens to the game on the radio and Jenn does his housecleaning jobs next week. *They make plans for a family meeting to talk about scheduling and car rules.	

COMMUNITY NEGOTIATION 3A: THE CURFEW CONTROVERSY

THE PROBLEM:

This highly urbanized city of 600,000 is concerned about the easy availability of drugs, the increased incidence of gang and street crime, and a high drop-out rate among young people who seem to have too much time on their hands to "do nothing" but "get in trouble". The city council is strongly supporting a local ordinance that would establish a **curfew for young people 18 and under — 11 P.M. on Sundays through Thursdays and 12 A.M. on Fridays and Saturdays.**

Criticism of the ordinance has come from parents, students, the American Civil Liberties Union, and the African-American community. There are enough votes for the ordinance to pass in the city council, but the council knows it will have to have broad based support for the measure to be effective. Therefore, **the city council has set up a meeting with important constituencies to modify the ordinance if necessary and add other provisions which might meet the needs of these constituencies.** All the constituencies are concerned about:

* *Increased gang activity and gang violence.
* *Neighborhoods that are increasingly unsafe, especially late at night.
* *Too few safe recreational and social opportunities for young people.
* *Too much emphasis on punishment and not enough emphasis on drug and violence prevention.

ROLES:

Two community relations police lieutenants who want the ordinance to stand just the way it is.

The mayor's community liaison who is most interested in reaching an agreement that everyone can live with.

Three high school student leaders, two whites, one opposed and one in favor, and one African-American who is opposed to the ordinance.

Two parents, one white business owner who favors the ordinance and one African-American lawyer who is undecided.

COMMUNITY NEGOTIATION 3B: THE LOST PLAYGROUND

THE PROBLEM:

A local developer has bought three adjacent properties to build a small shopping center that would serve an older subdivision nearby. While two of the properties are an old Catholic school and a closed restaurant, the other property is a community playground that kids have used for 40 years. While many residents like the idea of convenient services (pizza delivery, office supplies and printing, dry cleaners, drug store, ice cream shop), many young families and some long time residents strongly object to turning a recreational space into commercial property. A path connects the back end of the playground to the subdivision, so this has been a very safe place for kids to play. However, now that the majority of the population is childless and older, there is less investment in keeping the playground. The property taxes on the new shopping center will provide revenues for a community recycling program that will provide weekly pickups for all residents. The Zoning Commission is holding a hearing for local residents to present their views and then will hold their own meeting to decide whether or not to grant a permit for the project. They have the option of negotiating conditions for the permit with the developer.

Divide the class into two sections: 1) Those who are citizens speaking up at the hearing; and 2) Those who are members of the Zoning Board. This gives all students an opportunity to be both participants and observers who can comment on the proceedings.

ROLES FOR HEARINGS: Developer, potential shop owners, residents for and against, environmental activists, young families with children, director of recycling project, community comptroller

ROLES FOR MEETING: The developer and the Zoning Board (which is evenly split about granting a permit for the new shopping center). Several key members would like to negotiate with the developer to find a way

NEGOTIATION STRATEGIES

CONFLICT

CONFLICT BETWEEN WHOM?	CONFLICT OVER WHAT?	CONDITIONS WHICH REVEAL CONFLICT?
POSITIVE GOAL: To be able to____	NEGATIVE GOAL: To stop or prevent____	
GROUP	GROUP	
POSITIONS/DEMANDS	POSITIONS/DEMANDS	
INTERESTS/NEEDS	INTERESTS/NEEDS	
IMPORTANT VALUES	IMPORTANT VALUES	
CLARIFYING QUESTIONS		
PROBLEM-SOLVING QUESTION		
COMMON CONCERNS AND INTERESTS		
ALTERNATIVE SOLUTIONS	OBSTACLES	

SPECIFIC POINTS WHICH YOU THINK MUST BE INCLUDED IN THE AGREEMENT TO MAKE IT MUTUALLY SATISFACTORY

TRADE-OFFS

If --------------gets--------------then--------------gets--------------

If --------------gets--------------then--------------gets--------------

Agreement in Principle:

WHEN YOU ARE EXPERIENCING CONFLICT AND WANT TO NEGOTIATE......

1. **Initiate a conversation** — " I feel_____ about _____. This is a conflict for me. Can we make time to talk about it?"

2. **Pick your battles carefully**—Do you have the time, energy, and good will to resolve the conflict? Is this a time when it's better to postpone a conversation, "agree to disagree", or "let it go"?

3. Step back and ask, **"Who owns the problem?"** If it bothers you and doesn't bother or affect anyone else, ask yourself whether it's worth raising the issue.

4. Remember, that at least one party in the conflict is probably feeling disempowered, scared, hurt, put down, or mistreated.

5. Be aware of your body language and your tone of voice.

6. Ask clarifying questions to get more information and more clarity (Can you say that in another way? What happened? Is there anything else I should know that will help me understand?)

7. Use assertion messages — "I feel_____when
   _____(specific feeling)
   _____because_____.
   (behavior)   (the consequence)
   I would like you to..... (I need you to)_____." Give the other person time to respond and think about what you've said. Then say it again in another way if you think what you said wasn't acknowledged or understood.

8. Communicate clearly what you want and need.

9. **Say "No"** when you really mean it.

10. Let the other person know your limits. Disclose what you think you can and cannot do. Disclose any constraints on possible solutions.

11. Remember **negative feelings do not magically disappear**. If you need to vent before you begin to work through the conflict let your

231

partner know that you're committed to resolving the conflict, **but first**, you need to say what you feel and have those feelings heard.

12. Communicate to the other person that you are really listening. Paraphrase and acknowledge the **substance** of what a person is saying as well as acknowledging and reflecting the **feelings** of the person— "You sound frustrated about the deadline you've been given. It sounds like you don't feel you've had enough time to do the job well."

13. **Avoid** sentences that begin with **"You........!!!"** and **"Why.....??"** "You" statements and "why" questions immediately put the other person on the defensive, leaving him or her no room to "save face" or explain without being judged or accused.

14. **Avoid assumptions**—ask for the information you need to more clearly understand the other person's position, perspective, wants, or needs.

15. What's on the table that's negotiable? non-negotiable?

16. Do a **reality check** to make sure that you are still talking about the same issue, that you have a shared understanding of the problem and what you want to resolve.

17. When you set a time to talk - **agree on time limits** for the conversation - let each other know what "old baggage" you don't want brought up in this conversation.

18. Use a **24 hour rule** - wait a day to think about what's been said, what solutions have been suggested—then come back to review and make a decision.

19. Use a **1 - 10 scale**—Ask, "How important is this on a 1 - 10 scale?" If one says 10 and the other says 2, offer to do "My turn, your turn", do it by yourself, or negotiate a chit for the future.

Chapter 5: Dealing with Anger and Violence

ACTIVITY 1: WHY AND HOW DO CONFLICTS ESCALATE?

PURPOSE: Students will identify verbal and nonverbal responses which escalate conflicts, focusing particularly on responses that intensify feelings of anger.

LEARNING STRATEGIES: Role-plays, brainstorming, whole group discussion

TIME: 30 minutes

MATERIALS: Newsprint, markers

SUGGESTED INSTRUCTIONS:

1. Ask students how they know what they're seeing or hearing is a conflict? You might want to make a T-chart to keep posted while you're exploring the escalation of conflict.

WHEN THERE'S A CONFLICT....	
WHAT YOU HEAR	**WHAT YOU SEE**
YELLING	"IN-YOUR-FACE"
HIGH-PITCHED VOICES	CONFRONTATION
NAME-CALLING	RIGID BODY LANGUAGE
INSULTS	POINTING FINGERS
CRYING	PHYSICAL FIGHTING
ABUSIVE LANGUAGE	ANGRY FACIAL
INTERRUPTING	EXPRESSIONS

Conflict between people can grow and intensify unless it is resolved or managed. Have students think back over the arguments and fights they've had at school, with friends, at home. Explore the reasons why conflicts sometimes get out of hand.

2. Draw a staircase on the board or newsprint like the one below. Remind students what an "escalator" is and how that word is related to "escalate." (On an escalator, once you take your first step, you automatically keep "escalating" — you don't go in the opposite direction without considerable effort.)

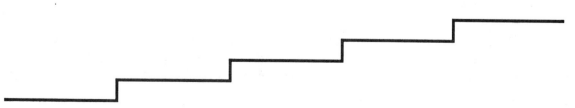

3. Explain that everyone is going to participate in a "hassle line" to further explore how conflicts escalate. Ask students to each find a partner and form two lines facing each other. The whole process is called a hassle line. Each line will take the role of a student involved in the a conflict.

Say to students in Line 1: *"It's lunchtime. The cafeteria is serving burgers and fries today. You are wearing the new white silk baseball jacket that you just got for your birthday. Your favorite aunt gave it to you. You know it cost a lot, and your Mom didn't really want you to wear it to school. You love this jacket! As you go though the cafeteria line, you know you're looking good! You're heading for the catsup dispenser to put lots of catsup on your fries, when.........*

Say to students in Line 2: *"You appear out of nowhere. You're in a big hurry because you have to take a make-up test in 10 minutes. Your teacher said this was the only time you could take your English test. You are racing to the catsup dispenser and step in front of another person standing there. That's you!* (Point to the students in line 1). *You slam down the handle and OOPS! Catsup goes all over your new white silk baseball jacket."* (Point to students in Line 1.)

Say to everyone: *"You and the person facing you will role-play what happens next. The first person to speak is the person in Line 1 who now has catsup all over the front of her brand new jacket. You will have two minutes to interact. One ground rule to remember: no physical fighting. When I say 'Curtain,' begin. When I say 'Freeze,' stop talking and freeze where you are."* It will get fairly loud, so make sure you have the door closed! Try to observe how different students respond to the situation. After you say *"Freeze,"* ask students to sit down and focus their attention on the escalator you've drawn.

4. Write the initial conflict on the bottom step of the escalator and the final outcome on the top step. Give students names in the scenario to clarify who did what.

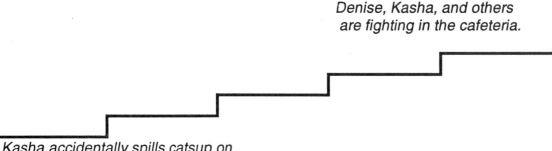

Denise, Kasha, and others are fighting in the cafeteria.

Kasha accidentally spills catsup on Denise's new white silk baseball jacket.

5. Ask students what happened in the hassle line. Generate a list of responses and reactions which escalated the conflict. What did people say and do that worsened the situation? Write responses on the escalator. Be sure to discuss spoken language and body language.
Some common responses :

Kasha blames Denise.	Denise blames Kasha.
They both trade insults and then begin shoving each other.	Kasha ignores what happens and tries to walk away.
Denise screams at Kasha and calls her names.	Kasha freezes and doesn't say anything.
Denise is upset and angry and Kasha ignores her feelings completely.	Kasha tries to make a joke out of what happened.

6. Focus the next part of the discussion on feelings. What were students feeling in the beginning, in the middle, and at the end of the role-play? Ask students who felt angry to share what their partners said and did that intensified their anger.

7. Ask a student to do the role-play with you two more times to demonstrate what happens when someone's feelings aren't acknowledged.

   First, you take the role of the "splatterer," saying things like, "So what? It's not my problem. Don't be such a baby! Forget you - I've got my own problems." Say anything that shows that you are completely ignoring the other person's feelings. After a minute of this harangue, ask the student how s/he is feeling. Ask if the angry feelings intensified. Ask what the "splatterer" could have said that would have helped the "splatee" feel somewhat calmer and less upset.

   Second, take the role of the "splatee" and ask the student to apologize immediately and offer lots of suggestions for what to do about the jacket. You say things like, "I don't want to hear it! I don't care what you can do - look at my jacket. You've ruined it! I don't want your solutions. Look what you've done! I just got this! My mother's going to kill me!" Ask the class, "The student tried to apologize and to offer suggestions. Both of these sound like good ideas. Why didn't they work?" Again, focus on the fact that the "splatee's" feelings were never acknowledged by the other person.

8. Summarize by saying that anger is the hardest emotion to control and manage in ourselves, and it's the most challenging emotion to defuse in someone else. Let students know that the next activities you do together will focus on anger.

The escalator exercise is adapted from *Elementary Perspectives*, William J. Kreidler

Activity 2: Who And What Makes You Angry?

PURPOSE: Students will explore who and what makes them angry and become more aware of their own anger cues and triggers.

LEARNING STRATEGIES: Brainstorming, paired dialogues, written reflection

TIME: One class period

MATERIALS: Newsprint, markers, note cards, and pencils

SUGGESTED INSTRUCTIONS:

1. First, brainstorm a list of **What and Who Make You Angry?** Ask students to be very specific and put all of their ideas on newsprint.

2. Explore the different causes of anger (when someone hurts, criticizes, or embarrasses us; when we are denied what we want or when our needs are not met; when we judge some behaviors as offensive or morally wrong; when we can't control a situation; when events that are beyond our control affect us in negative ways; when we witness or experience injustice, prejudice, or violence).

3. Ask students, "Are there situations when anger is healthy response? Are there situations when anger can be counterproductive?" Remind students that anger is a normal emotion. **Anger is a feeling. What we choose to do with our anger is the behavior (which can be helpful or harmful and have positive or negative consequences).** Everyone expresses and deals with anger differently. Think about situations in which one person "flies off the handle" while another person "writes it off."

4. Give each student a note card and ask them to write "Anger Triggers" on the top and jot down four or five behaviors, words, or phrases which set them off. Ask students to pair with a partner. Give each student about two minutes to share their triggers. Then give students about ten minutes to discuss these questions:
   - What kind of body language makes you angry?
   - How do you know when you're angry? What are the physical cues that send you a signal?
   - How do you usually react to your triggers?
   - Do you have a "long fuse" or "short fuse"?

5. Invite students to do some whole group sharing after paired dialogues and conclude by noting that our triggers can give us warning signs to stop and think about what we want to do next when we're angry.

   ✐ **Assessment:** Ask students for oral or written feedback about this activity.
   1. What was something you learned about yourself?
   2. In what way do you have a better understanding of anger?
   3. How did the paired dialogue work for you? What did you like about it?

ACTIVITY 3: ANGER MOUNTAIN: WHAT HAPPENS WHEN YOU GET ANGRY?

PURPOSE: Students will learn how anger affects our physiological and mental capacities.

LEARNING STRATEGIES: Whole class discussion

TIME: 20 minutes

MATERIALS: Handout 5:3

SUGGESTED INSTRUCTIONS:

1. Ask students if they've ever experienced angry moments when they had trouble thinking about what to say, what to do - times when the anger seemed to blot out all the things that they would have wanted to say or do. Ask students if they ever replayed the angry moment afterwards like a movie, deleting things you wanted to take back and editing in all the things that would have helped you stay in control or prevent an outburst that left people feeling hurt and more angry. Share some experiences where anger was a run-away feeling that had negative consequences. Be prepared to share a story yourself to start the conversation moving.

2. Pass out copies of **Handout 5:3** to every student. This graphic illustration is a useful tool to help students better understand what happens when they get angry. When your "hot button" gets pushed, you only have about 8 seconds when you are both mentally and physiologically alert before the physical responses to anger kick in and take over. In other words, You have about 8 seconds before you think STUPID! Once your anger kicks in, you start climbing up "Anger Mountain." The rush of anger makes it hard to go down the mountain until your anger is spent.

   The handout can be a starting point for discussing impulsive behavior - the things we say and do without thinking when we start climbing up "Anger Mountain." The handout also provides an opportunity to discuss the feelings of regret and guilt that we often experience on our way down the mountain. This graphic helps students understand why it's important to learn techniques that help them manage their anger so they don't lose control.

ANGER MOUNTAIN

Body Reacts with Adrenalin Burst

Regret

Thinking Stops

Tiredness

Hot Button

8 Second Thinking Zone

MIND

BODY

Center for Peace Education/NC ESR, Adapted with Permission

Activity 4: Expressing Angry Feelings and Identifying Sources Of Anger

PURPOSE: Students will consider a broad range of angry feelings we experience and practice making feeling statements that identify sources of anger.

LEARNING STRATEGIES: Paired learning, whole group sharing, creative writing

TIME: One class period

MATERIALS: Handout 5:4, pencils

SUGGESTED INSTRUCTIONS:

1. It's helpful to recognize that we experience a **range of angry feelings** - we react according to how angry we feel. Pass out copies of **Handout 5:4: "Expressing Angry Feelings and Identifying Sources of Anger"** so that each pair of students has one copy. Ask pairs to agree on where to place the words on the steps of the anger continuum - from least angry at the bottom to most angry on the top.

2. Review the anger continuum with the whole class. Then discuss the difficulties that most of us have not only expressing our anger in nonviolent ways but also identifying exactly what makes us angry. One of the reasons this happens is that beneath the anger we often feel hurt, mistreated, unfairly judged, excluded, or rejected.

3. Ask students to work with their partners again, this time practicing variations of "I" statements, inserting a feeling word from the list and identifying an experience or situation in which they felt this particular emotion. Do a demonstration for the class before partners begin. Ask partners to take turns practicing using each statement at least twice.

4. You may want to focus group sharing on these questions:
   * Did any of you find that you made others angry in the same way that they make you angry? What were the similarities?
   * Does your reaction depend on the reaction of the other person? How?
   * Do things about the world make you as angry as conflicts between you and other people? How are these situations alike and different?

&Going Further: This is a good opportunity for students to do some creating writing. Some suggestions:
   1. If **anger** was a place, what would it look like?
   2. Write a story in which an explosion of anger alters a relationship forever.
   3. Write a monologue using two voices: one voice says the angry words you say to person you're angry with, and the other is the voice of **hurt** beneath the angry words.
   4. Take the point of view of an animal, an object, a part of the earth and express the anger that it feels towards people who mistreat it.
   5. Make a recipe - and when you stir it up, you've made **Big Time Angry!**

Expressing Angry Feelings and Identifying Sources Of Anger

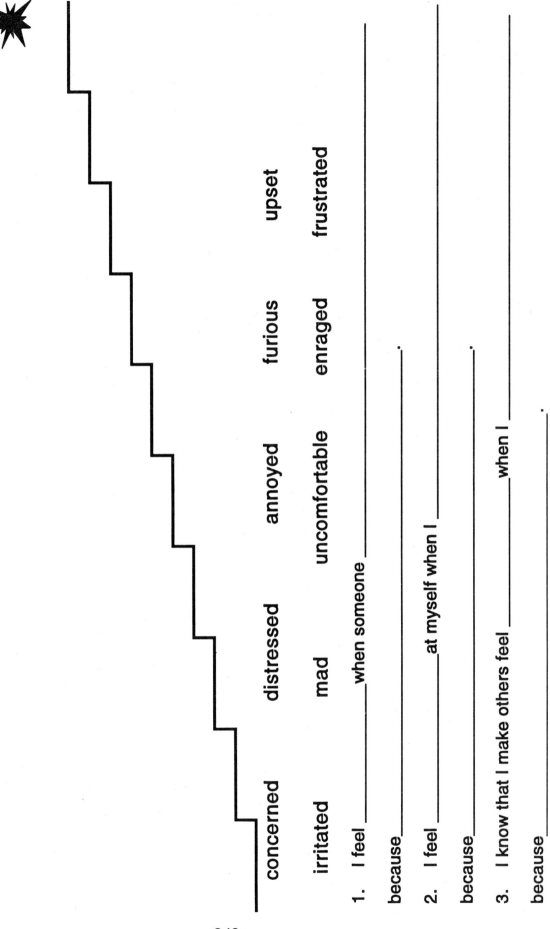

concerned   distressed   annoyed   furious   upset

irritated   mad   uncomfortable   enraged   frustrated

1. I feel _____ when someone _____

because _____ .

2. I feel _____ at myself when I _____

because _____ .

3. I know that I make others feel _____ when I _____

because _____ .

ACTIVITY 5: DEALING WITH ANGER CONSTRUCTIVELY

PURPOSE: Students will consider both positive and negative ways that people deal with anger and then identify what "anger reducers" work for them. Students will also participate in role-plays in which they practice expressing angry feelings in nonviolent ways.

LEARNING STRATEGIES: Whole group discussion, partner dialogues, role-play practice

TIME: One class period

MATERIALS: Handouts 5:5A , 5:5B, 5:5C, and 5:5D

SUGGESTED INSTRUCTIONS:

1. Using the previous list, **What and Who Make You Angry?** as a catalyst, brainstorm a new list of the **Ways People Deal With Their Anger.** Let students know that you are seeking an inclusive list (from destructive to constructive, violent to nonviolent, healthy to unhealthy responses and expressions of anger). Some common strategies:

   ➪ **Blow off steam; release angry energy** (Pound a pillow; jog; find a place to scream where you won't bother anyone)
   ➪ **Talk it out with the person you're angry with**
   ➪ **Talk to a friend who's not involved**
   ➪ **Chill out** (Take a few deep breaths; count to ten; go some place to be alone for a few minutes; listen to your favorite music)
   ➪ **Stuff it in** (Pretend nothing's wrong)
   ➪ **Do something risky** (Drink and drive; do drugs)
   ➪ **Get back at someone verbally** (Name-calling, sarcasm, "-dissing," intimidation and threats)
   ➪ **Do something constructive** (Write down your feelings, do some homework, organize a meeting to deal with the problem)
   ➪ **Displacement** (Pick a fight or start an argument with someone else; destroy somebody's stuff)
   ➪ **Do something that allows you to "escape"** (Read a book; watch T.V.; eat; play basketball; go out with friends)
   ➪ **Lighten up** (Make a joke of the situation; laugh it off)
   ➪ **Ignore the situation** (Say, "Forget it," and move on;)
   ➪ **Resort to physical aggression** (Hitting, fighting, killing)
   ➪ **Stop, think, and ask some questions** ("What just set me off? What do I really want to happen now? Do I want to get into a screaming match? Do I want to fight? Do I want to solve the problem? Do I just want the other person to hear my say? Am I willing to look for a solution?"
   ➪ **Tell myself, "I'm in charge of my own feelings"** (I can choose what I want to do right now. I don't want the other person to control what I do or say).
   ➪ **Keep my voice quiet and calm.**

⇨ Tell the other person how I feel, why I'm upset, and what I want to other person to do or to stop doing.

⇨ Say that I'm too angry to talk now, but I want to talk about it later.

⇨ Say an "I message" and give the other person a chance to respond and help problem solve.

2. Use any of these discussion questions for further exploration:

- Which strategies might make the situation worse?
- Which strategies may be self-destructive?
- Which strategies would give you a chance to stand up for yourself without being verbally abusive or physically aggressive?
- Which strategies would be hardest for you to use? Easiest to use?
- When emotions heat up, it's hard to get off the "escalator" — but it is possible! Anger leads to violence quicker than any other emotion. Managing your anger gives you more choices in the heat of the moment. Which strategies would help you to manage your anger so that you don't "lose it" and don't hurt others or yourself?

3. Pass out copies of **Handout 5:5A: "Anger Reducers"** to every student. Ask them to think about the discussion and look over the list as they choose the four or five strategies that will work for them to cool down their anger (top half of handout). Then ask students to think about the kinds of things they can say to themselves in that eight seconds after their "hot button" gets pushed so that they don't get on the escalator and regret losing control afterwards (bottom half of handout). Have students talk through their ideas with a partner.

4. **Role-play practice:** Demonstrate a role-play (you and a student volunteer) in which you choose to express your anger in a nonviolent way using one of the responses above. Then reverse and have the student play the role of the angry person. Debrief the role-play by asking class what they saw and heard that appeared to help people calm down and gain some control over their feelings. Give students copies of **Handout 5:5B: "Defusing Anger"** to review before practicing role-plays. Divide class in pairs and have them practice using situations and "Message Starters" on **Handout 5:5C: "When I'm Angry...."** and then reverse roles using the same situation. The role reversal is a crucial step in helping to develop empathy and an understanding of the other person's perspective.

⚓ **Going Further:** The terms, *"Fight, flight, or flow"*, can also be used to describe our reactions to anger. **Handout 5:5D** shows the behaviors, payoffs, and problems associated with each choice we can make.

Anger Reducers

What I can do to cool down my own anger:

I can _____

I can _____

I can _____

I can _____

Here are things I can say to myself so that I don't do something stupid in the heat of an angry moment.

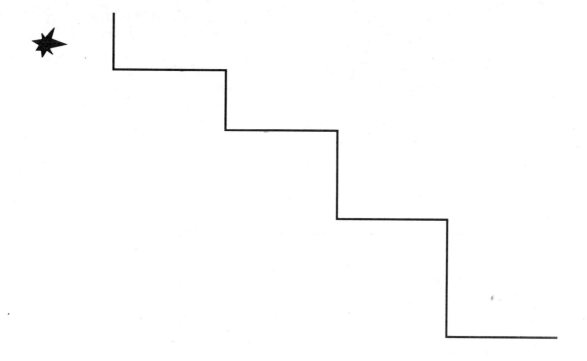

WHEN I'M ANGRY......

Choose the situation:

1. _____has just returned your favorite videotape and it's broken.

2. _____has told someone about a very personal crisis in your family that you didn't want anyone else to know about.

3. _____has neglected to thank you for the fifth time after you've helped her/him to study all semester.

4. _____did not invite you to a big party. You thought you were good friends.

5. _____is spreading rumors about your boyfriend/girlfriend because s/he likes him/her too.

6. _____copied your homework without even asking.

7. _____keeps calling you by an old childhood name just to bug you.

8. _____uses racial slurs throughout casual conversation.

9. _____has never apologized for picking you up late at school three days this week.

10. _____accidentally knocked your books off your desk as s/he was rushing to the next class.

11. _____always seems to be whispering about you with friends when you walk passed in the hall.

12. _____forgot to bring in the money s/he owes you again. You really need it today.

13. _____keeps asking you to skip school so you can go hangout with friends who don't go to school.

14. _____borrowed your history book and has lost it.

15. _____gives you "the look" every time you see him/her in class.

16. _____was playing around and knocked over your art project.

Choose What You Want to Say:

I feel _____when you_____because_____.

I feel _____when you_____. I want you to_____.

I am really angry about_____. I don't want to talk about it now. Can we deal with it later?

I feel _____when you_____. Can you_____so that I can_____?

Defusing Anger

Changing your mindset/beliefs:

From (Destructive)
- injustice, it's not fair
- blaming, it's your fault
- righteousness, I deserve better
- you should or you must
- it's so awful I can't stand it

To (Constructive)
- acceptance, bad things happen
- empathy, s/he couldn't help it
- I can't fight every battle
- humor and silliness

By:
- Identifying your beliefs about anger.

- Distinguishing between beliefs that are constructive and those that are destructive.

- Changing the statements we make to ourselves when we are provoked: "Stay cool;" "How can I solve this problem?" "Bottom line—I can always walk away."

Controlling your body's reactions:

From (Destructive)
- pulse racing
- pupils dilating
- palms & brow sweaty
- muscles tightening

To (Constructive)
- heart rate slowing
- muscles relaxed
- breathing slow and even

By:
- Identifying your triggers.

- Centering.

- Counting to 10.

- Taking deep breaths.

- Consciously relaxing your muscles.

Changing your behavior:

From (Destructive)
- yelling
- sulking/pouting
- arguing while angry
- hitting/throwing things
- accusing

To (Constructive)
- calming yourself
- listening
- paraphrasing and reflecting
- asserting

By:
- Changing your minutes/beliefs.

- Controlling your bodily reactions.

- Asking for time, disengaging if you need to.

- Using non-violent communication skills.

- Practice, practice, practice!

Comparing Fight, Flight, and Flow Behaviors

	Fight	Flight	Flow
Description	You express your feelings, needs, & ideas at the expense of others; you stand up for your own rights but ignore the rights of others; you try to dominate, even humiliate others.	You do not express your feelings, needs, & ideas; you ignore your own rights and allow others to infringe on them.	You express your feelings, needs, & ideas and stand up for your own ideas in ways that do not violate the rights of others.
Qualities	• hostile • self-defeating	• inhibited • self-denying	• expressive • self-enhancing
Feelings Produced	• anger • self-righteousness • guilt (later on) • isolation	• anger • depression • anxiety • resentment	• confidence • self-esteem
Payoff	Vents anger and achieves goals in the short run	Avoids unpleasant situations	Usually achieves goals; even if it doesn't, increases sense of self-worth because you were straightforward; improves self-confidence & leads to freer, more honest relationships with others
Problems	Distances self from others; increases defensiveness in others	Needs are not met; anger builds up; feelings of low self-worth arise	As they arise you can meet them in caring, constructive ways

Center for Peace Education/NC-ESR•118-A East Main Street•Carrboro, NC•919-929-9821

Activity 6: When Someone Else Is Angry.....

PURPOSE: Students will learn techniques to diffuse and difuse anger that they can use when they are in a situation where the other person is angry. They will practice these techniques in several role-plays.

LEARNING STRATEGIES: Whole group discussion, role-play practice

TIME: 30 minutes

MATERIALS: Handouts 5:6A, 5:6B, pencils

SUGGESTED INSTRUCTIONS:

1. Ask students this question: *"When you are really angry and you are with someone else, what do you NOT want someone to do or say?"* or *"When you're angry, what do people do or say that makes you feel even angrier?"* Brainstorm a list of students' responses.

2. Ask for a student volunteer to participate in a role-play with you in which the student can get really angry and upset about something. Use a situation from **Handout 5:6B** if the students can't think of something quickly. The student's role is to really stay with the angry feelings and express them. Your role is to use as many of the responses below as possible which discount or diminish the student's feelings.

    -   Tell the person, "I know how you feel."
    -   Say, "You shouldn't be angry. It's not that big of a deal."
    -   Give the person all kinds of advice and suggestions.
    -   Insist that "Everything will work out. Don't worry about it. You'll be fine."
    -   Make a joke of what happened.

3. When you freeze the role-play, ask the student how s/he felt during the role-play. What responses made the student even more angry? Ask the student what s/he would have wanted you to do or say instead? Ask the class to suggest how they would like others to respond to them when they are really upset. Brainstorm a list of suggestions to this question, **When it's the other person who is very upset, angry, or hostile what can you do?**

249

Identify some key first steps to defusing the situation (stay calm; don't raise your voice; respect the other person's comfort zone - don't get too close; focus your complete attention on the other person and listen; don't argue or interrupt).

Explore alternative responses that might help the angry person cool down and regain their balance. Some possibilities:

- Give the other person "space" to be angry or frustrated - let the other person vent while you keep listening attentively.
- Acknowledge and reflect the other person's feelings. Paraphrase what the other person is saying. Encourage the other person to keep talking.
- Make a quick apology. Saying "I'm sorry" eliminates a lot of stupid hassles when it's not worth your time and trouble to "get into it."
- If the other person has become calmer, you might volunteer to work on the problem together or ask some open-ended questions.

4. **Preparing role-plays:** Use the model on **Handout 5:6A** to develop role-plays which come from students' own experiences with other students, teachers, or parents.

5. **Role-play practice demonstration:** Ask two students to do a demonstration first, using the role play on **Handout 5:6A** or one that you've developed with students. You might want to "freeze" the demonstration at different points to get feedback from the role-players and the students who are watching it. You might also invite students to take turns in the role of the "defuser" as they try out different strategies to use with the angry person.

6. **Role-play practice:** Pass out copies of **Handout 5:6B: "When Someone Else is Angry....."** to each person. Ask students to take turns being the angry person and the skillful communicator. The person who is angry chooses the situation that has sparked the anger.

Here is one way students can give instant feedback to each other is by using a pen or pencil. Have the skillful communicator hold a pen or pencil. When the angry person is feeling an internal change (i.e., "I'm not quite so angry. I don't have to yell so much because someone is really listening. I think I've regained some self-control"), the angry person takes the pen or pencil from the "skillful communicator" to let her/him know that what s/he is saying and doing is working. When the pen or pencil has been passed, switch roles.

✐ **Assessment: Debriefing questions** to explore with the whole class orally or to use for written reflection:
  - How did it feel to be yelled at and try to stay calm?
  - What did your partner do and say that helped you to calm down?
  - Did any of you begin talking about the problem that was the source of the anger? How did that work for you?
  - What was the most challenging part of this exercise?
  - What's one thing you want to remember from today's activities?

☝ **Going Further:** Ask students to think about one person with whom they argue a lot. Pass out note cards to each student and ask them to write down two or three things they've done in the past that keep the argument going so that both people end up being very angry and two or three things that they want to try the next time they feel an angry confrontation coming on with this person.

WHEN SOMEONE ELSE IS ANGRY......

Person A: Choose a situation to role-play that will make it easy for you to get visibly angry. Be dramatic - yell, blame, accuse!

1. You have been grounded for a week and will miss a concert you really wanted to go to.

2. You got a D on a test you had really studied for.

3. Your Mom won't lend you money for the new _____ you want to buy.

4. There is a group at school who is constantly making fun of the slower kids who are "mainstreamed" in the school.

5. A friend is spreading rumors about your boyfriend/girlfriend because s/he likes him/her too.

6. A friend copied your homework without even asking and now you're both in trouble.

7. Your parents refuse to change your curfew on weekends because they're afraid you won't be safe if you stay out too late.

8. The essay you just wrote fell on the floor and_____ just stepped on it.

9. You think that your math teacher is picking on you because you dress sort of weird and your hair has a purple streak.

10. You're ready to fight a person who keeps teasing you and will not leave you along.

11. You are sick and tired of hearing the gunshots at night and waking up to hear about another kid being killled.

12. _____ is always borrowing your stuff without asking.

13. You are constantly pressured by friends to drink when you don't want to. You hate the pressure.

14. Kids in your homeroom make fun of you because you're smart and like school.

15. Your parents are making you go on a family trip that you think will be really boring.

16. In American Lit. class you read nothing except stuff written by dead white males.

Person B: Your goal is to help diffuse the person's anger so that the other person can cool down to the point of talking calmly and possibly beginning to think about what to do about the problem.

1. <u>Listen</u> attentively while the other person vents.
2. Don't get defensive. Stay calm. Keep your focus on the other person. Encourage the other person to keep talking.
3. Paraphrase and reflect the other person's feelings:
   You feel_____because_____. You sound_____.
   I can see that you're upset with me because_____.

252

Activity 7: Violence In America: Introductory Lessons and Starting Points

PURPOSE: The four introductory activities which follow give students the opportunity to help frame how they want to discuss and study the issue of violence in America.

Teachers' Note: Since this issue touches us all in significant ways, it seems appropriate to check out what kinds of feelings, beliefs, perceptions, and experiences students bring to this issue before you move ahead. However you choose to explore this issue, your role as an encouraging listener and facilitator will likely be welcomed as students struggle to make meaning of the violent society in which they live.

7A. Ideas for Journal Writing, Paired Dialogues and Discussion

TIME: At your discretion; can be written in class or for a homework assignment.

MATERIALS: Students' journals

SUGGESTED QUESTIONS:

1. Think about your first personal encounter with violence growing up. What happened? How did it change your view of yourself, other people, the world you live in?
2. How would you define a violent act? What constitutes a violent act?
3. What messages about violence were part of your growing up? Did everyone who was important to you give you the same message?
4. Do you think you live in a violent society? How do you know that you do or don't?
5. Do you think the United States is more violent now than it was 20 years ago? 50 years ago? 150 years ago?
6. Should children be hit? Why or why not? How? When?
7. If it ever okay to physically hurt another person? Where do you draw the line?
8. Why are people violent? What makes some people more prone to commit violent acts than others?
9. How does violence in society affect how you live? How does it shape what you can and cannot do? How does it influence choices you make?
10. Write about a violent incident that you witnessed or experienced. What sparked it? What happened? How did you feel when it happened? Afterwards? Was the violence predictable or unexpected?

7B. Deciding What to Talk About, Research, and Investigate:

TIME: One class period

MATERIALS: Newsprint, markers, three note cards for each student

SUGGESTED INSTRUCTIONS:

1. Make a web chart putting the word "violence" in the center. Ask students what words and phrases, topics and issues come to mind when they hear the word "violence." Students can use the web chart to frame questions about things they want to know more about.

2. Post the journal questions on newsprint and invite students to add other questions to the list. This could be done as a whole class or in small groups as long as all questions are put on newsprint. You might want to separate questions into several categories. Some possibilities:

   - Questions about violence, culture, and society
   - Questions which help you build a data base of information
   - Questions about violence, human behavior, and psychology
   - Kids, families, and violence
   - Questions about violence from a historical perspective
   - Possible opinion, survey, and interview questions.

2. Give each student three note cards. On note cards #1 ask students to write their names, "Questions to Discuss," and three questions that they would want to hear their classmates discuss. On note cards #2 ask students to write their names, "Questions to Investigate," and three questions that they think would be the most interesting and important to find out more about. On note cards #3 ask students to write their names, "Fact-finding Questions," and two questions they want to research.

3. These question preferences and students' journals will give you a good "read" on directions and themes to explore with your students.

7C.   A FishBowl Conversation About Violence

TIME: One to two class periods

MATERIALS: None

SUGGESTED INSTRUCTIONS:

1. Post several of the questions that students wanted to talk about the most. Invite five to seven students to participate in the fishbowl, making a circle in the middle of the room. Have the rest of the students form another circle around the fishbowl. This is an opportunity for students in the fishbowl to share their perspectives and for the audience to listen in interested silence.

    Here are the ground rules:
    1. Choose one question to begin the dialogue.
    2. Do a "go-around" in which each student responds to the question without being interrupted.
    3. After the "go-around," students in the fishbowl can ask clarifying questions to get a better understanding each other's perspectives.
    4. At this time, you can invite one or two students at a time to take the places of students in the fishbowl.

You may want to keep notes of the conversation so that you can come back to particularly compelling issues at a later time in discussion with the whole class.

7D. Where Do You Stand? (A Walking Opinion Poll)

TIME: 20 to 30 minutes

MATERIALS: Masking tape and signs which say, "strongly agree," "agree, not sure / mixed feelings," "disagree," "strongly disagree"

SUGGESTED INSTRUCTIONS:

1. Place masking tape and signs on the floor of your classroom from one side to the other so that students can move easily to stand next to any of the signs.

2.. From journals, question preferences, and the fishbowl, select out some of the more controversial issues and reframe them as opinion statements that offer strong recommendations for what we should do about violence or a distinct perspective on how we should think about violence and violent behavior. You may want to "muddy the water" by changing the statements slightly to see if students' opinions shift.
Here are some examples that have emerged:

   - Handguns should be banned.
   - Children who are violent learn violence at home, firsthand.
   - The United States is rooted in violence. Our society is no more violent now than it was two hundred years ago.
   - Violence on television should be limited to nighttime hours.
   - Censoring any kind of violent entertainment is a violation of our first amendment rights.
   - A certain percentage of the population is genetically more violent that the rest of us. They will commit violent acts regardless of race, class, family background, and environment.
   - Capital punishment should be abolished.
   - Capital punishment should be limited to cases of first-degree murder.
   - Capital punishment should be enforced for all murder cases.
   - When people feel unsafe and threatened, they are more likely to perceive other people as hostile and potential enemies.

2. Explain to students that they will participate in a walking opinion poll. Each time students hear a statement they are move to the place on the continuum that matches their opinion from "strongly agree" to "strongly disagree." Remind students that this is not the time to debate and grill each other. Rather, this is a way to check out what people are thinking and get a sense of the different ways people perceive an issue.

3. When students are standing where they want to be, ask several students to share why they placed themselves where they are.

ACTIVITY 8: DEFINING AND DESCRIBING VIOLENCE

PURPOSE: Students will develop definitions of violence and describe the kinds of violence that people experience on interpersonal, community, and institutional levels.

LEARNING STRATEGIES: Reading for understanding, cooperative learning, descriptive analysis

TIME: One class period

MATERIALS: **Handout 5:8**, newspapers, weekly newsmagazines

SUGGESTED INSTRUCTIONS:

1. Ask students to work in groups of three. Their group task is twofold:
   a. Come to agreement on a definition of violence in your group. Write it on your sheet of newsprint.
   b. How would you categorize different acts of violence? Brainstorm a list of categories that would describe different types of violence. Write these on your sheet of newsprint.

2. Post the newsprint and compare students' responses. With the whole class generate examples of violence and aggressive behavior. Ask students to think about the characteristics of violence and aggression. What constitutes a violent act? In other words, how do you <u>know</u> when you see or experience violence?

3. Pass out copies of **Handout 5:8: "Defining Violence"** to every student. Read Richard Gregg's definition of violence carefully, soliciting examples and illustrations of violent acts as you read. Ask students if they agree or disagree with this definition—parts of it or all of it? Read through the rest of the handout, referring back to examples that students generated in #2. Do their examples fit any of the types of violence mentioned?

4. Bring newspapers and weekly newsmagazines to class, and/or ask students to bring them from home. Divide class into groups of three. Using **Handout 5:8** as a guide, ask each group to find at least ten articles, photographs, cartoons, and newsclippings that illustrate the various types of violence described in the handout. Have students share their findings in class. Did students find more articles about one type of violence than another? Are some kinds of violence invisible or simply not covered by the media very much?

☞Going Further:
- Investigate violent incidents described in news and magazine articles by using a conflict analysis strategy to identify sources of the violence and the history of the conflict. (See Chap. 3, **Handout   **)

- Make a bulletin board of students' investigations in #4.

DEFINING VIOLENCE

VIOLENCE—force used to injure, hurt, threaten or take advantage of someone

> "Violence can be seen as destructive communication. Any adequate definition must include physical, verbal, symbolic, psychological, and spiritual displays of hostility and hatred. The definition must include both our acts and our inactions and that which is done directly to people or indirectly to them through what they esteem.
>
> Violence should then include physical acts against another (a range of acts from personal attack to war that violate human autonomy and integrity); verbal attacks that demean and humiliate; symbolic acts that evoke fear and hostility; psychological attitudes that deny one's humanity and equality (legal, institutional, and moral); spiritual postures that communicate racism, inferiority, and worthlessness (beliefs and values that demean and categorize). Violence then becomes a dynamic rather than merely an act." (1)

DIRECT VIOLENCE—war, batterings, assaults, murder, rape, child abuse (2)

INDIRECT VIOLENCE—economic structures which produce extreme inequalities which result in unequal life chances/repression of freedom of choice/repression of human (civil) rights (2)

INTERPERSONAL VIOLENCE—violence that occurs between two or more people, including *stranger violence* between people who don't know each other, *sexual violence* where sex is forced on an unwilling person, or *acquaintance violence* between people who know each other (3)

COMMUNITY VIOLENCE—violence that takes place on a large scale within a particular community (rioting, police violence, gang warfare) (3)

INSTITUTIONALIZED VIOLENCE—institutionalized power used to deprive individuals and group of basic needs and rights (1)

INDIVIDUAL AGGRESSION—innate propensity for fighting, a predisposition toward threatening behavior which can be verbally and physically violent (4)

1. Gregg, *The Power of Non-violence*
2. Brock-Utne, *Reader in Peace Studies*
3. Prothrow-Stith, *Violence Prevention*
4. Andreski, *Origins of War*

Activity 9: Kids and Violence: What Are The Facts? What Do Kids Say?

PURPOSE: This activity examines societal violence as it affects children and teens. Students will assess what they know from a survey on kids and violence and discuss the implications of the date from the survey. Student will also read excerpts from interviews and writings in which children and teens talk about how violence affects their lives.

LEARNING STRATEGIES: Reading for understanding, critical analysis, cooperative learning, whole group discussion

TIME: Two to three class periods

MATERIALS: Handouts 5:9A , 5:9B, pencils

SUGGESTED INSTRUCTIONS:

1. Pass out **Handout 5:9A: "Kids and Violence - What Do You Know?"** Ask students to read the questions and "guesstimate" their answers from the choices on the right side of the handout.

2. Review and discuss the answers with students.

   ANSWERS: 1. 3,000; 2. 75%; 3. 75%; 4. 8,000 and 100,000; 5. $20 and $200; 6. 60,000; 7. 75 million and 200 million; 8. 4 million; 9. 300,000; 10. 2nd and 1st (auto accidents, homicide, and suicide are the three leading causes of death among adolescents); 11. $60 billion; 12. relationship with a victim, poverty, drugs

3. The following questions can be used as discussion starters after reviewing the answers.

   - Are there any statistics that you find particularly disturbing or surprising?

   - What kind of picture do these statistics give us of the United States? What do these statistics tell us about our "national character"?

   - The number of firearms, the number of violent deaths, the number of homicides involving firearms, and the number of reported cases of child abuse and neglect are many, many times higher in the United States than in other industrialized countries.

How can we account for these striking differences? Are Americans addicted to violence? Is American culture so rooted to its violent beginnings as a nation that it cannot adapt?

- Do you think that most Americans consider violence a serious problem? Why or why not?

- Are some social conditions more likely to induce more violent behavior? Is violence ever a "social adaptation" a "a mode of survival"?

4. You might want to make **"When Killers Come to Class: Violence in Schools"** (From *U.S. News and World Report*) to read and discuss with students. Focus particularly on the research and survey data. Does it confirm or refute the facts in **Handout 5:9A**? Where do your students stand on the survey questions in this article?

5. Make enough copies of **Handout 5:9B "Kids Write and Talk About Violence"** so that each group of five students has one complete set of readings (pp. 1 - 5) and two copies of the questions. The readings are excerpts from *Voices From the Future: Our Children Tell Us About Violence in America*, by Children's Express (Crown Publishers, 1993), a Washington-based news service, reported and edited by teenagers. The instructions which follow suggest offer one way of responding to the readings.

   a. Have students in each group decide which excerpt they want to read: page one, two, three, or four. Give students about ten minutes to read their excerpts.

   b. Ask one person in each group to be a facilitator who asks questions from the **Handout 5:9B, page 6**, and ask one person to be the recorder who writes down the groups responses to the questions.

   c. When students have finished reading, ask each student to summarize the excerpt using suggestions on the handout. You might suggest doing this as a "go-around" where each student takes a turn talking without being interrupted.

   d. Heve the group talk through the rest of the questions on the handout.

   e. Give students about twenty to thirty minutes in their groups.

6. As a whole class, choose two or three of the questions to discuss and compare students' responses and reactions.

7. Pass out copies of **Handout 5:9B: page 7, "Children's Express Editors Speak Out!"** to every student. Explain that these are excerpts from a roundtable discussion with the teen editors who interviewed students whose stories you read about. Ask students to read the handout silently, marking at least three comments with a ☑ where they strongly agree, marking two comments with an ☒ where they strongly disagree, and writing other comments or questions that come to mind in the margins.

8. Discuss the editors' comments as a whole class reminding students to refer back to their notes. Finally, as a closure to this activity, you might want to raise some of these questions:

- Was it a good idea for students to write this book? Why or why not?

- What value does this book have in the national debate about violence and teens?

- Whom would you recommend this book to?

- If you were going to write a book like this from the perspective of your own community, whose stories would be important to include?

☞ Going Further:
- Use the previous question as a foundation for interviewing various people in your community, focusing on how their lives are affected by violence.

- Invite people from various agencies to come and talk to your class about teens and violence. You might include people from the local police, a date rape program, a child abuse hot line, a battered women's shelter, and other service agencies.

✎ Assessment: Topics for Writing
1. What was your initial reaction to the survey and the students' stories?
2. How has your thinking about violence or violent teens changed after this activity?
3. What are two or three things that you think every teen should know about kids and violence?
4. What is one thing your school could do to raise awareness of this issue among teachers and students?
5. What would you identify as three strategies, policies, or attitudes that could help reduce family and teen violence?

KIDS AND VIOLENCE: WHAT DO YOU KNOW ABOUT IT?

Read each question and make your best guess from the choices given.	Choices	Correct Answer
1. In 1989, almost _____ children, ages 10 to 19 died from homicide.	a. 450 b. 1,500 c. 3,000	
2. About _____ % of the casualties in the civil and border wars of the last decade are women and children.	a. 35% b. 55% c. 75%	
3. Guns are a factor in over _____% of adolescent homicides.	a. 25% b. 50% c. 75%	
4. By the sixth grade, the average kid in the U.S. has witnessed _____ murders and _____ other acts of violence on television.	a. 500 b. 2,500 c. 8,000 a. 20,000 b. 50,000 c. 100,000	
5. You can buy a used handgun for $_____ and a new semi-automatic pistol, for $_____.	a. $20 b. $40 c. $60 a. $100 b. $200 c. $300	

6. Over _____ Americans have been killed by firearms in the last two years (more than the number of U.S. soldiers killed in the Vietnam War).	a. 40,000 b. 60,000 c. 80,000	
7. There are _____ million handguns and a total of _____ million firearms presently circulating in the United States.	a. 25 b. 50 c. 75 d. 100 e. 200 f. 300	
8. U.S. manufacturers produce _____ million new guns for a civilian use every year.	a. 2 million b. 4 million c. 6 million	
9. Every month nearly _____ high school students are physically attacked.	a. 150,000 b. 300,000 c. 500,000	
10. Among whites, ages 15 to 19, homicide is the _____ leading cause of death. Among African-Americans, ages 15 to 19, homicide is the _____ leading cause of death.	a. 1st b. 2nd c. 3rd	
11. The Centers for Disease Control's Injury Division estimates that violent injuries cost the U.S. about $_____.	a. $60 million b. $600 million c. $60 billion	
12. Which three factors are most frequently associated with a homicide?	a. relationship with the victim b. being a gang member c. drugs d. poverty e. sexual assault	

Sources: *The Atlantic* (January 1993); *Deadly Consequences,* Deborah Prothrow-Stith, *Fateful Choices,* Fred Hechinger; *Fortune Magazine* (August 10, 1992)

SONIA, 19, NEW YORK CITY

My name is Sonia. I'm half Filipina...I was a violent child. My whole family used to fight all the time...Someone told me once that I was ready to push and shove no matter what happened. I liked all that physical aggression...I was ready to fight...I just wanted to get back at people. I wasn't thinking of how I could de-escalate or integrate what other people were doing...

Coming from wanting to be in fights all the time, it was hard to come here at first. You know, you got praise for being in fights and I was proud of it. I used to be proud to come home with bruises, which is really very silly. Now I would enter a dialogue. I would ask, What's happening here? If the other person was close to me, I'd start walking side by side, so that we're not in a confrontational position... I have learned how to do this because I interned with the Resolving Conflict Creatively program when I as at "City as School" High School...We try to decrease violence by learning techniques in active listening, which means paraphrasing, restating the facts, listening nonviolently, not interrupting, not calling someone names, and body language...

Through our actions, through our words, we show that we're serious about what we're doing and that we are actual examples of what it is we're talking about. We're modeling a peaceful, nonviolent approach. You can be assertive, too - you're not giving up your values, you're not giving up your way of thinking. You're not giving up anything. But you are learning to talk about your differences...

There is violence all over. Violence is a continuum, from being ignored to psychological abuse to physical abuse to sexual abuse - it's all out there. Just walking down the street, a girl gets lots of comments. Someone's looking at you or shouting..."Hey *mamasita*." That's violence...to a woman....

Someone once told me an eye for an eye makes the whole world blind. I think that basically capsulizes what it is that we're trying to express and create...You can't reciprocate hate and violence with hate and violence. You've got to reciprocate instead with love and understanding, because my children would do it to their children and their children would do it to their children...

I feel like I'm making a difference. At first I just wanted to change masses of people, but I know first you have to change and be open to change yourself. I think what helps make a difference is just relating to people differently. I'm listening a lot more and I'm trying to be nonjudgemental...I'm making a difference in my life because I feel better about myself. As I begin to empower myself, others are doing it as well. I see it more when...my little cousins...do it. They feel safe, I know they feel safe around me...

I'm not thinking anymore of how I can manipulate someone or get them back. I'm still an angry youth, I'm angry at what goes on in our world. This violence, this abuse, this shouldn't be happening. We shouldn't be living like this. There's no reason why we should live like this,...there are alternatives. It's really up to us to make a difference. It's up to every person individually to make a collective difference...We really need to work hard together and support each other because we can't do it alone. That way is just futile.

BIG DADDY, 16, INDIANAPOLIS

In my neighborhood, people are getting shot, getting killed, running around. People selling dope every day. They say average life span for a young black male is twenty-one years. Violence is definitely on the rise 'cause ain't nothing getting better. It's probably just always gonna get worse until you teach your kids to do better. Teach your kids.

I'd put more things like community centers, where the most violence comes from. I'd fix up the basketball courts...give them something to do...McDonald's ain't kicking it no more on that four-fifty an hour, so you might as well go sell some dope....violence was probably meant to be here. He wouldn't have put it here if it weren't...wouldn't be writing this book if there was no violence....look at out little kids growing up...how can they call the officer Mr. Friendly when they got guns all over? If you just go around popping each other, I don't think it'll never change 'cause that's all kids see nowadays. Just that.

Some people make you resort to violence...you gotta show people violence...and prove to them that what you mean is business. Like that war Bush started...that wasn't necessary. Send all them people over there for something that they had nothing to do with....I don't expect that much out of life...Like they say, I might not live over twenty-one. Ain't nothing much to expect. I just try to have fun and enjoy life to the fullest...

I experience violence a lot, a whole lot. It's a lot of violence in my family...I'm locked up for possession. Yeah, there's a lot of violence...probably 'cause of the neighborhood....I ain't ashamed to admit it. I sell, dope...People think most dope dudes carry guns...but..you can talk your way out of anything. You can survive without a gun...

I think that life is what you can make out of it....Drugs plays a major role...in our problems today...So I don't mess with that stuff. I don't give kids nothing...
The reason why I do the things I do is because we ain't never had it good. I do the things I do so I can get paid, so I can look out for myself and help my mother...We ain't all bad...

If I could change anything about my life, I wouldn't be locked up...But if you think about it, this is a summer camp. This is supposed to be Department of Corrections...I been here twice...This ain't nothing...When I get out there I probably be back again. It just don't show me no reason to change except for being lock up. But being locked up in here, what do I gotta worry about? I mean nothing...

I fight to solve mostly all my problems, either argumentative or physically. I love it. It's exciting. If I see somebody fighting, I be saying, Get him, kick him, beat him up...It don't really bother me, it don't make me sad or nothing. I get a kick out of it...

Just 'cause we in here don't mean we all bad. Some of it come from what we live in and what we used to, what we adapted to...Some of it is out way of life. People look at me like, He's a menace to society. They say we don't do nothing to society but pollute it. But maybe that's all I know and nobody tried to teach me better...

KIM,17

I was born in Korea and I came here over twelve years ago...We don't really have crimes or anything in this neighborhood, but...there's a lot of victims of the riot. Many were hurt.

My dad's supermarket got all burned down. There's nothing left after the riot. That's the only thing they have, that's all of their money invested and everything. His whole American dream is all burned down the drain now. And the problem is that our insurance company said they don't have enough money and they can't cover what we lost. So now we don't know what to do. We're pretty much angry. And sort of scared....I know a lot of Koreans, a lot of victims of the riots, that might turn against the blacks...But my dad is very open-minded. And I agree. I don't think we have to blame it on the blacks.

I think the whole society is to blame, and I'm angry. The whole community, and the majority is white, they totally ignore the issue because it's not involving them. I'm angry at that. There's so many killed, so many families ruined. There's so many things going wrong and they don't even care for it, they don't sympathize with what's happening, with the blacks or the Koreans. And I'm angry about that.

How can the government just let that happen? They could have done something...but they just stand back and let us kill each other off. .We have to solve it all ourselves....You know, it wasn't just the Rodney King verdict, it all built up with that Korean woman who had a liquor store and who shot that fifteen-year-old black girl. I think that...just built up all that anger and finally there was the verdict that triggered it. Then it all just went up.

I think that shooting was way too much. She had no right to kill that black girl...I used to help out when my parents had a liquor store...and there's a lot of kids who just come in and they're expert. They steal like crazy. You have to give them a chance, you sort of trust them, but they do it...I guess, that no one taught them right from wrong...But I bet that it's scary for a Korean lady who probably can't talk to them in English...I'm sure she was scared and she wasn't thinking straight and she pulled the trigger...

I'm angry because there's been so many people with liquor stores getting killed. And the thing is, it's always a black person pretty much. We have so many cases where the blacks or the Mexicans shot the Korean person, but they never show that. The media, the public...They're always on the black side because they think they need more support...

Still, I feel closer to my black friends since the riots...I have no problems with blacks...I think they're really good. I mean, they're like any other people. At my church there was a lot of blacks coming in or we'd go to black churches and try to break the barrier. So I guess we became a lot closer that way. This is the first time we're really actually trying to understand one another. I think it's good.

But for our family, I don't think we'll set up our store in the same place again because I think my parents would be too scared. Because of the racial tension. I mean, there's a lot of good ones, but there's still a lot of them who do not like Koreans, or the other way around. It's really difficult. I wish people would know that not all Koreans are prejudiced against blacks. I want people to understand that we're trying to open up to blacks. It's hard because we were never opposed to them in the first place. I wish that we could be closer...

266

MARIA, 16

CE: Do you hang out a lot?

MARIA: I go to a lot of parties. Sometimes they're all right, but when them gangsters start coming, well, the party ends and that's it. You can't party no more because they'll all start shooting....There's a lot of gang-banging in my neighborhood and the walls are really nasty. It's so stupid 'cause when one writes, then the other ones come and cross it out...And they just kill each other when they see them...You hear the shots. That's it...

When I was little, actually, I used to kick back with the Bloods. When I used to go to the park, they were always there. It was scary 'cause they wear red, and if anyone passes wearing blue, you just see everybody running, hiding, 'cause if they don't hide, they just get shot.

I live with my mom and my dad, but he's not really like my dad 'cause he be drinking all the time....I ran away from the house so many times. I go to a party, to a movie, to them drive-ins, get drunk, smoke, that's it...Out of all the times I ran away, they only called the police one time. But they didn't catch me. The police don't even bother looking for you. I came back on my own...

CE: Who do you think is responsible for the LA riots?

MARIA: The police. How is they just gonna beat on Rodney King like that and not do nothing about it? Them cops always be trying to beat up on somebody. All the time. And you don't ever see no whites getting beat up on. You only see blacks and Mexicans right there on the floor. That's all. They're all gangsters, with all them drive-by shootings and the killings and all.

CE: Do you know anyone that got killed?

MARIA: All my homeboys. Like five or six of them from the Seminoles. The youngest one was fifteen...They stopped going to school and started gang-banging and they just died. They shot them. Their enemies...Their moms were just crying and crying, like at the funeral and afterwards. Practically never was the dad there, though, only the moms...I guess they [the dads] just got tired, they leave, they don't care. Out of all the funerals, I never seen a father right there, crying...

CE: What is missing in this community?

MARIA: Police...They need to stop the gangs. If it wasn't for no gangs, there would have been a lot of people here still. We need to have more sports, too, more things for the teenagers so they wouldn't be in gangs. That's why they need gangs, 'cause there ain't nothing to do. They might as well just go jump somebody or kill somebody. They just do it so that they can think they're hard. So they could have their respect all the time.

CE: What was it like during the riot?...all the fires and people dying...Were you scared?

MARIA: I wasn't scared 'cause it happens all the time. You always hear about people dying...

CE: Don't people ever talk or think about their future?

MARIA: No. They don't have a future.

FRANKLIN, 17, ATLANTA

I come from New York, but I've been down to Atlanta for about a year...When I was in New York, we had schools that was kind of mixed. But when I came down here, they opened up this new school and they had a big old...fight with white people against black people just because they was white and black. I was all in the middle of that, but I wasn't hittin' nobody because that was is in your mind, it's not physical...

In New York, it's real bad. You know, niggers be shooting every night, doing ruthless, bad stuff. When I was there Thanksgiving they shot this kid, unloaded a gun on his head. Thanksgiving. Because he was selling weed. He wanted to get out of the business. And they shot him. I knew him. He had a baby on the way.

This new school ain't nothing compared to New York 'cause the white kids, they try to stay to their business. It's still segregated...They try to say that it's not, but the white kids stay on one side of the hall and the black kids is on the other side of the hall, even when you go to class...in New York, niggers getting shot in school over girls and stupid stuff...

You know, we can't say, Well, it's society's fault. society did this shit to me. If society give you a gun, it's up to you whether or not you're going to use that gun...It's up to you to say, Well, am I going to go out here and shoot this nigger or am I going to just put it down? It's always up to you....Me, I read a lot and I got to start praying again 'cause that really what lease a lot of the tension. You get your mind off things and try to do for you and your people. There ain't nobody else gonna do for you but yourself...

Now, on the racial stuff, I'm a separatist. I don't believe in integration. I believe Martin Luther King fuck us up when he mixed us with white people....All people of color, they came out of the cage and then they anted to rule the world. And that's what they doing. They rule three-fourths of the world. Now, we don't want to say we gonna take over the world and put the white man in slavery. Then we be just as dirty as he is. So we do it and we rule everything equally, with equality. You know that's what peace stands for. Please Educate All Children Equally.

The white man let the devil use him too much, and it's a lot of black people that let the devil use them too much, too...I gotta change that, 'cause we all chosen...to do something down here on Earth. I ain't sitting here waiting to die to go to heaven neither, 'cause I don't believe in heaven and I don't believe in hell. That's all a state of mind...We in hell right now. What else can this be? This sure ain't no damn paradise. We in hell and we gotta create heaven on Earth...

The black man need to rule to Earth again. I'm not racist or nothing like that, but I know what time is. I'm not saying I hate white people, 'cause I don't hate white people. I hate the things they have done. Just like we have slavery in our genes, they have that taskmaster in their genes. Even if they don't want to do it consciously, they want to do it subconsciously, just like black people want to be slave subconsciously. White people want to be our taskmasters. Actions speak louder than words. Look at history and look a today. People can't see that there's hope for black people.

As it is now, everybody is just dog eat dog...Everybody's worried about number one. I'm number one. I got to do this, I got to do that, I, I, I...What about everybody else?

Questions for Readings From:
VOICES FROM THE FUTURE

Names of students in your group _____

1. After you read your excerpts, do a "go-around" in which each of you takes about two minutes to summarize the excerpt you read, giving the following information:
   a. Name of the teenager being interviewed; age; place where student grew up; location of the interview.
   b. How has violence affected this person's life? How does s/he feel about her experiences?
   c. How does this person see the future? What one piece of advice would this person give to parents? to other teens?
   d. What were your feelings and reactions as you read about this person?

Questions to be answered by the whole group.

2. As a group, agree on two things that seem to be missing from these young people's lives.

   _____

3. What are the two most important things that you think their parents could have done differently?

   _____

4. These teens' stories don't end at the bottom of the page. What are the costs to society if nearly a quarter of its children grow up unable or unwilling to live functioning, productive lives that don't bring harm to themselves or the larger community?

   _____

5. Are there ways in which communities can support families to help prevent these tragedies? What kinds of interventions or opportunities might have helped these teens when they were growing up?

   _____

Children's Express Editors Speak Out

CHANDA: They wanted to be kids, but something was preventing them from doing that. They didn't know how to deal with that, other than being violent. They didn't know any alternative.

AMY: Every time I'd interview someone, I'd ask, "Who's your role model, who do you look up to?" And usually they'd say, My big brother, he's in a gang, he beats up people every day. And I was like, Don't you look up to your parents? And they'd say stuff like, My mom sleeps all day or my dad sells drugs. I just can't imagine having anyone to look up to who's a positive influence in your life.

CAT: The majority of times you're going to turn out better if you have a really healthy, decent background where you feel like you've got support from your family or support from someone else, than if you feel like you're all alone and you've always been all alone through your whole life and you've had to assert independence since you were two or since your were born...You can't struggle your whole life and expect to turn out a healthy member of society.

SHANE: Growing up in New York City, there's always stuff about violence on the news. You walk down the street and see people lying in gutters and you learn to look away. It's just much easier to pretend they're not there. But after you talk to just a few people in that situation, you learn that everyone has their own story...Everyone has a reason. So now, when I'm walking down the street and I see someone sleeping there or something., I think more about it. I try to wonder what brought them there. I can't just walk by anymore...

WENDY: There's always going to be violence. There was some violence twenty years ago, there was violence fifty years ago, but when violence starts to take over, it's a scary thing.

CHANDA: There's so many things going on that maybe some of these kids feel suffocated, like they're in a whirlwind, they're in a cyclone and they can't get out. Their frustration leads to murdering someone or robbing a store...and they can't deal with it.

ROLANDO: I say we do have hope. It's never too late. Never say never. To all the young kids out there, just think about what you're doing and do the right thing. Don't mess up. You have a whole life ahead of you.

Activity 10: Investigating Violence In America

PURPOSE: This activity introduces some additional questions that students may want to investigate and highlights source materials that you may want to read and discuss with the whole class or provide for students to use for small group or individual investigation.

LEARNING STRATEGIES: Reading for understanding, discussion

TIME: Optional

MATERIALS: Handout 5:10 is a list of readings and books that you may want to use with your class for group reading and discussion or for independent research. The selections that are starred (✱) are highly readable and focus particularly on adolescent violence.

SUGGESTED QUESTIONS TO INVESTIGATE:

- Why do some people seem to be more violent than others? Does our predisposition toward violence depend on how we are raised in our families? What community we live in? Can human beings learn to control violent behaviors?

- When discipline is violent (hitting, slapping, verbal abuse), what kinds of messages do children receive? Do these messages carry over to adulthood? How does childhood abuse produce a cycle of violence in the family and in the individuals who are members of that family?

- Is human aggression an innate or learned behavior? Are humans more inherently competitive or cooperative? Why do you think most people think violence is inevitable?

- What are the sociobiological foundations of aggression? Does the problem lie in our animal heritage, in our genes? Have we progressed because only the most aggressive have survived?

- Is a cultural predisposition toward violence and aggression a result of living in permanent hierarchical settlements (where a few people have most of the wealth, status, and power)? Is aggression inevitable when human groups claim permanent territories and borders?

- What messages do most Americans get about aggression and violence? Is aggressive behavior related to "getting ahead," "looking out for Number One"? Is our drive to compete linked to aggressive behavior? Are Americans generally rewarded for aggressive behavior?

Sources For Reading, Research, and Investigation

Addams, Jane	"War is Not a Natural Activity," *The Centennial Reader*
Ardrey, Robert	The Territorial Imperative
Arendt, Hannah	On Violence
Bailey, Ronald	Violence and Aggression
Bender, David	War and Human Nature: Opposing Viewpoints
Bondurant, Joan	Conquest of Violence
Ellul, Jacques	Propaganda
Fromm, Erich	The Anatomy of Human Destructiveness
Gandhi, M. K.	Non-Violent Resistance
Harris, Marvin	Our Kind
Keen, Sam	Faces of the Enemy
Kohn, Alfie	The Brighter Side of Human Nature
Kohn, Alfie	No Contest: The Case Against Competition
Lackner, Stephan	Peaceable Nature
Leakey, Richard	"Is it Our Culture, Not Our Genes, The Makes Us Killers?" *Smithsonian*, Nov. 1977
Lorenz, Konrad	On Aggression
Mead, Margaret	"Warfare Is Only an Invention — Not a Biological Necessity," *Asia*, vol. 40, no. 8, pp. 402-405
Merton, Thomas	The Non-Violent Alternative
Montagu, Ashley	Man and Aggression and Learning Non-Aggression
Morris, Desmond	The Naked Ape
Nagler, Michael	America Without Violence
Nesbitt, William	Human Nature and War: An Anthology of Readings
Pilbeam, David	"The Naked Ape: An Idea We Could Live Without," *The Pleasures of Anthropology*
Ross, Marc Howard	"Childrearing and War in Different Cultures," *Making War/Making Peace*
Rubinoff, Lionel	"In Nomine Diaboli: The Voices of Evil," *Strategies Against Violence*
Sanford, Nevitt & Bruno Leone	Sanctions for Evil
Prothrow-Stith, Deborah	Deadly Consequences

ACTIVITY 11:   PERSPECTIVES ON VIOLENCE

PURPOSE: This activity introduces students to the words and ideas of prominent people who have spoken and written passionately about the subject of violence.

LEARNING STRATEGIES: Critical reading and writing, whole group discussion

TIME: A few minutes or an entire class period

MATERIALS: Handout 5:11

SUGGESTED INSTRUCTIONS:

Pass out **Handout 5:11; "What People Say About Violence and Aggression"** or select several to use separately as starting points for discussion, journal writing or further investigation. Some ideas:

- Ask students to choose two quotes to analyze which reveal contrasting <u>assumptions and values</u>.

- Ask students to write about or discuss quotations with which they strongly agree and disagree.

- Ask students to discuss a quotation which speaks to them, one they think reflects what they are thinking more closely that any other.

- Select quotations to use for practice in critical reading and reasoning skills:

  a. <u>Paraphrasing</u> - Choose particular sentences to rewrite using your own words, while keeping the idea intact.
  b. <u>Summarizing</u> - Use some of the longish quotations to practice summarizing the main idea in one clear sentence.
  c. <u>Looking for Evidence</u> - Ask students to identify the kinds of evidence and data that would validate the truth as it is expressed in the quotation.
  d. <u>Looking for Loaded Language</u> - Ask students to look for prejudicial, pejorative, emotionally charged and exaggerated language that may contribute to overstating the case that the author is trying to make. Consider why writers might use this kind of language for persuasion. What makes this kind of language more successful or less successful?
  e. <u>Looking for What's Missing</u> - What an author chooses to say— what examples an author chooses to select—are more clearly understood when we examine what an author chooses to ignore, omit, or deny. Discuss a quotation that is less than convincing because of what is not acknowledged, or discuss a quotation written with absolute certainty, being aware of exceptions which refute that certainty.

WHAT PEOPLE SAY ABOUT VIOLENCE AND AGGRESSION

1. In so far as man is concerned, if competition, in its aggressive combative sense, ever had adaptive value among men, it is quite clear that it has no adaptive value whatever in the modern world.....Perhaps never before in the history of man has there been so high a premium upon the adaptive value of cooperative behavior.

   No human being has ever been born with aggressive or hostile impulses, and no one becomes aggressive or hostile without learning to do so.

2. In a competitive relationship, one is predisposed to have a suspicious, hostile, exploitative attitude toward the other, to be psychologically closed to the other, to be aggressive and defensive toward the other, to see the other as opposed to oneself and basically different. One is also predisposed to expect the other to have the same orientation.

3. One must marvel at the intellectual quality of a teacher who can't understand why children assault one another in the hallway, playground, and city street, when in the classroom the highest accolades are reserved for those who have beaten their peers. Classroom defeat is only the pebble that creates widening ripples of hostility.

4. Aggressiveness is the principal guarantor of survival...man is a predator whose natural instinct is to kill with a weapon.

   Our history reveals the development and contest of superior weapons as *Homo sapiens'* single, universal cultural preoccupation. Peoples may perish, nations dwindle, empires fall. Mankind as a whole has never in a single instance allowed local failure to impede the progress of the weapon, its most significant cultural endowment.

5. I need my enemy in my community. He keeps me alert, vital....But beyond what we specifically learn from our enemies, we need them emotionally; our psychic economy cannot get along will without them.

   Deeds of violence in our society are performed largely by those trying to establish their self-esteem, to defend their self-image, and to demonstrate that they, too, are significant...Violence arises not out of power but out of powerlessness.

6. Man is a beast of prey. I shall say it again and again...Conflict is the original fact of life, is life itself, and not the most pitiful pacifist is able entirely to uproot the pleasure this gives the most inmost soul.

7. Physical violence is the basis of authority....Government is an association of men who do violence to the rest of us.

8. The tendency to identify manhood with a capacity for physical violence has a long history in America.

9. Violence alone, violence committed by the people, violence organized and educated by its leaders, makes it possible for the masses to understand social truths and gives the key to them.

10. The condition of man...is a condition of war of everyone against everyone.

11. Innate, aggressive potentials must surely be part of human nature....I propose that bands and villages make war because they find themselves in competition for resources....These resources become scarce as a result of being depleted or as a result of rising population. Local groups face the prospect of reducing the rate of population growth or reducing their level of consumption. War offers a tempting solution. If one group can succeed in driving away its neighbors or thinning its ranks, there will be more resources for the victors...Groups can rationally accept the risk of battlefield fatalities in return for the chance to improve their living conditions.

12. Nonviolence is the answer to the crucial political and moral questions of our time; the need for man to overcome oppression and violence without resorting to oppression and violence. Man must evolve for all human conflict a method which rejects revenge, aggression, and retaliation. The foundation of such a method is love.

13. Violence is necessary; it is as American as cherry pie.

14. In order to rationalize the blizzard of cruelty and aggression in contemporary society, it is helpful to believe that is not always possible to control open anger, rivalry, and jealousy. This rationalization mutes feelings of guilt and dilutes a sense of personal responsibility for hurting others. The Japanese, by contrast, believe that each person can control his or her anger, and the differential frequency of violence in Tokyo and New York implies that if people believe that they can tame their aggressive impulses, they often do.

15. If our nature "at bottom" is to be aggressive—a nature which we can only struggle to inhibit—then why are so many hunter-gatherer cultures apparently devoid of aggression? Erich Fromm has pointed out that "the most primitive men are the least warlike and that warlikeness grows in proportion to civilization." If destructiveness were innate in man, the trend would have to be the opposite.

16. Drugs and gangs are surely major factors in spreading the epidemic of violence among young people, but the disintegration of the family, particularly but not exclusively in areas of urban poverty, is a major root of the crisis. The combination of such danger-prone conditions and one-parent homes under stress escalates child abuse of every kind—physical, psychological, and sexual.

    When children grow up as witnesses to aggression between family members, among neighbors, and among peers, they may conclude that to resort to brute force is an acceptable part of family and social life.

17. Our children are killing each other because we teach violence. We've got to do something to stop the slaughter....Many people don't think that violence can be avoided. They accept it as an inevitable part of life. We recognize anger as a normal and potentially constructive emotion. Students have legitimate reasons for their anger—they need to respond in healthy rather than unhealthy ways. But violence is, by and large, an unhealthy way to respond.

18. The television and movie industries do indeed bear a heavy responsibility for making violence appear an acceptable, even normal, way of life. This media conditioning begins when children are at an early age, virtually in infancy. Many cartoons to which very young children are regularly exposed, often without any adult presence, include violence that is meant to amuse. The problem often is not the violent action itself but rather the fact that it does not appear to cause pain or inflict lasting damage; the person or animal flattened by a fallen rock quickly recovers his original shape without any apparent consequences. Often, too, the violence is implicitly justified by being directed by the good guys against the villains. Whatever lessons about right and wrong these battles may teach, they fall short of any suggestion that conflicts can be resolved in nonviolent fashion.

19. Violence is a problem that begins at home. I believe that if all the children born in American learned at home how to manage anger and aggression nonviolently, our homicide and assault rates would decline by 50 percent—maybe 75 percent. Mothers and fathers rarely put guns in the hand of their children and tell them, "Go kill or be killed."

276

The destructive lessons that parents teach when they are physically and psychologically abusive to their children and when they allow their children to be physically and psychologically abusive to other, in conjunction with our society's glorification of violence, the ready availability of guns, and the drug culture are an explosive combination that set our children up to be the perpetrators and the victims of violence.

20. If people in a highly warlike society are likely to overestimate the propensity toward war in human nature, then it must be noted that the United States is one of the most warlike societies on the face of the planet, having intervened militarily around the world more than 150 times since 1850. Within such a society, the intellectual traditions supporting the view that aggression is more a function of nature than nurture have found a ready audience.

SOURCES:

1. Ashley Montagu
2. Martin Deutsch
3. Joseph Wax
4. Robert Ardrey
5. Rollo May
6. Oswald Spengler
7. Leo Tolstoy
8. Marshall Fishwick
9. Frantz Fanon
10. Thomas Hobbes
11. Marvin Harris
12 Martin Luther King, Jr.
13. H. "Rap" Brown
14. Jerome Kagan
15. Alfie Kohn
16. Fred Hechinger
17. Deborah Prothrow-Stith
18. Fred Hechinger
19. Deborah Prothow-Stith
20. Alfie Kohn

Activity 12: Monitoring Television Violence

PURPOSE: This activity helps students develop more critical eyes and ears as they watch violence on television. Students will develop a survey to monitor television violence and discuss their observations and conclusions.

LEARNING STRATEGIES: Cooperative learning, whole group discussion, observation and documentation

TIME: Two class periods

MATERIALS: Newsprint, markers (Optional: video clips of local news broadcasts)

SUGGESTED INSTRUCTIONS:

1. Brainstorm a list of television programs that are most popular with students. Do a quick survey of programs that are most popular with younger brothers and sisters.

2. Use any of the following questions to explore the television violence.

   - How is violence usually presented on television?

   - How do the images and language in advertising, television, and film make violence more acceptable?

   - How do violent television images affect us when we witness an actual incidence of violence?

   - Does television influence human behavior? Do you think that watching violence on television makes some people more aggressive than they would otherwise be?

3. Develop a survey to monitor violence on individual television programs. What do students think they should observe in each program? Do students want to make distinctions between what is seen on television and what is not shown (for example, the aftermath and consequences of a violent act).

   How do students want to qualify and differentiate between various acts of violence (verbal and physical / personal, community, and state-sponsored violence / direct and indirect / gratuitous, exaggerated, repetitious violence vs. violence that is necessary to the story line / violence that looks authentic vs. violence that is stylized, fantasized)?

278

How do they want to record their observations? Do they want to record situations in which an alternative nonviolent response is used instead to settle a dispute or disagreement?

4. After you have finalized the survey, ask students to pair up and ask each pair to choose one television program that they both want to monitor. This way they can compare their results for consistency.

5. When students have finished their monitoring, give each pair about 15 minutes to compare their results. Explain that each pair will present their observations to three other pairs.

6. Divide class into groups of four pairs each. Give each group newsprint and markers to record their findings. After all pairs have reported in each group, ask each group to write down three conclusions or generalizations about television programming.

7. Finally, post newsprint on the walls, and as a whole class review their observations, discoveries, and insights.

8. Encourage students to bring up new questions and concerns which have emerged from this exercise.

☞ Going Further:

1. **Monitoring Local News Broadcasts** Bring in several clips of the first fifteen minutes (without commercials) of local news broadcasts. Using the survey you developed, observe how violence is depicted and described on the local news. Is there any pattern in how violence are presented? What is shown and what isn't? How is violence sensationalized? Do you see gratuitous images of violence in the broadcast which are unnecessary to communicate the story but are used because they may titillate the audience? Do reporters inform the public about violence by presenting any of the facts and data that you have learned in these lessons? Do reporters communicate how violence has affected individuals, groups, neighborhoods, and the larger community? Do reporters investigate sources and root causes of violent acts that they broadcast?

   Are there contrasting stories presented which show other means of settling disputes or ways in which individuals and groups are trying to prevent and reduce violence in the community?

2. **"Violence Watch" Postcard Campaign** Students may want to develop criteria for a postcard campaign directed at local media. One postcard could designate a **thumbs down** ☟ for violent news stories poorly presented, with accompanying suggestions for how the story could have been presented differently. Another postcard could designate a **thumbs up** ☝ for news stories that give the public a fresh perspective, new information, or a more comprehensive understanding of violence in your local community, with specific feedback about what made the story more socially responsible.

Activity 13: Raising Awareness And Reducing Violence In Your Own Community

PURPOSE: Students will examine three common approaches to addressing interpersonal and community violence and research how people are working together to help reduce and prevent violence in their communities. Students will decide which efforts they think will be most cost-effective and bring about the best results. Finally students will consider project options for taking action in their own community.

LEARNING STRATEGIES: Investigative research, reading for understanding, group decision-making and collaborative problem solving

TIME: Several class periods and additional time for investigative research

MATERIALS: Handouts 5:13A, 5:13B, 5:13C; transparencies, overhead projector; newsprint; markers

SUGGESTED INSTRUCTIONS:

1. Pass out copies of **Handout 5:13A: "Reducing Violence in Local Communities."** Read and review the handout together, and take ten minutes to brainstorm other specific strategies and programs that students are aware of that could help reduce interpersonal and community violence. As you brainstorm, identify the approach that each suggestion reflects. Ask studenta why they think that most money is spent on law enforcement rather than prevention and intervention programs.

2. Pass out copies of **Handout 5:13B: "Violence Reduction: How Much Does It Cost?"** Explain to students that they will be using this list to make decisions about how to allocate community resources to reduce violence.

3. Divide students into small groups to do research. Each group member needs to decide what kind of research they want to do. Some suggestions:

   - Telephone interviews to find out about programs that currently exist in your own community.
   - Reading research (periodicals and books) that describes successful violence prevention and intervention programs around the country.
   - Field trips to interview people that coordinate programs into your community as well as people who participate in these programs.

281

You may want to brainstorm research suggestions with the whole class. Ask each group member to jot down what they want to research and the method they will use for finding out. Remind students that the purpose of research is to gather specific information about various programs that may help them decide how to allocate resources in their community.

4. Give each group out one copy of **Handout 5:13C: "Recommendations from the Task Force on Violence"** and one transparency students will fill in their final recommendations. Tell students: "You are members of your community's (or region's) Task Force on Violence. Through new state and federal funding, your city (or region) will receive an additional $10,000,000 dollars each year for the next five years. Your job is to recommend to the city (or regional) council how to spend this money." The guidelines for decision making are on the handout. Give the students at least 30 minutes to work in their groups.

5. Ask one student from each group to present their recommendations to the whole class, giving a brief explanation for the choices they made. Invite students to ask questions at this time. Use a transparency projector so the class can compare recommendations. Discuss and note differences and similarities in the recommendations.

6. Ask for one volunteer from each group to participate in a caucus at lunch or after school or while the rest of the class is engaged in another activity. The caucus group has the responsibility to make a final recommendation to the whole class that they think will receive the class's approval.

7. Ask one person from the caucus group to present the final recommendation. Decide how the class will reach agreement (straw poll, consensus, ballot).

8. When the class has reached agreement on their recommendations, ask them who they would like to give their recommendations to in their community. Ask for volunteers who are interested in drafting a cover letter, producing a final document, and telephoning appropriate community leaders and service providers with whom they would like to meet.

Reducing Violence In Local Communities

Public and private efforts to reduce and prevent violence usually reflect four different approaches:

1. **Prevention** — Stopping the violence before it happens
   - Reducing and eliminating the root causes of violence (lack of opportunity; discrimination; lack of resources to meet basic needs; generational family patterns of despair, hopelessness, irresponsibility, and alienation; neglect, abuse, and abandonment)
   - Conflict resolution, violence prevention, and mediation programs which teach nonviolent means for responding to conflict
   - Public education about violence, its personal costs, and costs to society
   - "Neighborhood Watch" and other crime prevention and personal safety programs
   - Comprehensive support programs and counseling for "at risk" parents, families, and children in schools and neighborhood centers

2. **Deterrence** — Using threats to prevent persons from taking actions that are harmful to individuals or the community (If you do A, I will do B). Deterrence depends on the credibility of the threat, the willingness to carry it out, and/or the belief that the threat will hurt the victimizer.
   - Community policing programs / More police officers on the streets
   - Metal detectors in schools
   - Capital punishment and mandatory prison sentences for violent crimes
   - Purchasing a firearm for protection

3. **Intervention and Rehabilitation** — After a violent act has been committed, using community resources to directly intervene with individuals in ways that help both victims and victimizers break the cycle of violence, support their efforts to change patterns of behavior, and provide initial resources and support to assist them in living productive, functional lives in their local communities.
   - "Boot camps" for youth offenders
   - Support programs for adolescents and families already entrenched in a cycle of violence
   - Intensive programs for youth who have received hospital emergency room services after incidents of gang violence
   - Shelters and programs for battered women and abused children

4. **Law Enforcement, Punishment, and Legal Restrictions and Regulations on Behavior and Weapons**
   - Gun control legislation / Bans on handguns and assault weapons
   - Community curfews restricting youth activity in the late evening hours on the streets and in public places
   - No bail for violent offenders / No probation for violent offenders
   - Trying violent youth offenders as adults
   - More prisons, more money, and personnel for law enforcement

Most of our "political capital" is expended on 2. and 3. Why do you think so little money and energy is spent on prevention? Ask students to generate a list of suggestions that they would recommend to reduce violence in the

VIOLENCE REDUCTION: HOW MUCH DOES IT COST?

Average Cost	Service
$40,000/yr	One police officer in one public school or one new police officer on the street
25,000/yr	Incarceration of one prison inmate
25,000/yr	Residential treatment for a violent youth offender
20,000/yr	Residential care for one abused child who is now a ward of the state
15,000/2mo	Treatment at a residential drug rehabilitation center and follow-up support
15,000/family	Participate in "Families First," a comprehensive family support program including health care, parenting support, counseling, child care, child development, and education/job training opportunities
12,000/yr	Foster care for one child
10,000	Development of comprehensive conflict resolution and school-based mediation program in one school
5,000/yr	Support services for alcohol and drug addicts now in recovery
2,500	One school metal detector
1,300/family	Participate in "family preservation" programs
500	Comprehensive school-based support programs for one "at-risk" teen (health care, social, and psychological services)
500/child	Comprehensive neighborhood-based youth programs

RECOMMENDATIONS FROM THE TASK FORCE ON VIOLENCE

Using information from **Handouts 5:13A and B**, your group has been given the task of recommending how to spend $10,000,000 in new revenues to reduce violence in your community. Your community will receive this amount of funding annually for the next five years. Here are the guidelines you must follow:

- Your choices must match targeted areas that have already been determined by state and federal officials:
  35% or $3,500,000 must be spent on Law Enforcement
  35% or $3,500,000 must be spent on Intervention and Rehabilitation efforts
  30% or $3,000,000 must be spent on Prevention and Deterrence efforts

- You must make the case that your choices are cost-effective: they must lead to greater safety and security in your community and must save taxpayers' money in the long run.

- You may not recommend more than <u>a total of five line items</u> in the final budget (<u>or fewer than three!</u>). Community leaders have already decided to focus their energies on implementing a few successful programs that can produce results rather than choosing to spread money and resources all over the map.

> **First,** take about 10 minutes to make your own recommendations independent of the group.
> **Second,** do a "go-around" in which each group member makes recommendations defending his/her choices.
> **Third,** reach a consensus (everyone in your group must agree) about final budget recommendations.
> **Finally,** write your final choices on the transparency and identify who will make your report to the whole class.

Draft Recommendations

Targeted Spending Categories	Your Choices	Final Choices of Your Group
Prevention and Deterrence		
Intervention and Rehabilitation		
Law Enforcement		

FINAL RECOMMENDATIONS FROM THE TASK FORCE ON VIOLENCE

Names of Group Members:

_____   _____

_____   _____

_____

Targeted Spending Categories	Final Choices of Your Group
Prevention and Deterrence	_____ _____
Intervention and Rehabilitation	_____ _____
Law Enforcement	_____ _____

Chapter 6: Perspectives on War and Peacemaking

Activity 1:   What Is War?

Activity 2:   Are Aggression and War in Our Genes?

Activity 3:   Perspectives on War

Activity 4:   Images and Language of War in Literature, Film, and Art

Activity 5:   Talking, Writing, and Drawing Peace

Activity 6:   Positive and Negative Concepts of Peace

Activity 7:   Images of Peace in the Media, Literature, and the Arts

Activity 8:   Perspectives on Peace

Activity 9:   What Is the Role of a Peacemaker

Activity 10: Anatomy of a Problem Solver/Peacemaker

Activity 11: Interviewing People About Peacemaking

Activity 12: Peacemakers at Work

Activity 13: Spotlight on Peacemakers: Past and Present

Activity 14: Interviewing and Celebrating Local Peacemakers

Activity 1: What Is War?

PURPOSE: Students will consider the kinds of human activity we define as war, what activities we might describe as warlike, and what activities are neither. Students will examine various definitions of war and types of warfare, especially as these descriptions relate to the kinds of war we are witnessing at the end of the twentieth century.

LEARNING STRATEGIES: Brainstorming, whole group discussion, reading for understanding, cooperative learning

TIME: One class period

MATERIALS: Handout 6:1, newsprint, markers, large paper, newspapers, tape

SUGGESTED INSTRUCTIONS:

1. Make a **web chart** placing the word "war" in the center. Ask students to brainstorm all the words and phrases that they think of when they hear the word "war."

2. Put the following list of items on the board or newsprint and ask students to consider whether they would categorize each item as "War," "Warlike," or "Neither:"

   Gang fight
   "War on Drugs"
   Intifadah uprisings of Palestinians in Gaza and the West Bank
   U.S. invasion of Panama in 1990
   Drug wars in Columbia
   "War on Poverty"
   Vietnam War
   Urban street violence
   Trade wars over tariffs and open markets

   Terrorist bombing of Pam Am Flight 407 over Scotland
   L. A. riots in 1992
   Protests in Tienamen Square in China in 1989
   Democratic Revolution in Russia in 1990
   The Cold War
   Armed conflict in Bosnia-Herzegovina
   Political chaos in Somalia
   Israeli bombing of nuclear facilities in Iraq in 1988

   Give students a few minutes to discuss the list with a partner before you open up discussion with the whole class. Make three lists as students select where they would place each item. Discuss what students perceive to be the differences between these activities and events.

3. Pass out copies of **Handout 6:1: "Defining War and Aggression"** to each student. Read through the definitions of war and the descriptions of various kinds of warfare carefully, soliciting examples and illustrations from students using the web charts, the list from #2, and current conflicts that students might be familiar with.

✎ **Assessment:** Divide students into groups of three. Ask students to use current newspapers and news magazines to make a collage of current conflicts, labeling them using descriptions from the handout.

289

Defining War and Aggression

INSTITUTIONALIZED AGGRESSION War-making by one state or insurgent group against another state or insurgent group (1)

It is the use of armed force by a state against the sovereignty, territorial integrity, or political independence of another state including:

1. invasion or attack by armed forces
2. bombardment or use of any other weapons
3. blockade of ports or coasts
4. attack on air forces or naval fleets (2)

Anthropologists warn us not to confuse the behavior of individuals with the behavior of nation-states. State-sponsored aggression or warmaking requires more than the potential inclination to fight that may characterize individual human beings. Among other things, war-making requires "a great deal of stimulation of martial ardor playing on vanity, fear of contempt, family attachment, group affiliation and loyalty, and so on."(1)

WAR ——Violent conflict between organized groups (3)
——The conditions which permit two or more hostile groups to carry on a conflict by armed force (4)
——A struggle for control of government within a governed society (2)
——A clash between major interests that is resolved by bloodshed (5)
——The continuation of politics by other means (5)
——Embraces more than politics: it is the expression of culture, in some societies the culture itself (8)

Types of Warfare:

"Low-intensity conflict" (insurgencies, organized terrorism, paramilitary crime, sabotage, and other forms of violence in a shadow area between peace and war) (6)

Limited war (wars involving one of the superpowers and a third party that is contained within a well-defined area (wars in Vietnam, Afghanistan, Korea) (7)

Regional wars (fought within or along the boundaries of contending states) (7)

Civil wars (struggle for power within a state) (7)

Wars of self-determination or national independence movements (7)

Total war (full mobilization of troops and use all available weapons and technology to defeat the enemy) (7)

Sources:
1. Andreski, *Origins of War*
2. United Nations
3. Glossup, *Confronting War*
4. Wright, *A Study of War*
5. von Clausewitz, *On War*
6. Kissinger, *Discriminate Deterrence*
7. Nye, *Hawks, Owls, and Doves*
8. Keegan, *A History of Warfare*

ACTIVITY 2: ARE AGGRESSION AND WAR IN OUR GENES?

PURPOSE: Students will read excerpts which present contrasting viewpoints about the nature of aggression and war, examine the positions found in each reading, and consider the implications of these positions.

LEARNING STRATEGIES: Reading for understanding, cooperative learning, whole group discussion

TIME: One class period

MATERIALS: Handouts 6:2A, 6:2B, pencils

SUGGESTED INSTRUCTIONS:

1. Pass out the first page of **Handout 6:2A Are Aggression and War in Our Genes?** Read together the first paragraph and the questions that follow. Explain that students will read excerpts that represent two contrasting perspectives on aggression and war. These questions can be used as a guide for reading the excerpts which follow.

2. Before students read, you might want to review words which are not defined in the readings:
   exploit (to use to the best advantage)
   maladaptive (not suited to a particular adaptation)
   intraspecies (within a species)
   natural selection (all species produce more than enough offspring to replace themselves, but in a given environment, some individuals with certain traits are more likely to survive and reproduce than others, passing on those favorable traits to the next generation)

3. Divide students into groups of four (two students in each group will receive copies of **Perspective #1** excerpts [sections 1 -- 5] and two in each group will receive copies of **Perspective #2** excerpts [sections 6 -- 9, A -- D]). Students will record their answers on **Handout 6:2B: "What Did You Find Out?"** for each section that they read.

Remind students that they will not find answers to every question in each section; however, they will have a pretty clear composite of each perspective from the collection of readings in each section. Have each group member share their findings with each other and then answer the summary questions at the bottom of the handout as a whole group. Remind someone in each group to record their responses to the summary questions.

4. As a class, review responses to the summary questions on **Handout 6:2B,** and then open up discussion to the original questions on the first page of **Handout 6:2A.**

Some points to include in discussion:
- New research, especially studies of identical twins who were raised in different households from birth, are leading many scientists to consider that genes not only control physical characteristics (like eye color, height, skin color) but also profoundly influence human behavior and personality; no one yet, however, has isolated an "aggressive" gene or an "introvert" gene. The controversial question is *how much* do genes influence our personality and behavior? Many scientists feel that people, like other animals, adapt to changing situations and pass on successful behaviors to the next generation, counterbalancing the genetic imprint from our chromosomes.

- There is common agreement in all among scientists that human beings, like other animals, have a predisposition toward aggressive behavior. However, sociobiologists are far more likely to see violent aggression and war as biologically based behaviors either to be controlled and suppressed or to be replaced with more ritualized nonlethal aggressive activities.

- Humanistic anthropologists and other behavioral scientists are more likely to identify the *expression* of aggressive behavior as something that is *learned* and *chosen.* They suggest that there is much greater interdependent relationship between biology and environment and culture.

- Where sociobiologists see *war as inevitable* (it's in our genes), behavioral scientists see *war only as a possibility* (the expression of war depends on a culture's values and political organization).

292

- Belief in one perspective or the other has enormous implications regarding what we choose to do or not do about violence and warmaking in our culture.

  If we are biological determinists and view violence and war as inevitable, we will think there's not much we can do about the crisis of violence. We may not even see it as a crisis. We will advocate public policy that stresses law enforcement and imprisonment. In other words, violence and warfare will always be here at a constant level—our goal should be to contain and deter violent behavior as much as possible, punish those who misbehave or harm others, and be prepared to win a war against any potential enemy. The role of leaders is to react quickly, manage effectively, and reduce the damage as much as possible.

  If we are scientific humanists we will place much more emphasis on the power to learn, unlearn, and change specific behaviors and the power to choose cooperative, nonviolent behaviors if these behaviors are valued and rewarded in a particular culture. We will advocate public policy that allocates more resources for prevention, reduction of environmental stressors that may intensify and increase aggression and violence, and development of skills that build and strengthen interpersonal, community, and global cooperation. The role of leaders is to model nonviolent, cooperative behaviors and attitudes through the language they use, the example they set, and the public values they advocate.

- **Some concerns about the popularization of the theory of biological determinism:** First, sociobiology does not reject the "nurture" aspect of human development; it is far more complex than popularizers make it out to be when theory is reduced to either nature or nurture. Second, many people feel that a simplistic understanding of sociobiology can lead to a conclusion that human actions are disconnected from personal responsibility for those actions (i.e. "My genes made me do it—I cannot be held personally accountable!"). Finally, critics are concerned that people can use biological determinism to support a world view in which a few are winners and many are losers, some can learn and many can't, and some groups are intellectually and morally superior to others and thus deserve more power, status, and resources—that who you are and who you can become is reduced to your genetic heritage.

Are Aggression And War In Our Genes?
Two Perspectives

Biologists, ethologists (who study the social behavior of animals), and anthropologists (who study human evolution, human diversity and variation, and human culture [culture is all learned behavior]) are all interested in the big questions about human nature:

1. How are humans alike and different from other animals?

2. What influences our behavior the most: our genes and the biological imprint of our animal ancestors, or our culture, what we learn after we are born?

3. What is humanly possible as a product of our culture, and what is humanly inevitable as a product of our biology?

4. Is there a biological and/or a cultural basis for aggression? Is there a biological and/or cultural basis for war?

Perspective #1

The new science of the 1960s brought with it the emerging field of sociobiology, the science of the biological basis of social behavior. Many scientists point to evidence that we behave like other animals and are driven by the same animal instincts. The heart of this controversy centers on whether human beings are "biologically programmed" to be aggressive and therefore make war with their own kind. Given the weapons in the hands of human beings, this is an extremely relevant question—and the answers to this question have very serious implications for the future of humankind.

1. **Raymond Dart**, an anthropologist from South Africa, discovered fossil remains in 1924 that he insisted were from a creature that was a "missing link" between apes and the earliest human beings. He theorized that human evolution came about because early hominids invented weapons that were used to kill prey. Hunting and killing were critical to human survival—the best hunters with an acute killing instinct would be favored in a process of natural selection. Consequently, the killing instinct would be genetically imprinted from one generation of hunters to the next.

    Dart's theory of the "killer ape" was very popular in the 1920s and 30s, at the same time that "social Darwinism" was very popular— the theory that the strongest and most competitive people are the most "fit" to survive and deserve to control the behavior and destiny of others.

2. **Konrad Lorenz**, the Nobel Prize-winning ethologist, suggests that aggressive behaviors are found in many vertebrates; aggressive behavior, specifically on the part of males, allows the species to have enough space to exploit the resources it needs or to select a mate. Lorenz sees aggression as an adaptive behavior; animals are aggressive so that they have a better chance of survival. Lorenz also notes that animals engage in ritualized aggression (rams locking horns, for example) which stops the aggressive behavior from becoming lethal (i.e., one animal actually kills another of the same species).

    Lorenz warned that aggression is not only "in our genes," but that for human beings, aggression is "maladaptive." In other words, humans have not successfully developed ritualized behaviors that replace the kind of lethal aggression that expresses itself in warfare. Lorenz suggested that contact competitive sports like football are a way to discharge aggressive energy.

3. **Robert Ardrey**, who wrote *African Genesis* and *The Territorial Imperative*, argues that human beings' innate aggression and territoriality are a basic foundation for war. He writes, "We have to recognize that the conditions that give rise to war—the separation of animals into social groups, the 'right' of each group to its own area, and the evolution of an enmity complex (hostility toward the enemy) to defend such areas—were on earth long before man made his appearance".

Ardrey insists that "the drive to maintain and defend territory" is not the cause, but the *condition* of human war. According to Ardrey, in order to learn more about why humans make war, we need to learn much more about our biology. The cultures in which wars are fought are of less importance in understanding human aggression and war-making.

4. **Lionel Tiger** and **Robin Fox,** anthropologists and authors of *The Imperial Animal,* argue that "aggression in the human species is the same as aggression in any other animal species." There is no killer instinct that makes the human species any different from other animals. Aggression and competition are necessary forces in the evolutionary process of natural selection. "One animal has to strive to outdo another for nest sites, territory, food, mates, dominance, so that selection can take place." Tiger and Fox see violent aggression against predators as a positive force which protects that species from the outside and nonviolent aggression and competition as a way of preserving the species from within. They regard violence as innate, but suggest that as humans we have endless choices of how to use this violence.

    The most radical part of Tiger's and Fox's thesis is their theory that war-making is an inherently male endeavor. "War is not a human action but a male action; war is not a human problem but a male problem. Only males governed, only males hunted, and out of this lopsided sexual fact emerged another: only males cooperated to fight." Tiger and Fox agree with other sociobiologists that the male hormone testosterone is linked to heightened levels of aggression. They insist that "organized predatory violence has always been a male monopoly, whether practiced against game animals or those enemy humans defined as 'not-men.' This is the important step toward human warfare."

5. **Sigmund Freud**, the pioneering psychoanalyst, writes in *Civilization and Its Discontents,* "The existence of this tendency to aggression.... is the factor that disturbs our relations with our neighbors and makes it necessary for culture to institute its high demands. Civilized society is perpetually menaced with disintegration through this primary hostility of men toward one another....The fateful question of the human species seems to me to be whether and to what extent the cultural process developed in it will succeed in mastering the derangements of communal life caused by the human instinct of aggression and self-destruction."

Sources: Ardrey, Robert, *African Genesis*; Campbell, Bernard, *Humankind Emerging*; Freud, Sigmund, *Civilization and Its Discontents*; Kohn, Alfie, *The Brighter Side of Human Nature*; Tiger, Lionel, and Fox, Robin, *The Imperial Animal*; and Weiss, Mark, *Human Biology and Behavior*

Perspective #2

Many anthropologists and scientists (**S.L. Washburn, Margaret Mead, Richard Leakey, Ashley Montagu,** among them) reject the limitations of "biological determinism" arguing that human behavior is too complex to attribute personality and behavioral traits such as aggression to any specific genes. They reject that human beings are genetically programmed to be killers citing evidence that human evolutionary history reflects greater expression of sharing behaviors and cooperation than deadly aggression and competition.

6. From "War and Human Nature," in *Anthropology and Contemporary Human Problems,* John H. Bodley

> Aggression must be clearly distinguished from war; whereas aggression per se might be understandable to some extent in biological terms, warfare is a cultural phenomenon carried on between cultural groups....it should be clear that during most of humanity's existence, war, as usually defined, simply did not exist until the evolution of centralized political organization, even though humanity's biological inheritance must have remained constant.

7. From "The Naked Ape: An Idea We Could Live Without," **David Pilbeam,** in *The Pleasures of Anthropology*, edited by Morris Freilich

> The closest we can come to a concept of "natural man" would indicate that our ancestors were, like other primates, capable of being aggressive, but they would have been socialized culturally in such a way as to reduce as far as possible the manifestation of aggression. This control through learning is much more efficient in man than in other primates, because we are cultural creatures— with the ability to attach positive values to aggression-controlling behaviors.

The issue is whether we choose to use them.

Pilbeam points to the !Kung Bushmen in the Kalahari of Southern Africa who encourage peaceful cooperation and provide the young with nonviolent role models. On the other hand, he notes that the Yanomamo Indians of Brazil value "a high capacity for rage and a willingness to use violence"; consequently, they encourage young boys "to argue, fight, and be generally belligerent."

Pilbeam suggests that American culture provides the young, especially young males, with a variety of violent, aggressive role models. All of these behaviors are learned. Cultural values will determine whether cooperative, nonviolent behaviors or competitive, aggressive behaviors will dominate.

8. From "Sociopsychological Aspects of the Nuclear Arms Race," **Jerome Frank**, M.D., American Psychiatric Association

Although it is undeniable that programs of violence are imbedded in the central nervous system, there is no direct link between them and complex social behaviors such as waging war. Innate patterns of scratching, biting, and kicking have nothing to do with launching a nuclear missile. Waging war must be learned afresh by every generation. We cannot claim that because he is violent, human sacrifice in religious rites is inevitable, or that because man is innately carnivorous, cannibalism is inevitable. Human survival, to be sure, now demands the creation of less lethal psychological equivalents for war, but in principle this is not beyond the bounds of possibility.

9. From "The Seville Statement on Violence," submitted by 20 scientists from 12 nations at a **UNESCO** (United Nations Educational, Scientific, and Cultural Organization) conference in Seville, Spain, on May 16, 1986.

A. IT IS SCIENTIFICALLY INCORRECT to say that we have inherited a tendency to make war from our animal ancestors. Although fighting occurs widely throughout the animal species, only a few cases of destructive intraspecies fighting between organized groups have ever been reported among naturally living species, and none of these involve the use of tools designed to be weapons. Normal predatory feeding upon other species cannot be equated with intraspecies violence. Warfare is a peculiarly human phenomenon and does not occur in other animals.

The fact that warfare has changed so much over time indicates that it is a product of culture. Its biological connection is primarily through language which makes possible the coordination of groups, the transmission of technology, and the use of tools. War is biologically possible, but it is not inevitable. There are cultures which have not engaged in war for centuries, and there are cultures which have engaged in war frequently at some times, and not others.

B. IT IS SCIENTIFICALLY INCORRECT to say that war or any other violent behavior is genetically programmed into our human nature. While genes are involved at all levels of nervous system function, they provide a developmental potential that can be actualized only in conjunction with the ecological and social environment. Except for rare pathologies, genes do not produce individuals necessarily predisposed to violence. Neither do they produce the opposite.

C. IT IS SCIENTIFICALLY INCORRECT to say that in the course of human evolution there has been a selection for aggressive behavior more than for other kinds of behavior. In all well-studied species, status within the group is achieved by the ability to cooperate and to fulfill social functions relevant to the structure of that group. "Dominance" involves social bondings and affiliations; it is not simply a matter of the possession and use of superior physical power, although it does involve aggressive behaviors.

Where genetic selection for aggressive behavior has been artificially instituted in animals, it has rapidly succeeded in producing hyper-aggressive individuals; this indicates that aggression was not maximally selected under natural conditions. When such experimentally created hyperaggressive animals are present in a social group, they either disrupt its social structure or are driven out. Violence is neither in our evolutionary legacy nor in our genes.

D. IT IS SCIENTIFICALLY INCORRECT to say that war is caused by "instinct" or any single motivation. The emergence of modern warfare has been a journey from the importance of emotional and motivational factors to the importance of intellectual factors. Modern war involves institutional use of personal characteristics such as obedience, suggestibility, and idealism; social skills such as language; and rational considerations such as cost-calculation, planning, and information processing. The technology of modern war has exaggerated traits associated with violence in the training of armies and in generating support for war in the general population. As a result of this exaggeration, such traits are often mistaken to be the causes of war rather than the consequences of preparing for and making war.

We conclude that biology does not condemn humanity to war, and that humanity can be freed from the bondage of biological pessimism. Just as "wars begin in the minds of men," peace also begins in our minds. The same species that invented war is capable of inventing peace. The responsibility lies with each of us.

WHAT DID YOU FIND OUT?

Name _____   Sections I am reading _____

Answer these questions for each section:

	Perspective # ___	Perspective # ___	Perspective # ___
	Section	Section	Section
1. How are humans like other animals?			
2. How are humans different from other animals?			
3. Which influences our behavior more—genes or culture? Evidence?			
4. Is there a **biological / cultural** basis for aggression? One or both? Evidence?			
5. Is there a **biological / cultural** basis for violence and killing? One or both? Evidence?			
6. Is there a **biological / cultural** basis for war? One or both? Evidence?			
7. What can humans do to prevent and reduce war?			

Summary Questions: 1. Identify areas of agreement in both perspectives. 2. Identify areas of disagreement between perspectives. 3. How would public policy efforts to deal with aggression and violence—prevention, law-enforcement, punishment—differ for advocates of each perspective? 4. Does one perspective make more sense to your group? Why?

300

ACTIVITY 3: PERSPECTIVES ON WAR

PURPOSE: This activity introduces students to the words and ideas of prominent people who have spoken and written passionately about the subject of war.

LEARNING STRATEGIES: Critical reading and writing, whole group discussion

TIME: A few minutes or an entire class period.

MATERIALS: Handout 6:3

SUGGESTED INSTRUCTIONS:

Pass out **Handout 6:3: "What People Say About War"** or select several quotations to use separately as starting points for discussion, journal writing or further investigation. Some ideas:

- Ask students to choose two quotations to analyze which reveal contrasting <u>assumptions and values</u>.

- Ask students to write about or discuss quotations with which they strongly agree and disagree.

- Ask students to discuss a quotation which speaks to them, one they think reflects what they are thinking more closely that any other one.

- Select quotations to practice critical reading and reasoning skills:

  a. <u>Paraphrasing</u> - Choose particular sentences to rewrite using your own words, while keeping the idea intact.
  b. <u>Summarizing</u> - Use some of the longish quotations to practice summarizing the main idea in one clear sentence.
  c. <u>Looking for Evidence</u> - Ask students to identify the kinds of evidence and data that would validate the truth as it is expressed in the quotation.
  d. <u>Looking for Loaded Language</u> - Ask students to look for prejudicial, pejorative, emotionally charged and exaggerated language that may contribute to overstating the case that the author is trying to make. Consider why writers might use this kind of language to persuade. What makes this kind of language more successful or less successful?
  e. <u>Looking for What's Missing</u> - What an author chooses to say—what examples an author selects—are more clearly understood when we examine what an author chooses to ignore, omit, or deny. Discuss a quotation that is less than convincing because of what is not acknowledged or discuss a quotation written with absolute certainty, while being aware of exceptions which refute that certainty.

WHAT PEOPLE SAY ABOUT WAR

1. Peace through strength is a fallacy, for peace is not simply the absence of a nuclear holocaust. Peace is not a nation which has seen its teenage suicide rate more than double in the past two decades. Peace is not a nation in which more people die every 2 years of gunshot wounds than died in the entire Vietnam War. And peace is not here in Washington—where after leading the Nation in murders last year, children are beginning to show the same psychological trauma as children in Belfast, Northern Ireland.

2. As a woman, I can't go to war and I refuse to send anyone else... You can no more win a war than you can win an earthquake.

3. It is sometimes said that war is a natural condition of man. As a military man, I do not believe it....I do believe breathing, eating, loving, caring, are natural conditions of man. People don't make war, governments do....And our governments appear willing to accept war, even nuclear war, as a natural event....There is not one nation in the world where the people want war.

4. I have known war as few men now living know it. Its very destructiveness on both friend and foe has rendered it useless as a means of settling international disputes.

5. After all, war isn't that effective. In every case, at least one side loses, which is only 50% effective, if you're lucky. The winner pays a very large price, as well.

6. We are ready to kill to keep our automobiles running. We're ready to kill to keep up our materialistic, wasteful economy... I am sick and tired of 18-year-olds being coerced into bearing the burden of the failure of politicians to face the tough economic choices.

7. ...We will never have peace...so long as people go on manufacturing death and trying to sell it.

8. It is always immoral to start a war....Diplomatic and other nonviolent means should always be used to resolve conflicts and fend off aggression....If nonviolent methods fail, and one nation unjustly attacks another, the victim nation has as a last resort the right and

duty to use violent means to defend itself within certain moral limits.....The military response to any attack may not exceed the limits of legitimate self-defense.

This means that the damage inflicted and the costs incurred must be proportionate to the good expected by the taking up of arms. The wholesale slaughter of civilians in large population centers is simply immoral, whether the destruction is intentional or unintentional, direct or indirect, no matter what weapons system is used.

9. Nothing in human history is more obscene than the cool discussion of competing nuclear strategies by apocalyptic game-players. All sorts of scenarios are being put forward about the circumstances under which we would drop bombs on the Soviet Union and the Soviet Union would drop bombs on us, as though both countries were involved in nothing more than a super backgammon game. The strategists in both countries need to be reminded that they are not playing with poker chips but with human lives and the whole human future.

10. My suggestion is quite simple. Put the codes that are needed to fire nuclear weapons in a little capsule, and then implant that capsule right next to the heart of a volunteer. The volunteer would carry with him a big, heavy butcher knife as he accompanied the President. If ever the President wanted to fire nuclear weapons, the only way he could do so would be for him to first, with his own hands, kill one human being. The President says, "George, I'm sorry but tens of millions must die." He has to look at someone and realize what death is—what an innocent death is. Blood on the White House carpet. It's really brought home. When I suggested this to friends in the Pentagon, they said, "My God, that's terrible. Having to kill someone would distort the President's judgment. He might never push the button."

11. So far, war has been the only force that can discipline a whole community, and until an equivalent discipline is organized, I believe that war must have its way.

12. The warring state permits itself every such misdeed, every such act of violence, as would disgrace the individual man. It practices not only the accepted strategies, but also deliberate lying and deception against the enemy....[It maintains] an excess of secrecy, and a censorship of news and expressions of opinion....It absolves itself from the guarantees and contracts it had formed with other states, and makes unabashed confession of its rapacity and lust for power, which

303

the private individual is then called upon to sanction in the name of patriotism.

13. There are no warlike peoples—just warlike leaders.

14. It would indeed be a tragedy if the history of the human race proved to be nothing more than the story of an ape playing with a box of matches on a petrol dump.

15. Human war has been the most successful of all our cultural traditions.

16. A man who experiences no genuine satisfaction in life does not want peace...Men court war to escape meaninglessness and boredom, to be relieved of fear and frustration.

17. ...and they shall beat their swords into plowshares, and their spears into pruning hooks; nation shall not lift up sword against nation, neither shall they learn war any more.

18. Force—that is, physical force, for moral force has no existence save as expressed in the state and the law—is thus the *means* of war; to impose our will on the enemy is its *object*. To secure that object we must render the enemy powerless; and that, in theory, is the aim of warfare.

19. In general, those who plan do not kill and those who kill do not plan. The men who planned the saturation bombings, free-fire zones, defoliation, crop destruction, and assassination programs in the Vietnam War never personally killed anyone.

20. War is a permanent feature of our life, surviving from one historical period to another regardless of all change in social and political systems, in religions, ethics, intellectual and technical standards. These systems have simply altered the nature of war.

21. Where human societies are organized for the purpose of carrying on war (and there are few which are not), there is always the danger that war will occur.

22. Despite the horrors, futility and destructiveness of war, there are nevertheless certain virtues and truths associated with it which humanity cannot afford to lose.

There is in all hearts a desire to live a significant life, to serve a great idea and sacrifice oneself for the noble cause, to feel the thrill of spiritual unity with one's fellows and to act in accordance therewith. We all wish for strenuous action and the exercise of courage and fortitude, to be carried away by the enthusiasm of daring. We all love to undergo a common discipline and hardship for the sake of a fine ideal; to be in good effective order; to be strong, generous and self-reliant; to be physically fit, with body, mind and soul harmoniously working together for a great purpose, thus becoming a channel of immense energies. Under such conditions, the whole personality is alert, conscious, unified and living profoundly, richly and exaltedly.

23. The Warrior Caste has the ability to reproduce itself from one generation to the next. Only women can produce children, of course; but—more to the point—only wars can produce warriors. One war leads to the next, in part because each war incubates the warriors who will fight the next, or, I should say, create, the next.

Our task—we who cherish "daily life" and life itself—is to end the millennia-old reign of the Warrior Caste. There are two parts to this task. One is to uproot the woman-hating, patriarchal consciousness that leads some men to find transcendence and even joy in war. That will take time, though we have made a decent start. The other part is to remember that war itself is the crucible in which new warriors are created. If we cannot stop the warriors' fevered obsessions, and bring these men back into the human fold, we can at least try to stop their wars.

Authors:
1. Senator Mark Hatfield
2. Jeanette Rankin
3. Rear Admiral Gene R. LaRoque
4. General Douglas MacArthur
5. Gene Sharp
6. Senator Mark Hatfield
7. Edna St. Vincent Millay
8. Statement of the Catholic Bishops on the Just War Theory
9. Norman Cousins
10. Roger Fisher
11. William James
12. Richard Barnett
13. Ralph Bunche
14. David Ormsby Gore
15. Robert Ardrey
16. Nel F.S. Ferre
17. *Isaiah 2:4*
18. Carl Von Clausewitz
19. Richard J. Barnet
20. Urpo Harva
21. John Paul Scott
22. Richard B. Gregg
23. Barbara Ehrenreich

Activity 4: Images And Language Of War In Literature, Film, Music, And Art

PURPOSE: This activity presents some key questions that students might address in discussions about the theme of war as portrayed in literature and the arts. A bibliography of resources is included.

LEARNING STRATEGIES: Reading for understanding, critical analysis, whole group discussion, independent writing

TIME: Optional

MATERIALS: Any of the resources cited in the bibliography

SUGGESTED QUESTIONS FOR DISCUSSION AND JOURNAL REFLECTIONS:

1. Our earliest literature contains visceral images of war and physical conflict (*Gilgamesh, The Iliad, The Old Testament*). Why is war such a compelling subject of literature in the past and the present? Are there experiences in the human condition that only warfare provides? Do you agree with this statement? "Despite its destructive character, war persists because it has served many of men's needs in terms of providing security, excitement, fellowship in a great cause, cooperative effort, and many other things human beings want, need or think they need. Because of this, war must be looked upon as another human institution, which, as long as it serves human needs will persist." (Nesbitt, Abromowitz, and Bloomstein, *Teaching Youth About Conflict and War*)

2. Is warfare a "male domain"? Are we most familiar with war-making images because most of our images throughout history have been produced by males? If war is the dominant metaphor in men's thinking, is it also the dominant metaphor in women's thinking? If not, what images do you perceive as dominant metaphors in women's thinking? In literature, what kinds of images are contrasted with war-making images (hearth and home, domestic tranquillity, fertile fields ready for harvest, community and family harmony, the birth of a child)? Are these images necessarily male or female metaphors?

3. A veteran of Vietnam acknowledged the horror of the war but also spoke about images of war that "delight the eye" (the streak of napalm scorching the earth, the bursting of bombs, a bridge or building exploding into a million matchsticks). Why do we find these images compelling and captivating? Think about children's action toys, Saturday cartoons, action/adventure films, and comic books. Are warlike behavior and violence the most dominant images for many children? Can other behaviors and images offer excitement, drama, high risk and adventure? Are the media images children most often see the preferred images of children or the preferred images of the adults who produce them and advertise them?

4. Explore the relationship between individuals and the collective institution of war. How do authors connect our attraction to war with the "roots of war within us"? What makes us so willing to go to war? Why is patriotism so closely connected to "dying for one's country—making the ultimate sacrifice"?

5. How do authors use different literary styles and devices to depict war?

   Romance/Heroism —*For Whom The Bell Tolls* — Ernest Hemingway
   Irony —"Dulce et Decorum Est," Wilfred Owen
   Cynicism —*The Quiet American*, Graham Greene
   Naturalism —*The Red Badge Of Courage* — Stephen Crane
   Realism —The Good War: An Oral History Of World War II, Studs Terkel
   Fantasy/Science Fiction —Dune, Frank Herbert

6. How do writers' own experiences shape their perceptions of war and choice of point of view? How might the stories and accounts of war be different if the author is a journalist, a combat veteran, a civilian who is witness to the ravages of war, a civilian whose country is at war thousands of miles away, a historian, a parent whose son has died in war, an adolescent, a government propagandist? How does an author manipulate a reader's feelings through the choice of point of view?

7. Explore the differences in literature, art, and film that depict war as a humanizing or dehumanizing experience. Does some literature reveal how people are moved to virtue, a "call to conscience," self-discovery, and empathy through their war experiences? Does other literature reveal how people are moved to demonize the enemy, make an enemy less than human in order to kill him, depersonalize war, and disconnect feelings from war? Does some war literature offer the reader a range of characters who experience different feelings about war?

8. How does literature and art depict the "human costs of war"? Do the experiences of suffering, sorrow, and devastation make us more human? Do we know less of life without the experience or memory of war? How can we know of suffering, sacrifice, and violent death if we have not experienced it? How do war experiences shape a nation's and culture's attitudes about war? (Think about how many American wars have been fought on foreign soil in comparison to European, African, and Asian wars fought on their home fronts. Do Americans perceive war more optimistically (and perceive "winning" as a clearer, more achievable outcome) because the U.S. has not experienced the long-term destruction and devastation of 20th century war within its own territory?)

9. How do loaded and biased language, euphemisms, and abstract, neutralized, depersonalized terms make war more attractive or repellent, more or less psychologically acceptable, and more distant or connected to our own experiences?

10. What do literature and art teach us about war that textbooks and documents do not?

RESOURCES:

1. Refer to the interdisciplinary humanities unit "War and Peace in Ancient Greece and the 20th Century" for other literature suggestions (on page in Appendix A).

2. The following list of literary, film, video, and art resources are especially appropriate for grades 9 through 12. You may want to select excerpts from some of the longer literary works to use in class depending on your time constraints.

ART

Bruckner, D. J. R.	Art Against War (400 years of protest art)
Hodgson, Pat	The War Illustrators (20th century)
Keegan, John	The Nature of War (Anthology of paintings)
	A History of Warfare (Cultural history of war)
Kollwitz, Kathe	Prints and Drawings (World War I)
Phillips, Robert	Political Graphics: Art as a Weapon
Yenne, William	German War Art: 1939-1945

DRAMA

Euripides	The Trojan Women

FICTON

Caputo, Phillip	A Rumor of War (Vietnam)
Del Vecchio, John	The 13th Valley (Vietnam)
Fussell, Paul	The Norton Book of Modern War
Gioseffi, Daniela	Women on War (anthology by women from every continent)
Haldeman, Joe	War Year (Vietnam)
Hemingway, Ernest	For Whom the Bell Tolls (Spanish Civil War)
Herr, Michael	Dispatches (Vietnam)
Kosinski, Jerzy	The Painted Bird (WW II Eastern Europe)
Remarque, Erich Maria	All Quiet on the Western Front (World War I)

Trumbo, Dalton	Johnny Got His Gun (World War I)
Tuchman, Barbara	The March of Folly (From Troy to Vietnam)
	The Guns of August (beginning of WW I)
Walsh, Patricia	Forever Sad the Hearts (Nurse's Vietnam experience)
Wharton, William	A Midnight Clear (World War II)

MUSIC

Denisoff, R. S.	Songs of Protest, War, and Peace
Dolf, Edward	Sound Off! Soldier Songs from the Revolution to

NONFICTION

Baker, Mark	Nam
Broyles, William	"Why Men Love War" *Making War/Making Peace*
Emerson, Gloria	Winners and losers: Battles, Retreats, Gains, Losses and Ruins from the Vietnam War
Fields, Rick	The Code of the Warrior (Samurai, Knights, and Plains Indians)
Fussell, Paul	The Norton Book of Modern War
Gioseffi, Daniela	Women on War (anthology by women from every continent)
Gray, J. Glenn	The Warriors (Historical overview)
Hachiya, Michihiko	Hiroshima Diary: The Journal of a Japanese Physician *Making War/Making Peace*
Higgins, Marguerite	War in Korea: Report of a Woman Combat Correspondent
Keegan, John	The Face of Battle (Historical overview)
Kovic, Ron	Born on the Fourth of July (Vietnam)
Larteguy, Jean	The Face of War (Vietnam)
Lawson, Don	Youth and War (Vietnam)
Lifton, Robert Jay	In a Dark Time (Poetry and writings on living in the nuclear age)
Nixon, Barbara	Raiders Overhead: A Diary of the London Blitz

Rosenblatt, Roger	Children of War (Children in war zones of the 80's)
Saint-Exupery, Antoine de	Wind, Sand, and Stars (Essays)
Santoli, Al	Everything We Had (Vietnam)
	To Bear Any Burden: The Vietnam War and Its Aftermath, in the Words of Americans and Southeast Asians
Tolstoy, Leo	Letter to a Non-Commissioned Officer
Townsend, Peter	The Smallest Pawns in the Game (How affects children, 1940-1978)
Trooboff, Peter	Law and Responsbility in Warfare: The Vietnam Experience
Turkel, Studs	The Good War: An Oral History of World ' Two
Walzer, Michael	Just and Unjust Wars
Weil, Simone	Reflections on War
Wouk, Herman	War and Remembrance (World War II)
Editors of Yank Weekly	Yank: The Story of World War II as Writte the Soldiers

POETRY

Auden, W.H.	The Shield of Achilles
Brooke, Rupert	1914 (five sonnets)
Cohn, Carol	"Nuclear Language and How We Learned to Pat the Bomb" *Making War/Making Peace*
Fussell, Paul	The Norton Book of Modern War
Gioseffi, Daniela	Women on War (anthology by women from every continent)
Harrison, Michael	Peace and War (Poetry Anthology)
Lifton, Robert Jay	In a Dark Time (Poetry and writings on living in the nuclear age)
Richards, Grant	Swords and Plowshares (Poetry anthology)
Stallworthy, John	The Oxford Book of War Poetry
Twain, Mark	"The War Prayer"
Weil, Simone	Winning Hearts and Minds: War Poems of Vietnam Veterans

VIDEOS AND FILM

In the Minds of Men (29 min.) Looks at
the universal suffering caused by
wars in the 20th century

Unforgettable Fire (15 min.) Recollection
of Hiroshima survivors

An Essay on War (23 min.) Why we
wage it, how we justify it, and how
nations and individuals are affected
by it

The Hat: Is This War Necessary? (18
min.) Two enemy soldiers meet and.
. . .)

Neighbors (9 min.) Allegory about
boundaries

Total War (26 min.)

Report from Beirut: Summer of 1982 (20
min.)

Sad Song of Yellow Skin (60 min.) The
people of Saigon after the war
    Suffer the Little Children (53 min.)
        Northern Ireland in 1971

WAR (video series produced by Gwynne
Dyer)

ACTIVITY 5: TALKING, WRITING, AND DRAWING PEACE

PURPOSE: Students will explore what they think "peace is...." using a variety of media.

LEARNING STRATEGIES: Drawing, reflective writing, class discussion

TIME: Two class periods

MATERIALS: Drawing paper, markers or crayons, newsprint

SUGGESTED INSTRUCTIONS:

Defining Peace:
1. Begin by asking students to write a definition of peace. When you discuss students' definitions, try to clarify what peace *isn't* as a way to more specifically describe what peace *is*. Write a collective definition on newsprint to keep for the next part of the activity.

Drawing Peace:
2. Divide students into groups of three or four. Give each group a large piece of newsprint and markers or crayons. Explain that their task is to cover the paper with their images of peace by drawing pictures, symbols, and cartoons. Their murals should help answer the question, "What does peace look like?"

3.. Put students' murals next to the class's collective definition and compare them. Are they similar or different? For now, have students just describe what they see and don't see. Interpretation and analysis come later.

Writing Peace:
4. Ask students to choose one question to write about from the suggestions which follow:
   - Describe a scene or situation you think of as peaceful.

   - Write about something you were doing when you experienced peace.

   - What comes to mind when you hear the phrase "a world at peace"?

   - Write about a time when:
     ~You felt at peace with yourself.
     ~You felt inspired and excited.
     ~You you were completely involved in what you were doing and the time just disappeared.
     ~You worked with a group of people and accomplished something that nobody thought you would.
     ~You felt like you overcame a difficult challenge by yourself.

313

~You helped someone get through a tough time.
~You and your family felt very close and connected.
~You stood up for what you believed.
~You took the time to really try to understand and listen to someone whose ideas and opinions were very different from your own.

5. Invite students to share what they wrote with the class. Then briefly review the class's collective definition of peace and look again at the images they drew. Have students summarize their collective vision of what peace is.

Talking Peace:
6. What follows are some questions and issues to consider in a class discussion about peace after students have done the previous activities:

- Explore the substance, tone, and feeling of students' words and images. Are they passive, dull, pastoral, static, repetitive, positive or negative, dynamic, exciting, powerful? For many children the images of peace that they are familiar with are either "corny" and boring (flowers, peace signs, shaking hands, etc.) or alienating (a noisy protest, a person being arrested, etc.).

- Think about why the concept of peace receives either negative press or no press. We seldom hear about peace or see images of peace which are connected to action. Instead, peace is most often present as a "still life" after all the action has taken place!

- Introduce students to the idea that peace can involve the same kind of focused action and dynamic tension that we experience in most conflicts—the difference lies in the purpose of our actions (destructive, life-diminishing or contructive, life-enhancing) and how we use that tension (violently or nonviolently).

- Contrast students' images of the words "peace" and "peaceful" with "peacemaking" and "peacekeeping?" Record a list of words and phrases that illustrate how they interpret these two sets of words differently. Can peace be perceived as a struggle that involves excitement, dynamic action, risk taking, and intense, deeply felt experiences?

  Make a list of verbs which can replace the phrases, "make peace" and "keep the peace." In other words, what would you see a person, group, or nation *doing* if they were making the peace or keeping the peace?

314

ACTIVITY 6: POSITIVE AND NEGATIVE CONCEPTS OF PEACE

PURPOSE: Students are first introduced to the concepts of positive and negative peace. Then they explore how these concepts imply different political and social commitments and policies. Students apply their understanding of these concepts by creating "positive peace" collages.

LEARNING STRATEGIES: Whole group discussion, reading for understanding, cooperative learning, reflective writing

TIME: One class period

MATERIALS: Handout 6:6, large drawing paper, magazines, newspapers, tape, glue

SUGGESTED INSTRUCTIONS FOR DISCUSSION ON POSITIVE AND NEGATIVE PEACE:

1. Introduce the concepts of positive and negative peace using any of the questions and discussion notes which follow:

   A. Peace as merely the absence of war and physical violence **negative peace.** Many would say the major goal of peace is to stop war or at least reduce and limit the threat and effects of war and physical violence. Explore with students whether this strategy can actually prevent wars in the future or merely contain them. Does these strategies get at the root causes of war and violence? Does real peacemaking require nonviolent resolution of conflict?

   Images of negative peace tend to address immediate symptoms and conditions of war and the use and effects of force and weapons. These images often shout or lament, "War is bad and we must stop it."

   B. If students agree that war is **not peace** (war is violent, destructive, life-diminishing), what kinds of activities are **peace** (nonviolent, constructive, life-enhancing)? What kinds of attitudes promote peace and enhance the quality of life?

315

Does peace involve the creation of a more just, equitable, and ecologically balanced world? Can peace mean doing nothing—not willingly harming anyone, but not getting involved? Can peace be possible if pervasive poverty exists?

C. **Positive peace** involves efforts to reduce and eliminate the root causes of war and violence through greater social equality and justice. A commitment to positive peace addresses the question, "What do we do, and how do we change ourselves to make real peace possible?"

Images of positive peace often depict two parallel worlds — the present struggles to achieve justice and equality in this world and the imagined world we have not yet created. Positive peace integrates our power to act now with our hopes and visions for the future.

D. Can there be an oppressive, coercive "peace" that is worse than the state of war (for example, the Chinese occupation of Tibet, the Israeli occupation of the West Bank and the Gaza Strip, or the Soviet domination of Warsaw Pact nations after World War II)?

Can there be an oppressive, coercive peace that is better than a peace in which there is no institutionalized warfare but a high level of interpersonal violence is tolerated? (For example, consider China, which has a repressive government and a very low incidence of interpersonal violence, and the United States, which has a free democratic government and the highest level of interpersonal violence in the industrialized world.)

You might want to explore the writings of peacemakers (Martin Luther King, M.K. Gandhi, Jane Addams) who concluded that war can no longer serve any moral purpose even against totalitarianism.

2. Pass out copies of **Handout 6:6: "What Is Peace?"** Read it with students, reviewing the differences between negative and positive peace. Solicit examples from personal experience, current events, literature, the media, which illustrate these concepts.

Are there any definitions that are new to students? Which activities are more reactive (efforts to act after something has happened)? Which activities are more proactive (efforts to act before something happens)? When groups and governments do commit resources to "peace," which of these activities get the most the most attention and resources? Why do you think this is so?

SUGGESTED INSTRUCTIONS FOR MAKING A "POSITIVE PEACE" COLLAGE:

1. Using newspaper clippings, photographs, and magazines, make collages of words, headlines, stories, and images which illustrate the concept of positive peace. Using **Handout 6:6** as a reference, generate examples of specific projects, activities, jobs, and/or behaviors that illustrate the idea of positive peace. Students can work individually or in pairs to complete the project.
2. Have students share their collages with the class, pointing out two or three things on their collages that they want to highlight.

✐ **Assessment:** After students have shared their collages, invite students to discuss or write about the following questions, which lie at the core of the concept of positive peace:

- What do you think are the major obstacles to achieving positive peace?

- What kinds of changes would human beings need to make in what they value and what they do to make real peace possible?

- What kinds of changes can we each make within ourselves which move us toward achieving positive peace in our personal lives?

WHAT IS PEACE?

NEGATIVE PEACE is the absence of direct violence (physical, verbal, and psychological) between individuals, groups, and governments. (1)

Efforts to achieve negative peace emphasize:
Managing interpersonal and organizational conflict in order to control, contain, and reduce actual and potential violence.

Reducing the incidence of war by eliminating the extreme dangers of the war system and limiting war through international crisis management. (2)

Preventing war through strategic deterrence and arms control (3)

The concept of **NEGATIVE PEACE** addresses immediate symptoms, the conditions of war, and the use and effects of force and weapons. Words and images which reveal the horror of war and its aftermath are often used by writers, artists, and citizen groups in their efforts to stop it.

POSITIVE PEACE is more than the absence of violence; it is the presence of **social justice** through equal opportunity, a fair distribution of power and resources, equal protection and impartial enforcement of law. (1)

Efforts to achieve positive peace emphasize:
- **Establishing peace through world order** by supporting international law, compliance with multilateral treaties, use of international courts, and nonviolent resolution of disputes, participation in international organizations, trade, and communication. (4)

- **Establishing social equality and justice, economic equity, ecological balance; protecting citizens from attack, and meeting basic human needs.** (5)
- **Establishing a civil peace** which provides the constitutional and legal means necessary to settle differences nonviolently (6)

- **Eliminating indirect violence** which shortens the life span of people, sustains unequal life chances, or reduces quality of life for any citizen (7)

- **Practicing conflict resolution** as a foundation for building peaceful interpersonal and institutional relationships.

The concept of **POSITIVE PEACE** involves the elimination of the root causes of war, violence, and injustice and the conscious effort to build a society which reflects these commitments. Positive peace assumes an interconnectedness of all life.

SOURCES:

1. Galtung, *Reader in Peace Studies*

2. Nye, *Hawks, Owls, and Doves*

3. Morgan, *Deterrence*

4. Mendlovitz, *On the Creation of a Just World Order*

5. Reardon, *Reader in Peace Studies*

6. Adler, *Haves Without Have-Nots*

7. Brock-Utne, *Reader in Peace Studies*

ACTIVITY 7: IMAGES OF PEACE IN THE MEDIA, LITERATURE, AND THE ARTS

PURPOSE: Students will explore how peace is portrayed in media, literature, and the arts.

LEARNING STRATEGIES: Observation and data collection, whole group discussion, reading for understanding

TIME: Optional, depending on the resources you choose to use in class

MATERIALS: Any of the resources listed on **Handout 6:7**

SUGGESTED INSTRUCTIONS:

Investigating Images of Peace in the Media:

1. Explore how the media helps to shape our images of peace. What news gets covered by the media? What doesn't? What entertainment programs get on the air? What kinds of programs are not on commerical television? To what degree does the media cover individuals, groups, and governments actually resolving conflicts and disagreements using peaceful processes? How often do we see stories which convey images of positive peace?

2. For a homework assignment, ask students to choose a television news or entertainment program to monitor for images of peace. Ask students to use three criteria to record what they see and hear:

   A. Record incidents and situations in which people are actively engaging in a peaceful, nonviolent process to resolve a conflict or work out their differences.

   B. Record activities in which people are actively involved in building a more peaceful society.

   C. Record incidents or situations in which people could have been shown actively resolving conflicts or working out their differences peacefully, but producers and directors made decisions to show something else instead.

3. Have students share their data with the class. Discuss the criteria which you think might be most important to producers and directors in selecting what news gets covered and what situations are filmed in entertainment programs.

319

If it is true that for the news media, "News is conflict" and for the scriptwriter, "There's no plot without a conflict," is it likely that the images of conflict and peace will change in the media? Could the media portray conflict differently and still attract an audience?

Exploring Images of Peace in Literature, Film, and Art

Choose any of the works listed on **Handout 6:7: "Positive and Negative Images of Peace in Literature, Film, and Art"** to read, watch, or view and compare and contrast.

Use any of the following questions as starting points for discussion:

- Explore literature, biographies, and autobiographies in which people struggle for personal and social peace. What obstacles do people face? What sustains them when the peace they are seeking seems out of reach?

- Explore the role of writers and artists as agents of change in society. There is a rich tradition of protest art against war, tyranny, and injustice. Is this art the art of propaganda? Is propaganda against war good? Propaganda for war bad? Is there any danger in communicating simplistic messages about war and peace? What's the difference between protest grounded in despair and nihilism and protest driven by hope and empowerment?

- Explore the idea of peacemakers as visionaries, those whose ideas and schemes are not practical or possible in the present. Consider this quote from Robert Lifton (*In a Dark Time*), "Human wisdom has been the wisdom of the seer: the poet, the painter, or peasant revolutionary, who when the current worldview failed, turned the kaleidoscope of his or her imagination until familiar things took on a wholly different pattern."

  Are visionaries more motivated by despair or hope? How do they use power? How do they reach their audiences and affect change? Are all peacemakers visionaries? Are all visionaries peacemakers? Is there a difference between visionaries and inventors?

Positive And Negative Images Of Peace In Literature, Film And Art

H--->High School   M--->Middle School   E--->Elementary

MEDIUM	NEGATIVE PEACE IMAGE	POSITIVE PEACE IMAGE
Poem(H) Poem(M/H)	"The Village Wife's Lament," Hewlett	"Day of These Days," Laurie Lee "Peace Prayers," Harper-San Fransisco
	Complete poems of Wilfred Owen, W.W. Norton	
Painting Painting	"Guernica," Picasso	"Peaceable Kingdom," Henri Rousseau
	"The War Spirit at Home," Lily Spencer	"Peasants Enjoying a Siesta," Van Gogh
Photography Photography	Hearts of Darkness, Don McCullin	The Family of Man, Edward Steichen
	Children of War, Children of Peace, Robert Capa	Loving, Ann Morris
Photography	War Torn, Susan Varmazen	
Film Short(H)		We, the Children, Unicef
	"Life On Earth Perhaps," Video Project	The Turning Point (video project)
Play(M/H)		
Essay(H)	"A Walk in the Woods," Lee Blessing	"I Never Saw Another Butterfly," Clesete Raspanti
		Chief Seattle's Message
Short Story(M)	Pres. Eisenhower's Farewell Address to the Nation	"Tender Warriors," Dorothy Sterling
Fable(E/M/H)	"The Enemy," Pearl Buck	The Lorax, Dr. Seuss
Illustrated Stories (E/M/H)	"The Last Flower," James Thurber	The General, Janet Charders Peace Begins With You, Katherine Scholes
	The Bomb and the General, Umberto Eco	Wheel on the School, Meindert De Jong
	The Wall, Eve Bunting	
	Sadako and the Thousand Paper Cranes, Eleanor Coerr	

Literature of War and Peace Series: SPICE, Stanford, CA
I. ". . . . what they are running from, and to, and why." (fables)
II. Survival and Afterward ("By the Waters of Babylon)
III. Why War? (poetry)
IV. "A man's bound to fight for what he believes in." (short stories)
V. The Individual and the State.

ACTIVITY 8: PERSPECTIVES ON PEACE

PURPOSE: Students will read how writers, artists, political leaders, and citizens define and image peace.

LEARNING STRATEGIES: Critical reading and writing, class discussion

TIME: A few minutes or an entire class period

MATERIALS: Handout 6:8

SUGGESTED INSTRUCTIONS:

Pass out copies of **Handout 6:8: "What People Say About Peace"** or select several quotations to use separately. The quotations can be used as a springboard for the following activities:

1. Ask students to read the quotations, selecting two or three that they like the best. Divide students into groups of five. Have students participate in "round robins," each taking a minute or two to discuss a quotation that most closely reflects their idea of peace.

2. Identify several quotations that describe ideas and activities more closely associated with negative or positive concepts of peace.

3. Make a list of root causes—both attitudes and actions—of violence, war, and "non-peace" that are mentioned in the quotations.

4. Choose any of the quotations to use as a premise or thesis for an extended essay which develops the ideas contained in the quotation.

5. Read and discuss the quotations that specifically address the concept of non-violence (12, 14, 15, 16, 17, 19) and explore the writings of these peacemakers.

6. Find newsclippings, cartoons, photographs, articles which illustrate the main idea contained in the quotation.

7. Use any of the ideas listed in Activity 3 in this chapter.

WHAT PEOPLE SAY ABOUT PEACE

1. Those who cherish their freedom and recognize and respect the equal right of their neighbors to be free and live in peace must work together for the triumph of law and moral principles in order that peace, justice, and confidence may prevail in the world.

2. Every gun that is made, every warship launched, every rocket fired signifies, in the final sense, a theft from those who hunger and are not fed, those who are cold and are not clothed. This world in arms is not spending money alone. It is spending the sweat of its laborers, the genius of its scientists, the hopes of its children. . . . this is not a way of life in any true sense.

3. To be free of bondage or restraint, to live under a government based on the consent of the citizens, these are basic among all freedoms. . . . and this is the reason why a democracy is from every possible humane point of view the best form of government. . . . What so many human beings in the modern world have failed to understand is that *freedom* is the greatest of all trusts.

4. We are all members of one family, yesterday, today, and tomorrow. We know we shall find peace only where we find justice — only where we find respect for all human beings, only where all human beings have the right to a decent living for themselves and their families.

5. Injustice anywhere is a threat to justice everywhere. We are caught in an inescapable network of mutuality, tied in a single garment of destiny.

6. The broad ultimate requirements of survival. . . . are in essence. . . . global disarmament, both nuclear and conventional, and the invention of political means by which the world can peacefully settle the issues that throughout history it has settled by war.

7. We need an Academy of Peace, not to do away with conflict, but to learn and teach how to creatively manage conflict.

8. I think that people want peace so much that one of these days government had better get out of their way and let them have it.

9. Mankind has grown strong in eternal struggle and it will perish through eternal peace.

323

10. Is not peace, in the last analysis, basically a matter of human rights—the right to live out our lives without fear of devastation—the right to breathe air as nature provided it—the right of future generations to a healthy existence?

11. The strength of the United States serves to protect the American people and helps preserve the peace. We need strength to deter attack, to support the causes of freedom, and to work for a peaceful world.

12. If you succumb to the temptation of using violence in the struggle, unborn generations will be the recipients of a long and desolate night of bitterness, and your chief legacy to the future will be an endless reign of meaningless chaos.

13. Think of what a world we could build if the power unleashed in war were applied to constructive tasks! One tenth of the energy that the various belligerents spent in the war, a fraction of the money they exploded in hand grenades and poison gas, would suffice to raise the standard of living in every country and avert the economic catastrophe of worldwide unemployment. We must be prepared to make the same heroic sacrifices for the cause of peace.

14. It is the enemy who can truly teach us to practice the virtues of compassion and tolerance.

15. Only when peace lives within each of us, will it live outside of us. We must be the wombs for a new harmony. When it is small, peace is fragile. Like a baby, it needs nurturing attention. We must protect peace from violence and perversion if it is to grow. We must be strong to do this. But force, even in the name of honor, is always tragic. Instead, we must use the strength of wisdom and conscience. Only that power can nurture peace in this difficult time.

16. Whatever may be the result, there is always in me a conscious struggle for following the law of nonviolence deliberately and ceaselessly. Such a struggle leaves one stronger for it. Nonviolence is a weapon of the strong. My experience, daily growing stronger and richer, tells me that there is not peace for individuals or for nations without practicing truth and nonviolence to the uttermost extent possible for 'man.'

17. My personal trials have also taught me the value of unmerited suffering. As my sufferings mounted I soon realized that there were two ways that I could respond to my situation: either to react with bitterness or seek to transform the suffering into a creative force.

18. Peace is not the product of a victory or command. It has no finishing line, no final deadline, no fixed definition of achievement. Peace is a never-ending process, the work of many decisions by many people in many countries. It is an attitude, a way of life, a way of solving problems and resolving conflicts. It cannot be forced on the smallest nation or enforced by the largest. it cannot ignore our differences or overlook our common interests. It requires us to work and live together.

19. My experience has been that the poor know violence more intimately than most people because it has been a part of their lives, whether the violence of the gun or the violence of want and need. I don't subscribe to the belief that nonviolence is cowardice. When people are involved in something constructive, trying to bring about change, they tend to be less violent than those who are not engaged in rebuilding or in anything creative. Non-violence forces one to be creative; it forces any leader to go to the people and get them involved so that they can come forth with new ideas.

20. I suggest our best metaphor for peace is an ancient one—the wrestling match. The Greeks visualized peace as a form of loving combat, a contest, or "agon" between well-matched and respectful opponents. They applied the word "agon" equally to a wrestling match or a verbal dialogue. Their highest vision was of a world in which the impulse to war might be gentled in an arena where men and women competed for glory. They thought of conflict as creative and strengthening so long as it was rule-governed.

   Politics is a playing field. I see enemies facing each other honestly to further their legitimate interests and value systems.

21. From the break of day till sunset glow, I toil. I dig my well, I plow my field, and earn my food and drink. What care I who rules the land if I am left in peace?

22. Peace is not the product of terror or fear.
    Peace is not the silence of cemeteries.
    Peace is not the silent result of violent repression.
    Peace is the generous, tranquil contribution of all to the good of all.
    Peace is dynamism. Peace is generosity. It is right and it is duty.

23. Football is war's most apt metaphor. Football thinking prevails where diplomacy is abandoned: Team 1 vs. Team 2, defense vs. offense, winner vs. loser. Air strikes are likened to touchdowns. Borders are gridiron substitutes. Bunkers hold huddles underground. Generals are coaches and soldiers are players. We who watch on television are the

cheerleaders. Pass the popcorn.

Rejecting war means rejecting the idea that someone has to win and someone has to lose. It means understanding that football is a game,

that is no substitute for careful thinking and common sense with risky business at hand. Football is not war and war is not football.

Peace means imagining a way to work out differences through dialogue and negotiation. It means valuing other children as much as our own, citing casualties in one figure without distinguishing between nationalities. Peace is envisioning a solution to the unsolvable. It means thinking the unthinkable, that we might just call a halt, yesterday to war.

Authors:

1. Franklin D. Roosevelt
2. Dwight D. Eisenhower
3. Ashley Montagu
4. Anonymous
5. Martin Luther King, Jr.
6. Jonathan Schell
7. Father Theodore Hesburgh
8. Dwight D. Eisenhower
9. Adolf Hitler
10. John F. Kennedy
11. Caspar Weinberger
12. Martin Luther King, Jr.
13. Albert Einstein
14. The Dalai Lama
15. Deng Ming Dao
16. M. K. Gandhi
17. Martin Luther King, Jr.
18. Oscar Arias Sanchez
19. Cesar Chavez
20. Sam Keen
21. Anonymous Chinese poet
22. Oscar Romero
23. Mary E. Hunt

Activity 9: What Is The Role Of A Peacemaker?

PURPOSE: Students will brainstorm a list of peacemakers and discuss what peacemakers do and the roles that they play in families, school, and society.

LEARNING STRATEGIES: Brainstorming, class discussion

TIME: One class period

MATERIALS: Newsprint, markers

SUGGESTED INSTRUCTIONS:

1. Using newsprint, brainstorm two lists with the whole class:
   a. What do peacemakers do?
   b. Name people whom you would describe as peacemakers (living or dead) from your community, across the country, and around the world.

2. In discussing the lists, consider the following questions:

   • Does everyone play the role of a peacemaker sometimes?

     Which students and adults play the role of peacemaker at school? What do they do in this role? What makes it hard to be a school peacemaker? Why is it worth doing?

   • Explore the kinds of activities involved in personal, community, and global peacemaking? How are these efforts similar and different?

   • Are peacemakers always visible? Why or why not?

   • What do you know about any of the peacemakers on your list? Do they share any common qualities of character? What are they?

   • What kinds of struggles do peacemakers face? How is a struggle for personal peace different than a struggle for community or world peace? How are these struggles connected? Can an unpeaceful person make peace in the world? Why or why not?

     If **peacemaking is a struggle,** what makes this kind of struggle different from war or violent conflict? What is the goal of the struggle? Some would argue that moral courage is required in war. Do you agree? Does peacemaking require the same or a different kind of moral courage?

Activity 10: Anatomy Of A Problem Solver/Peacemaker

PURPOSE: Students will brainstorm a list of qualities needed in a problem solver/peacemaker and draw and label their own image of such a person.

LEARNING STRATEGIES: Brainstorming, drawing

TIME: One class period

MATERIALS: Handout 6:10

SUGGESTED INSTRUCTIONS:

1. Discuss with students the skills, attributes, and attitudes that they think people need to be good problem solvers\peacemakers. Make a list of their responses.

   Richard Gregg, author of *The Power of Non-violence*, has noted that peacemaking and nonviolent resistance can have the same qualities of character and dynamics that nations honor in war-making in that both war-making and peacemaking involve:

   1. A psychological and moral aim
   2. Discipline that is instinctive and also holds emotional power for participants
   3. A high regard for strategy and planning
   4. A method for settling major disputes and conflicts
   5. The requirements of courage, dynamic energy, capacity to endure fatigue and suffering, self-sacrifice, self-control, chivalry, charm, and action
   6. An opportunity for service to a larger idea or principle

   Do you agree with his assessment? Why or why not?

2, Ask students if they can think of parts of the body that would be associated with particular characteristics that they've mentioned. Brainstorm a list of things the body can do that could be linked to skills that people need to be effective peacemakers. You can use **Handout 6:10: "The Anatomy of a Problem Solver/Peacemaker"** as a guide for generating lists.

3. Invite students to draw posters of their own images of a peacemaker, labeling body parts that they would associate with specific skills and attitudes that people need to be effective problem solvers\peacemakers.

4. Have students share their posters with the rest of the class and the larger school community.

5. Enlarge **Handout 6:10B: "Anatomy of a Problem Solver/Peacemaker"** to poster size and post in your classroom as a reminder of skills you and your students are practicing daily.

The Anatomy of a Problem Solver/Peacemaker

Anatomy

Big ears
Heart
Big eyes
Strong hands
Big feet
Brain
Mouth
Wink
Knees
Smile
Fingers
Thick skin
Swivel neck
Big "reach"
Voice box
Thumbs up!
Nose

Stuff You Wear or Carry With You

Loose clothing
Light bulb
Eraser
Shoes
A STOP sign
Paper and pencil
Quarter
"Conflict Toolbox"
A signed agreement/treaty
Band-Aids
"Talking stick"
Umbrella
Fan

Skills, Behaviors, and Characteristics of a Problem Solver/ Peacemaker/Mediator

Step into someone else's shoes
Think before you act
Express your feelings
Dialogue / talk it through
Listen! Listen! Listen! (Sikiliza!)
Brainstorm solutions
Step lightly. Follow disputants' concerns and feelings
Don't jump to conclusions
A firm handshake
Being fair / not taking sides
Paraphrase, reflect, summarize
Warmth and caring
A calm voice
Stay grounded when others are upset
Win-Win solutions
Helping hand
Good ideas and questions
Patience
Creativity (Kuumba!)
Cool down
Correcting mistakes
Forgiveness
"Put-ups" not "put-downs"
See all perspectives / respect for different points of view
Be flexible
Use humor to lighten up
Provide protection to ensure safety
Observe and "read" people

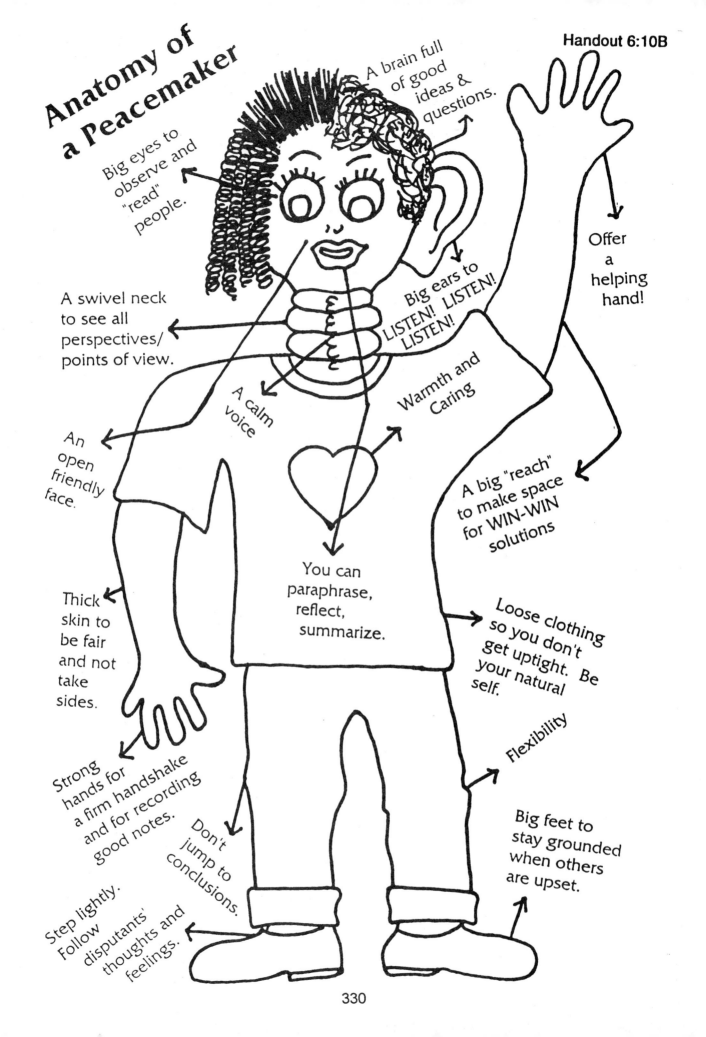

ACTIVITY 11: INTERVIEWING PEOPLE ABOUT PEACEMAKING

PURPOSE: Students will develop a survey to use when they interview their peer and adults to find out their views about peacemakers and peacemaking.

LEARNING STRATEGIES: Interviewing and data collection, small group and whole class discussion

TIME: One class period

MATERIALS: Handout 6:11

SUGGESTED INSTRUCTIONS:

1. Generate questions that could be part of a survey that students use to interview people about peacemaking, or you can use the questions on **Handout 6:11**. Discuss who might be interesting for students to interview. Brainstorm ideas for how to get a broad sample of people to be interviewed (children, teens, parents, grandparents, school staff, people whom you or your parents work with, etc.) Suggest to students that they can do face-to-face interviews or telephone interviews. Ask each student to interview six people.

2. When students have completed their interviews, divide class into groups of four or five and have students share their interview data in small groups. Ask one student in each group to be the summarizer who will report back to whole class, highlighting:

   • The most common responses on the surveys.

   • Two or three of the most interesting or surprising responses from the interviews.

PEACEMAKER INTERVIEWS

Name of interviewer_____

Person Interviewed_____Age ____

1. What kinds of activities do peacemakers do? _____

_____

2. What qualities of character are important for a peacemaker?

_____

3. Share one experience where you played the role of a peacemaker.

_____

_____

4. Identify three or four peacemakers that come to mind_____

_____

- -

Person Interviewed_____Age ____

1. What kinds of activities do peacemakers do? _____

_____

2. What qualities of character are important for a peacemaker?

_____

3. Share one experience where you played the role of a peacemaker.

_____

_____

4. Identify three or four peacemakers that come to mind_____

_____

Activity 12: Peacemakers At Work

PURPOSE: Students will read about peacemakers from around the world and discuss the common qualities that these peacemakers seem to share.

LEARNING STRATEGIES: Cooperative learning, reading for understanding

TIME: One class period

MATERIALS: Handout 6:12 A - F, newsprint, markers

SUGGESTED INSTRUCTIONS:

1. Explain that students will be reading about peacemakers from all over the world. Pass out copies of **Handout 6:12: "Peacemakers At Work"** to groups of three students each. (Each group will receive six pages—two pages of reading for each student.) Also, give each group two sheets of newsprint and two markers. Have students write the following headings on the newsprint.

What did peacemakers <u>do</u>?Why?	Personal Qualities of Peacemakers

2. Explain that each student in the group will read two of the six pages about peacemakers. After everyone is finished reading, one person in each group will record their findings on the newsprint. Make sure that students understand that in answering the "why" question, they are identifying the reasons for their efforts. In other words, what did the peacemakers want to accomplish?

3. Post the newsprint around the room, and give students a chance to look at each other's work. In a whole class discussion, look for responses that are repeated from one group to another. Summarize the actions, reasons, and personal qualities that were most frequently listed, and discuss the obstacles which made the work of peacemakers a struggle. Finally, think about the kinds of skills that enable a person to be an effective peacemaker.

PEACEMAKERS AT WORK

1. "On September 8, 1965, the mostly Filipino members of the Agricultural Workers Organizing Committee, AFL-CIO, struck the grape fields of Delano, California. They were joined one week later by the mostly Mexican-American members of the National Farm Workers Association, led by the Cesar Chavez. Thus began the first successful strike by farm workers for union recognition in American history."(1)

2. In the 1970s and 80s, women "organized to change the way the public, the media, and the law ignored and even glamorized violence against women. Around the country they began projects against rape, wife beating, pornography, and child abuse and set up local self-help centers and shelters for victims of rape and domestic violence."(1)

3. "The people affiliated with *The Catholic Worker*, including many workers, students, and poor who came to volunteer, felt that they could not write about issues without participating in them. In 1935, they picketed the German consulate to protest the treatment of European Jews. Catholic Workers went to Arkansas to support the Tenant Farmers Union and helped with the formation of the National Maritime Union in 1936."(1)

4. "Susan B. Anthony, a Quaker and the leading organizer of the woman's movement for 50 years, and Elizabeth Cady Stanton, the movement's theoretician, organized the National Woman's Suffrage Association in 1869 in order to work for a federal amendment to guarantee women the right to vote." They also publicized other women's issues: "long hours and short pay for working women and grossly unfair divorce and inheritance laws."(1)

PEACEMAKERS AT WORK

5. The Fund for Women provided West African women with technical assistance to improve traditional methods for smoking fish in thatched huts over wood fires, a process too time-consuming which often resulted in hazardous fires. A group of women in Ghana invented a new type of oven which was inexpensive to build and smoked ten times the amount of fish with the same amount of fuel. They now have a food source which lasts up to nine months.(2)

6. Lee Tai-young, became South Korea's first woman lawyer in the 1950s and founded the Women's Legal Aid Center. Ms. Lee's goals were to "fight divorce and inheritance laws that were unfair to women" and support women's efforts to receive fair treatment in cases of adoption, unequal wages, rape, assault, and fraud. Ms. Lee added a "mobile legal aid unit" which reaches impoverished rural women in need of legal assistance.(2)

7. "In 1889, at the age of 29, Jane Addams started the Hull House, an organization that brought culture, friendship, pride, and many social and civic opportunities to thousands of poor immigrants in Chicago. She worked tirelessly for such social reforms as a child labor law, eight-hour workdays for women, and the first juvenile courts." Addams was later much criticized for her work with the Women's Peace Party and the Women's International League for Peace and Freedom which advocated mediation and economic sanctions rather than the use of force in the war in Europe.(3)

8. Linus Pauling was an American scientist involved in atomic weapons development during World War II. He founded the Emergency Committee of Atomic Scientists to "inform the public about the devastation that the powerful new weapons could cause." Although Pauling received a Nobel Prize in Chemistry in 1954, he was the target of much criticism for his dissenting views. Pauling raised concerns about the dangers of the hydrogen bomb and the hazards of nuclear fallout during nuclear weapons testing. He was awarded the Nobel Peace Prize for his efforts to stop nuclear testing.(3)

PEACEMAKERS AT WORK

9. In challenging the racist policies of Birmingham, Alabama, Dr. Martin Luther King switched tactics from simply trying to arouse the conscience of the people to a strategy of purposely creating a crisis and letting the advocates of hatred and bigotry expose themselves. King's conviction that the protesters should take suffering on themselves rather than inflict it on others was severely tested in Birmingham. Protest marches were met with shocking brutality as police attacked demonstrators with guard dogs and hoses."(3)

10. "The 'Toxic Avengers' were born when Jose Morales, a science teacher at the local youth center, noticed that barrels of hazardous waste had been dumped in a nearby vacant lot. He and his students sent samples of the waste to a lab to see if it was toxic. They protested against the company that had dumped the barrels, and it stopped the dumping. As a result of this project, a group called the Citizens' Committee for New York decided to donate money so the Toxic Avengers could do more work."(4)

11. Aruna Chandrasekhar "had read about the Exxon Valdez oil spill in the National Geographic magazine and thought kids would want to know how sea creatures were affected by it. She decided to write about otters because 'they've been hunted for their coats for many years, and they're almost extinct.' She wrote and illustrated *Oliver and the Oil Spill*, a book about otters trapped in an oil spill off the Pacific Coast." The book won first prize in a national writing contest.(4)

12. Lucille Thornbrugh recalled, "Being a woman was an obstacle as a union organizer. We would talk to the workers individually until we got enough of them together to hold a meeting. We would rent a motel room because we didn't want to jeopardize their jobs by meeting in a home....we would sign up all those present, then we would have "inside" organizers. Wen we won a union election, I stayed in town until they elected their officers and I had shown them how to conduct a meeting. Then I would call in a negotiator to help them draw up their contract and negotiate it with the employer.

I remember one of our organizers telling me about a group of very low-paid workers he had organized. I asked him about their contract. 'Contract, hell,' he said. 'First I have to teach them to read.' And he did just that, with blackboard and chalk at the labor hall. Today they have a good union."(5)

PEACEMAKERS AT WORK

13. Julian Bond, a civil rights activist, speaks fondly of the example his father, president of a black university in the 50s, set for him. "My father wasn't involved in the kind of activism that would get your name in the newspapers. He just set an example of responsibility, and I watched that. And I watched the way he dealt with institutions and the way pressures came down on him when he wanted Lincoln University to remain a national institution for the education of young black men, and the board of trustees wanted it to be a kind of local Pennsylvania school serving that surrounding community. Anyway, my father lost his job over that..."(5)

14. Stanford Pugsley is "the newest member of the Salt Lake City Board of Education. This 16-year-old honor student had the courage to put an obscure Utah law to the test. The 1986 law stated that any student who could collect the signatures of 500 peers could request appointment to the board as a non-voting member. Stan was the first to do it in Salt Lake City, and now he's serving a one-year term."(6)

15. "Picture 25 kids entering drug-infested city parks, organizing basketball games, staging concerts, and offering art instruction to reclaim the parks from crime and drug abusers. It's happening in mid-town Manhattan in New York City.

The idea was born in the heads of kids who protested the drug and prostitution traffic which frightened young people and families away form the parks. Beginning in 1988 with three parks in Manhattan, the program has expanded to include new neighborhoods. The 15 original staff members (aged 12-19), who are known as the Youth Force, invited other kids, police, and youth group leaders to be part of their planning committee. After papering their neighborhood with flyers about their programs, more than 1200 kids signed up to participate in their projects."(6)

PEACEMAKERS AT WORK

16. "Many towns and city councils in Europe take their responsibilities for young people seriously. Some 350 young people's councils operate in France.... Massy, a town of forty thousand inhabitants near Paris, managed to employ a youth worker to help set up their Children's Council in 1989. The town council works closely with the schools and school district authorities. The thirty-six young council members work in five committees, namely: living together, a clean environment, leisure and culture, safety, and information...."(7)

17. "A project at the Instituto Technico Commerciale in Rieti, Italy, involves a group of older students who discuss school life and health issues with 11- and 12-year-olds in small groups. The older pupils visit the younger ones in their classes once a month throughout the school term. The project aims to influence the younger pupils to adopt healthy lifestyles—in particular to avoid harmful substances such as tobacco, alcohol, and other drugs."(7)

18. "Ross Misher was only 13 years old when his father was murdered." An employee of his father's went out on a lunch break, bought a gun, and returned to work, killing Ross's father and himself. Ross said, "I think about the 59 other families that went through the same exact thing I did...60 a day, every day...If a person cannot wait a reasonable period of time to receive a gun, I don't think he needs it for the right reasons." Ross testified before a U.S. Senate Subcommittee in support of requiring a 'cooling-off' period for anyone purchasing a gun." Ross continued his campaign when he founded Students Against HandGun Violence at George Washington University.(6)

19. "For centuries, the white colonists' Indian program in Brazil was one of extermination only. 'Shoot the Indians on sight' was the general policy .... creating a situation where the Chevantes Indians answered white atrocities with their own atrocities. Onto this scene came Candide Rondon, an officer in the Brazilian army, who instituted a new military policy of not harming the Indians. After a long struggle, he persuaded the Brazilian government to establish the Indian Protection Service."(8)

PEACEMAKERS AT WORK

20. "Contrary to the occupation agreement in 1940, the Nazis displayed the swastika flag on a public building in Denmark. The Danish king, King Christian, demanded the flag's removal. The German military officials refused. The king said he would send a soldier to remove the flag. The reply was that they would shoot him. 'I am that soldier,' said the king. The flag cam down."(8)

21. "When half a million Soviet and Warsaw Pact troops invaded Czechoslovakia in August, 1968, they expected to take over the country easily—within a matter of a few days. Instead, they encountered massive nonviolent resistance by the people of Czechoslovakia. Even though spontaneous, the resistance movement was able to prevent the Soviet military takeover for a full eight months. The Soviets were forced to negotiate with the very Czech government officials they had planned to replace."(8)

22. One of the most famous events in the struggle for Indian independence from the British was the Salt March organized by Gandhi. "In defiance of the British police, volunteers walked to the ocean to get their own salt, rather than buying it from the British colonists. The New York Telegram reported on May 22, 1930, that the "scene was astonishing and baffling to the Western mind accustomed to see violence met by violence, to expect a blow to be returned and a fight result. During the morning I saw hundreds of blows inflicted by the police, but saw not a single blow returned by the volunteers. So far as I could observe the volunteers implicitly obeyed Gandhi's creed of nonviolence.... Much of the time the stolid native Surat police seemed reluctant to strike....Sometimes the scenes were so painful that I had to turn away momentarily."(8)

23. In August 1991, Russian citizens, armed with nothing more than candles and Russian flags, faced down Soviet soldiers and army tanks in front of the Russian Parliament as the world watched on television. After the failed August putsch by Soviet reactionaries was put down, Mikhail Gorbachev spoke of one lesson learned from these extraordinary events. "The irreversible character of the changes resulting from democracy and glasnost was confirmed. A real breakthrough has been made into a new life. Huge masses of people gained self-awareness as citizens, for whom freedom has become a supreme value despite all the hardship of their everyday life. It was those people who stood in the way of the conspirators, who disrupted their plot to return the country to the totalitarian past."(9)

SOURCES:

(1) *The Power of the People,* Robert Cooney and Helen Michalowski

(2) *Women in the Third World,* Maxine P. Fisher

(3) *The Peace Seekers,* Nathan Aaseng

(4) *Kid Heroes of the Environment,* The Earthwork Group

(5) *Refuse to Stand Silently By,* Eliot Wigginton

(6) *The Kids' Guide to Social Action,* Barbara Lewis

(7) *Social Education,* May, 1992

(8) *Alternatives to Violence,* Kathy Bickmore

(9) *The New York Times*

ACTIVITY 13: SPOTLIGHT ON PEACEMAKERS PAST AND PRESENT

PURPOSE: Students will choose one peacemaker to learn more about and present their research to the rest of the class.

LEARNING STRATEGIES: Individual research and writing, class presentations

TIME: One class period and out of class time for research

MATERIALS: Handout 6:13

SUGGESTED INSTRUCTIONS:

1. Ask students to choose one peacemaker to research. Look for videos, correspondence, speeches, autobiographies, and biographies that will give students a picture of how these people have spent their lives working to make the world a more just and peaceful place. **Handout 6:13: "Visionaries and Peacemakers"** is a list of writers, philosophers, religious leaders, Presidents, diplomats and negotiators, Nobel Peace Prize winners, military officers, organizations, community workers and mediators, international leaders, scientists, grassroots organizers, and young people who have made significant contributions to peacemaking around the world. Students might choose to interview or write to living peacemakers. Students might also want to research or write for information about organizations that work on peace and justice issues locally and globally.

   FOCUS QUESTIONS for research might include:

   a. Identify this person's vision of peace. What did this individual want to change?
   b, What obstacles made work as a peacemaker challenging or difficult?
   c. How did this person change the lives of individuals and the communities in which they worked?
   d. What attitudes, personal characteristics, and commitments made this individual unusual? What qualities helped them in their work?
   e. What projects, events, and writings are associated with this individual?
   f. What new ideas and strategies did this individual use in their work?
   g. Find one quotation which reflects this individual's perspective on peace and peacemaking.
   h. How would you convince the class that this person deserves the title of peacemaker?
   i. How do you think this person would respond to a current crisis that you are concerned about?

2. You and your students might want to plan a calendar of presentations throughout the year so that each student gets the opportunity to share their peacemaker's vision with the rest of the class.

Visionaries and Peacemakers

ADDAMS, JANE

BAEZ, JOAN

BALL, GEORGE

BEGIN, MENACHEM

BEN-GURION, DAVID

BERRIGAN, DANIEL

BIKO, STEVEN

BONHOEFFER, DIETRICH

BRANDT, WILLY

BROWER, DAVID

BUDDHA

BUNCHE, RALPH

CALDICOTT, HELEN

CARTER, JIMMY

CHAVEZ, CESAR

CHIEF JOSEPH

CHIEF SEATTLE

COFFIN, WILLIAM
  SLOANE

CORRIGAN, MAIREAD

DALAI LAMA

DAY, DOROTHY

DEBS, EUGENE V.

DELLUMS, RON

DEMING, BARBARA

DEWEY, JOHN

DOUGLASS, FREDERICK

DUMAS, LLOYD

DUNANT, JEAN-HENRI

EDELMAN, MARIAN
  WRIGHT

EINSTEIN, ALBERT

ESQUIVAL, ADOLFO
  PEREZ

FISHER, ROGER

FORSBERG, RANDALL

GANDHI, MAHATMA

GEORGE, SUSAN

GORBACHEV, MIKHAIL

GRUENING, ERNEST

GUTHRIE, WOODY

HAMER, FANNIE LOU

HAMMARSKJOLD, DAG

HATFIELD, MARK

HAVEL, VACLAV

HENDERSON, ARTHUR

HESCHEL, ABRAHAM

KANT, IMMANUEL

KELLY, PETRA

KING, MARTIN LUTHER

KING, CORETTA SCOTT

LAPPE, FRANCES MOORE

MACBRIDE, SEAN

MALCOLM X

MANDELA, NELSON

MARSHALL, GLEN
  GEORGE

MCGOVERN, GEORGE

MELMAN, SEYMOUR

MONTESSORI, MARIA

MORSE, WAYNE

MOTHER TERESA

MULLER, ROBERT

MYRDAL, ALVA

NERUDA, PABLO

OWEN, WILFRED

PAUL, ALICE

PAULING, LINUS

PENN, WILLIAM

POPE JOHN XXIII

REARDON, BETTY

RANKIN, JEANNETTE

ROBLES, ALFONSO
  GARCIA

ROMERO, OSCAR

ROOSEVELT, ELEANOR

RUSTIN, BAYARD

RUSSELL, BERTRAND

SADAT, ANWAR

SAGAN, CARL

SAKHAROV, ANDREI

SATO, EISAKU

SCHELL, JONATHAN

SCHUMACHER, E.F.

SCHWEICKART, RUSTY

SCHWEITZER, ALBERT

SHARP, GENE

SHRIVER, SARGENT

SIVARD, RUTH

SMITH, SAMANTHA

ST. FRANCIS OF ASSISI

TOLSTOY, LEO

THOMAS, EVAN

TRUTH, SOJOURNER

TRUMBO, DALTON

TUTU, BISHOP
  DESMOND

VANCE, CYRUS

WALESA, LECH

WARNKE, PAUL

YOUNG, ANDREW

WIESEL, ELIE

Activity 14: Interviewing And Celebrating Local Peacemakers

PURPOSE: This activity offers students the opportunity of finding out more about local peacemakers and activists by inviting them to class and sponsoring peacemaking awards to be given to people in your community.

LEARNING STRATEGIES: Class dialogue with invited guests, written reflection

TIME: Several class periods

MATERIALS: None

SUGGESTED INSTRUCTIONS:

1. As a discussion starter, write this quotation on the board:

   > Activism pays the rent on being alive and being here on the planet...If I weren't active politically, I would feel as if I were sitting back eating at the banquet without washing the dishes or preparing the food. It wouldn't feel right.
   >
   > Alice Walker

   What do you think Alice Walker means by the phrase, "Activism pays the rent..."? Explore the idea of "renting space" on the planet in the context of stewardship, caretaking, and the kind of world we leave to future generations.

2. Ask students what kinds of questions they might want to ask local activists and peacemakers. Make a list of their questions. Here are some questions that other students have asked:

   - Why do you do what you do? What is your vision of peace?
   - How has your work made your life different?

- What's the driving goal in your work? What are the obstacles that make it difficult to achieve this goal?
- What are the successes that make your work worth the struggle?
- What can ordinary citizens do to help make your vision a reality?

3. Invite local activists and peacemakerS to come to your class. Invite students to take responsibility to make arrangements for their visits, introduce them to the class, and write thank-you notes afterwards. You might want to invite a panel of people to come at one time who represent different visions of peacemaking in the community.

Assessment: After the visits, ask students to write down their reactions before you discuss them. What were new ideas, information, or insights for you? Did anyone particularly inspire you, confuse you, or offend you? Did anyone talk about things that are especially important to you? Were there any ideas that challenged your own opinions? Was there any one quality of character that any of the guests seem to share? What was it?

Going Further: Sponsor Local Peacemaker awards at your school or in your community. Invite students and adults to be part of a committee to develop criteria for awards and the process for selecting award recipients. Be sure to include children, teens, and adults in your consideration.

Chapter 7: Tools for Participation, Decision Making, and Problem Solving

Activity 1: Tinker Toys: A Communications Exercise

PURPOSE: After participating in a highly interactive team-building activity, students consider how the quality, type, and style of communication affects a group's ability to accomplish a task effectively.

LEARNING STRATEGIES: Collaborative problem solving, written reflection, and group discussion

TIME: 15 minutes to introduce exercise and roles; 30 minutes for exercise; 15 minutes for reflective writing; and 30 to 45 minutes for whole group debriefing

MATERIALS: **Handout 7:1**, enough tinker toys, Legos, or other building materials to make an original construction, and four or five identical replicas of the original construction

SUGGESTED INSTRUCTIONS:
1. In preparation for the exercise, you need to do the following ahead of time:
    a. Make copies of **Handout 7:1 Tinker Toy Roles** and cut apart the strips so that each group of five to seven students has a complete set of role strips.
    b. Make a construction out of tinker toys or other building materials. (You decide how complex the construction is and whether it is abstract or looks like a person, a vehicle, a building, etc.) Divide the rest of the tinker toys so that you have four or five sets of identical pieces for each team to build a replica of the original.
    c. You need to decide where you will do this activity in your school. You need to have access to the following spaces:
    - A construction site for each team. These can be located in the same large space or in separate rooms.

    - A hallway or room that can serve as the message center. The Messengers, who are only allowed to be in this space, should not be able to see either the construction sites or the original construction from the "message center".

    - An enclosed space where the original construction is located. Lookers and Feedbackers need to be able to go in and out of this area. One configuration could look like this:

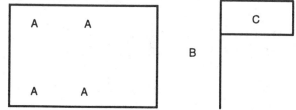

A-Construction Sites   B-Message Center   C-Location of Original

347

2. Explain to students that they will be working in teams of five to seven students. Their goal will be to create an exact replica of a tinker toy construction that only a few team members will be able to see. Here are the rules and guidelines for the exercise.

   a. Group members will need to decide the roles that each of them will take. Each group will receive role reminders so that students can remember what they can do and who they can talk to. *(See **Handout 7:1** for description of roles. Make enough copies so that each group gets a complete set of role strips. Write the roles and responsibilities on a piece of newsprint so that the class can see them as you explain them. Be sure to encourage questions so that students clearly understand what they can and cannot do.)*

   b. Each team will have about five minutes to organize themselves and about twenty minutes to build a replica of the original construction.

   c. You (the teacher or facilitator) will serve as a monitor, making sure that students are where they're supposed to be and doing what they're supposed to do.

   d. Invite students to keep asking you questions during the exercise. If team members aren't sure whether it's okay to do something they want to do, they can ask you. You can tell them "Yes" or "No." For example, someone might ask, "Can the Looker draw a picture of the original to give to the messenger?" You can answer, "Yes." Or someone might ask, "Can the Supplier bring pieces to the Messenger to see if they are the correct pieces to use?" You can again say, "Yes." If no one asks how to "stretch" the original rules, you don't tell!

   Important Note! You can simplify the exercise if it's appropriate by using fewer roles, creating more teams, and creating a smaller, simpler original construction. If you use fewer roles, you may want to use the Looker, the Messenger, and the Builder.

3. During the construction phase of the exercise, remind teams how much time they have at two or three different intervals. If some teams finish before others, they can observe other teams *in silence*. If some teams don't finish by the time you call "Time," encourage them to think about what made it difficult for them to accomplish the goal.

4. ✏ **Assessment:** After you have called "Time," ask students to go back to their seats and respond in writing to some or all of the following questions.

   Give students about ten or fifteen minutes to reflect and write.
   a. Did your team accomplish the goal of building an exact replica of the original construction? If so, write down what your team members did

that helped construct the replica successfully? If not, write down what team members did or did not do that made it difficult to complete the task.

(Be sure to congratulate teams who asked questions about the rules. Not making assumptions about what's okay and what's not is a critical element of effective group communication. The more questions you ask, the more you know.)

b. How did you decide who would take what roles in your team? *(Some team members decide by saying what they would like to do; others decide by saying what role they absolutely don't want to do.)*

c. Was your role what you expected it to be? What was easy/fun/hard/surprising about your role? What skills were particularly important for a person who takes your role?

d. Were there any roles that you think were more important than other roles? Were all roles equally important? Please explain.

e. Brainstorm a quick list of all the skills your team needed to use so that you could build your replica successfully. *(This is a good way to point out to students that real work in the real world isn't made up of homework assignments and separate academic subjects. Real work usually requires a person to combine lots of skills efficiently to get the job done!)*

f. How did the communication restrictions (*who* you could communicate with and *how* you could communicate) make this exercise challenging? How did these restrictions make your job much more complicated than it had to be? How would you change the rules and roles so that your task would have been easier to do? *(This is a good place to consider how people process information. Some people need to see it or write it down, some need to hear it or talk about it, others need to use it and do something with it! Most of us work more effectively if we can have information presented to us in several ways.)* You might also encourage students to point out other obstacles that make "getting the message" more difficult, for example:
   - When we don't have access to all the information we need
   - When we can't ask questions / When people respond by saying, "Uh huh", "Yes", or "No"
   - When we don't have a sense of the "big picture," when we only get pieces that we're not sure how to put together in a way that makes sense / When we don't know what the final outcome is supposed to look like
   - When directions are vague / When we don't get enough details
   - When we can't have back and forth conversation to make sure we get it

349

- When someone in the communication chain isn't clear, shuts down, or doesn't care if they're really understood

g. What did you learn about yourself as a worker and problem solver? What do you need to do a job well and work effectively in a group?

h. What did you like best about doing this exercise? What did you like least about this activity? *(Some students will usually say that they didn't like the restrictions, especially that they had to make an exact copy of someone else's model–they couldn't use their own ideas. It's worth exploring under what circumstances is it crucial to follow directions exactly and when it's okay to bend the rules or be more creative in figuring out solutions.)*

5. **Whole Class Debriefing:** Choose to discuss any of the questions in #4. Be sure to give yourself and your students enough time to debrief the activity. This activity isn't worth much (but a good time!) if students don't take away insights that they can apply to their own learning and their interactions with others, in and out of the classroom.

TINKER TOY ROLES

(only one person) Role: **Looker**	**What You Do:** You can only see the **original construction**. You **cannot** go to your team's building site.	**Who You Can Talk To:** You can only talk to the Messenger.
(only one person) Role: **Messenger**	**What You Do:** You must stay in the message center. You **cannot see either the original or the replica**.	**Who You Can Talk To:** You can talk to the Looker, the Builder, the Supplier in the message center.
(one or two people) Role: **Supplier**	**What You Do:** You can move between your construction site and the message center. You can distribute **no more that 6 tinker toy pieces** to the builders at a time.	**Who You Can Talk To:** You can talk to the Builder and the Messenger. You can ask "yes" or "no" questions to the Feedbacker.
(one or two people) Role: **Builder**	**What You Do:** You can move between your construction site and the message center. You build the replica with the Tinker Toys supplied by the supplier.	**Who You Can Talk To:** You can talk to the Messenger and the Supplier. You can ask "yes" or "no" questions to the Feedbacker.
(only one person) Role: **Feedbacker**	**What You Do:** You can go anywhere. You are the only one who can see **both the original and the replica**.	**Who You Can Talk To:** You can listen to the Builder and the Supplier, but you can only say, "Yes, that's right," or "No, that's wrong."

Activity 2: Making Group Talk Good Talk

PURPOSE: This activity offers students and teachers many strategies and ideas for how to make "group talk" open, thoughtful, and respectful.

LEARNING STRATEGIES: Whole group discussion, pair-share dialogues, group brainstorming, documented observation

TIME: Flexible! These ideas can be incorporated into any activity that you are doing in the classroom.

MATERIALS: Handout 7:2

SUGGESTED IDEAS AND STRATEGIES:
1. **Encourage students to become aware of the multiple factors which influence whether we truly hear others and whether we are heard and truly understood.**

   ① **Assumptions** - The quick predictions and automatic judgments we make based on our beliefs, perceptions and experiences. Assumptions frame how we see the world and view individuals and groups. Stereotypes often emerge from our assumptions. One way to "red flag" assumptions is to differentiate between what we observe and what we imagine.

   ② **Perceptions and Direct Experiences** - What we see, hear, think, and feel. The range, depth, and limitations of our experiences may open up or close down our capacity to listen.

   ③ **Values and Attitudes** - Our strongly held beliefs about human beings and how the world works. Our values reflect what we are told in our families, in our religious, educational, and social institutions—what we believe is right/wrong, good/bad, acceptable/not acceptable. Our values reflect what is really important to us and often filter what we hear and don't hear in a conversation.

   ④ **Communication Style** - The kinds of words we use and how we say things matters. Are we using sarcastic and judgmental language? Do we constantly interrupt? Do we insist that others talk exactly like we do? Do we give the other person enough time to get their thoughts together? Do we always have to have the last word? Our style can shut down or encourage conversation and problem solving. We need to be aware of both our verbal language and our body language.

2. Students Seem to Improve Their Listening Skills When:

① Teachers let students know ahead of time that listening is a vital part of a particular activity.

② Both teachers and students take turns monitoring conversations noting plus's and minus's. Students can help each other identify what's working in a good conversation and what they can do to improve their practice.

③ Teachers give students the opportunity to really talk, allowing enough time for students to engage in rich and complex conversations.

④ Teachers encourage students to ask questions which seek more information and understanding and discourage questions which are confrontational and judgmental.

⑤ Teachers and students intentionally practice various listening skills regularly in the classroom.

3. Multiply Conversations by Using Pair-Share Dialogues.

This is a simple technique to get everyone engaged in dialogue at the same time. Ideally it is a way to brainstorm, begin discussion of a compelling question, frame a topic of study, or assess what people know. Students pair up and bring their own knowledge, opinions and experiences to the topic at hand, one person speaking for about two minutes, and then the other partner speaking for about two minutes, thus reversing the roles of listener and speaker.

It is important to remind students that when they are in the role of listener, their goal is to encourage their partner to talk, *not to interrupt*! After the pair-share, ask some students to share their own thoughts or paraphrase their partner's thoughts. You might want to record responses on newsprint to keep a record of the continuum of students ideas and opinions.

4. Use Small Group "Go-Arounds" to Encourage Listening Attentively and Speaking Thoughtfully.

This is a another way to multiply the number of conversations and also ensure that students will hear multiple points of view. Divide students into small groups of four to seven students. You may want all groups to discuss the same issue or questions or invite groups to choose which two or three questions they want to discuss from a larger list of questions. In a "go-around," one student in the group responds to the chosen question without being interrupted. Then the next student responds to the same question with being interrupted. This process continues until all students have spoken to the question.

At this point, groups can respond to another question or participate in more back and forth conversation.

5. **Structured Dialogues Help Students Pay Closer Attention to How They Listen, What They Say, and How They Say It.**
Structured dialogues have the advantage of slowing down thinking and thus improve listening, ensuring that participants choose more carefully what they say and how they say it.
Some process suggestions:

① Limit the size of the group involved in a dialogue. If you can divide the group in half using two facilitators, there are more opportunities for each person to feel part of the dialogue.

② Sit so that everyone is facing each other.

③ Prepare a set of questions before hand that students have helped to generate. You may want to prioritize questions or identify three or four that students are eager to discuss.

④ Do at least one or "go-around" with an open-ended question where everyone who wants to respond gets to speak before the group begins raising questions or wants to participate in back and forth dialogue.

⑤ Sometimes it is helpful to have participants paraphrase what the previous speaker has said or summarize important points before the conversation goes in a new direction.

⑥ You might want to use a "fishbowl" when you have a large group. This technique is especially useful when emotions are heated and there are disparate perceptions of an issue or conflict. Ask five to seven students to begin the conversation in the center of the space. Make sure that this is a diverse group that reflects different perceptions, experiences, and opinions of the larger group. This group should sit in a circle. Everyone else sits in a circle around the fishbowl.

After all students in the fishbowl have had one or two times to speak in a "go-around" about a particular topic or question, you can invite others to take their places by tapping a student on the shoulder and moving into that student's spot in the fishbowl. (A variation is to invite students to "shadow" one of the students in the fishbowl by sitting behind the student and then speaking from the perspective of that student.)

⑦ If the dialogue becomes heated, stop for a minute and do a feeling/reality check. (How are people feeling about what's been said? How do others feel about _____? How do others see this issue? Who else wants to respond before we move on? Is there anyone else who has another opinion? Is there anyone else who agrees?)

⑧ Identify areas of agreement and disagreement. Look for common ground.

⑩ Finally, assess the quality and process of dialogue (orally and/or in writing) to summarize the substance and the direction of the conversation. (Were all points of view heard? respected? Were there new insights that shifted your thinking? What new ideas and facts complicated the issue for you? What did you learn about the topic/yourself/other individuals/other groups from this conversation?)

6. Generate Ground Rules and Make Agreements About How You Want People to Talk to Each Other and Treat Each Other During A Dialogue.
Some common suggestions:

① No interrupting. Allow people to have time to compose their thoughts and finish what they have to say.

② All participants have the right to pass if they choose not to speak to a particular question.

③ Keep issues and personalities separate. Discourage the use of statements that refer to specific people or attack "them." Discourage statements in which participants presume to speak for someone else.

④ Loaded or controversial language heats up tensions. The group may decide that participants can request that certain words be replaced with less emotionally charged language.

⑤ To encourage open and honest conversation, sometimes it is appropriate to request that the conversation doesn't "leave the table."

⑥ Encourage students to speak from their own experience, using "I" statements. *"I think........I've experienced..........I observe.......I feel....... I don't understand.......I see..........I hear........I like.......I prefer......"*

⑦ The facilitator's role is to ensure that mutually agreed to ground rules are maintained.

7. Discuss the Differences Between Dialogue and Debate.

Many students never talk because they always feel like they are in the middle of somebody else's contest! With the whole class, brainstorm a list of differences between *dialogue* and *debate*. Think about how goals differ and also how people attend and respond differently. Think about the advantages and disadvantages of each type of discourse. **Handout 7:2** is one way to compare and contrast dialogue and debate.

COMPARING DIALOGUE AND DEBATE

Dialogue is collaborative: two or more sides work together toward common understanding.	Debate is oppositional: two sides oppose each other and attempt to prove each other wrong.
In dialogue, finding common ground is the goal.	In debate, winning is the goal.
In dialogue, one listens to the other side(s) in order to understand, find meaning, and find agreement.	In debate, one listens to the other side in order to find flaws and to counter its arguments.
Dialogue enlarges and possibly changes a participant's point of view.	Debate affirms a participant's own point of view.
Dialogue complicates positions and issues.	Debate simplifies positions and issues.
Dialogue reveals assumptions for reevaluation.	Debate defends assumptions as truth.
Dialogue causes introspection on one's own position.	Debate causes critique of the other position.
It is acceptable to change one's position.	It is a sign of weakness and defeat to change one's position.
Dialogue is flexible in nature.	Debate is rigid in nature.
Dialogue stresses the skill of synthesis.	Debate stresses the skill of analysis.
Dialogue opens the possibility of reaching a better solution than either of the original solutions.	Debate defends one's own positions as the best solution and excludes other solutions.

Dialogue creates an open-minded attitude: an openness to being wrong and an openness to change.	Debate creates a closed-minded attitude and a determination to be right.
In dialogue, one submits one's best thinking knowing that other peoples' reflections will help improve it rather than destroy it.	In debate, one submits one's best thinking and defends it against challenges to show that it is right.
Dialogue calls for temporarily suspending one's beliefs.	Debate calls for investing wholeheartedly in one's beliefs.
In dialogue, one searches for basic agreements.	In debate, one searches for glaring differences.
In dialogue, one searches for strengths in the other position.	In debate, one searches for flaws and weaknesses in the other position.
Dialogue involves a real concern for the other person and seeks to not alienate or offend.	Debate involves a countering of the other position without focusing on feelings or relationship and often belittles or deprecates the other position.
Dialogue encourages de-polarization of an issue.	Debate encourages polarization of an issue.
In dialogue, everyone is part of the solution to the problem.	In debate, one person or viewpoint wins over the other.
Dialogue affirms the idea of people learning from each other.	Debate affirms the idea of people learning individually in competition with others.
Dialogue remains open-ended.	Debate implies a conclusion.

From *Perspectives*, Educators for Social Responsibility

ACTIVITY 3: CLASSROOM EXPECTATIONS, AGREEMENTS, AND CONTRACTS

PURPOSE: This activity introduces several ways that students can identify the kinds of skills, behaviors, and attitudes that are needed to create a positive learning climate and offers ideas for developing agreements that build effective working relationships in the classroom.

LEARNING STRATEGIES: Reflective writing, whole group brainstorming, discussion, and decision making

TIME: Flexible. *T-charts* can be generated in 10 minutes. Classroom contracts, on the other hand, may require three to five class periods.

MATERIALS: Newsprint, markers, **Handout 7:3**

SUGGESTED INSTRUCTIONS:
1. You might want to begin the new school year by asking students to write down their ideas in response to any of the following questions:
    a. What makes a safe classroom for you to be your best and learn your best?
    b. How do you want others to treat you in this classroom?
    c. What rights does every student have in a classroom?
    d. What responsibilities does every students have in a classroom?
    e. What do we do that helps the classroom community?
    f. What do we do that hurts the classroom community?
    g. What makes a good teacher? What does a good teacher do and say?
    h. What makes a good student? What does a good student do?
    i. What are the kinds of activities that help you learn?
    j. What makes learning fun for you?

2. After reading students' writing, decide together the key questions that would help you develop a classroom contract. Brainstorm responses to these questions. The ideas that you and your students have generated can form a foundation for a classroom contract. **Handout 7:3 Classroom Contract of Rights and Responsibilities** includes a sampling of agreements that students and teachers have developed together.

    Working out a classroom contract becomes an excellent tool for developing decision-making skills. **(See Activity 5: Making Good Decisions)**. Students need to agree on the decision-making model they will use to approve their final contract. Then you and your students can continue to modify the contract until it is in polished form for a final decision.

After everyone has agreed to the contract, both students and teacher sign the contract. You might want to suggest that students send the contract and a letter describing their work to key administrative staff in your school. Encourage staff to give feedback to your students.

3. *T-charts* are another way to help students focus on specific behaviors that help create a productive learning community or help them succeed in doing a specific task. For example, if the behavior you want students to practice is good listening, you can generate responses from students that help them to identify what they would see or do and what they would say or hear if students are practicing good listening. Post T-charts in the room so that both you and your students can monitor and assess whether students are actually practicing the desired behaviors in skillful ways. Some examples of skills and procedures to T-chart:

Working In A Group
Completing a Task By Yourself
Using Special Classroom Supplies
  and Materials
When You Don't Understand...
When You Can't Find What You
  Need.....
Studying For An Exam

Classroom Meeting
A Good Classroom Discussion
Showing Respect For Each Other
When You Need Help...
When You've Finished a Task Before
  Others
When There's Tension in the Class
  Over Assignments, Expectations

Example:

Good Listening	
What You See or Do	What You Say or Hear
Make eye contact; focus on the other person	Don't interrupt; let the other person finish completely what he or she is saying
Lean forward a little or nod	Restate what someone says
Try to sit still; don't fidget or play with stuff	Use encouragers like, "Uh huh"; "Tell me more"; "Yeah"
Be in interested silence with the other person; give the other person time to respond	Reflect what someone is feeling

"Sample" Classroom Contract of Rights and Responsibilities

Every Student Has The Following Rights In This Class:

1. The right to *learn*.
2. The right to *not be touched without permission*.
3. The right to *keep belongings and school work in the classroom without having them taken or messed up*.
4. The right to *not be embarrassed in class by students or teacher*.

Agreements that Help Create a Positive Learning Community	Positive Outcomes/Consequences (What Happens As a Result?)
1. *Listening to each other*	*We know what to do / What's been said*
2. *Cooperative participation in a group*	*Group task gets completed*
3. *Using 12" voices in a group*	*Many groups can work at the same time*
4. *Taking care of student-teacher problems in private*	*People can be calmer, more thoughtful; and more honest*
5. *Everyone is ready to start 5 min. after bell rings.*	*People have time to shift gears and settle in.*

Affirmations When Individuals or the Whole Class Respect the Rights of Others or Contribute Positively to the Classroom Community:

1. *A group cheer for someone*
2. *Negotiated independent study*
3. *Affirmation and appreciation notes and verbal "put-ups"*
4. *Recognition from Principal*
5. *Special "We Choose" activities, "No Homework" days, special agendas and community building activities which don't necessarily relate to course.*

Agreements About What Hurts the Classroom Community	Negative Effects/Consequences (What Happens As a Result?)
1. *Personal "Put-downs"*	*Hurts someone's feelings*
2. *Touching, pushing, shoving*	*Invades someone's personal space*
3. *Not listening to directions*	*Takes more time / Can't complete task*
4. *Making distracting noises and gestures when someone else has the floor.*	*It's harder to listen / It's distracting for the person who's speaking / It makes it harder to be serious about what you're saying*

Things to Do and Steps to Take When an Individual, Several Students, or the Whole Class Violate the Rights of Others or Hurt the Classroom Community:

1. *"Time Out" from regular classroom activities until ready to participate*
2. *Work out a contract to you get what you need without bothering others.*
2. *One-to-one time with teacher / Conference with student & parent*
3. *Classroom meeting to problem-solve*
4. *Take time to practice the skill / Give feedback on how class is doing*

This contract has been ratified by the students and teacher on _____
Names _____   _____   _____

Activity 4: Building Blocks For Cooperation: A Group Process And Problem-Solving Exercise

PURPOSE: The goal of this exercise is to enable students to think about how they work in groups and to identify the attitudes, roles, and behaviors that can help groups work cooperatively and effectively to solve problems.

LEARNING STRATEGIES: Interactive small group exercise, whole group sharing and discussion

TIME: One to two class periods depending on the amount of sharing and debriefing time you want to include

MATERIALS: Each team needs a large number of construction blocks in four or five colors (foam or wooden blocks, Legos, etc.), **Handout 7:4**.

SUGGESTED INSTRUCTIONS:
1. Divide class into teams of five to seven students. Mix the blocks up so that each pile of blocks has more of one color than the other colors.

2. **Instructions for each team:**
   A. Your team's challenge is to build as many towers as you can using as many of your blocks as you can.

   B. There are four rules for building towers.
      1) Each tower must be higher than the previous tower.
      2) The first tower must contain at least one block of each color. The pattern you use in the first tower will form your color sequence for the rest of your towers.
      3) You need to continue using the same color sequence as you build higher and higher towers.
      4) You can keep asking questions about what you can/can't do.
      5) Your negotiator can trade for blocks from other teams.

   C. You may want to show students examples of several towers in a row. Let students know that there are many ways to meet this challenge. For example, students can use single blocks to continue the pattern (#1, #2, #3) or they can continue their color sequence by using only one, two, or three colors per tower (#4) or one, two, or three blocks per tower (#5).

#1
- red
- green
- yellow
- blue

#2
- blue
- red
- green
- yellow
- blue

#3
- green
- yellow
- blue
- red
- green
- yellow

#4
- blue
- blue
- blue
- red
- red

#5
- green
- yellow
- yellow

D. Your team needs to decide who will be responsible for each role in your group. (Write roles on newsprint so everyone can see them or copy **Handout 7:4** .)

E. You will have five minutes to choose roles and decide on your plan. During this time you may not touch the blocks. Then you will have fifteen minutes to build.

F. Give each process observer a card with these questions on it:

> **How did the team decide who would take each role?**
> **Who made decisions?**
> **How did the team decide how to build the towers?**
> **What did people do or say that helped the group meet the challenge?**
> **Was there anything the team could have done differently to work more effectively together?**

3. **Debriefing:**
Ask process observers from each team to speak first. Then open the discussion to the whole class. Post questions on board or newsprint that you want to discuss:
- How did it feel to play your role? How did you contribute to the success of your group?

- Were you successful in meeting the goal of the exercise? How would you assess your group's effort, 1 to 10?

- What was fun/easy/frustrating/challenging about this exercise?

- Was your solution different than the others? Did asking questions help you come up with interesting solutions to specific challenges?

(For example, sometimes students run out of blocks. One time a student asked if she could use other colored objects [yellow pages, books, bottles] when their group ran out of blocks!)

- Was there any tension in the group? Did team members have to compromise? Work out differences? Did you feel competitive with other groups? Why or why not?

- What skills and attitudes helped you work well together? If you were not satisfied with how your team worked together, what would you do differently next time so that your team would be more successful? Make a T-chart:

A Good Team	
What You Hear or Say	*What You See or Do*

Roles For Tower Building

Facilitator - Person who begins the discussion and ensures that everyone has their say	**Question Asker and Summarizer** - Person who asks questions and summarizes ideas and suggestions from group
Negotiator - Person who can negotiate with other groups to trade for blocks that you need (you may have only a few yellow blocks, but more than enough red blocks)	**Gatekeeper** - Person who makes sure that group stays focused on goal (tracks time, color sequence, height of towers)
Encourager - Person who encourages students when they are making positive contributions to group / gives positive feedback to group	**Compromiser** - Person who can help group sort out conflicting ideas and help group reach decisions on what to do

Process Observer - Person who watches and listens instead of doing. This person jots notes about how group accomplishes the task and how the group works together and then reports back to whole class at end of exercise

Activity 5: Making Good Decisions

PURPOSE: In this activity students explore the realm of daily decision-making, discuss the elements that make a a good decision, and identify and practice four ways of making decisions.

LEARNING STRATEGIES: Whole class discussion, partner dialogues, reading for understanding, group decision making, and observation/research

TIME: Two class periods

MATERIALS: Handouts 7:5A and 7:5B, newsprint, markers

Teacher Notes*:

Decision making around the real choices that affect students lives puts young people in a process where truly significant learning is taking place, at whatever developmental level. The most important factors identified in studies of how people learn—respect, immediacy and relevance, are all present. Since most decisions are not made in isolation, decision making also provides ample opportunity for communication and conflict resolution skills to be practiced. Students experience controversy and choice handled either constructively or destructively and then look at the results. They practice making decisions both under time restraints as well as when they are given all the time they feel they need. In encouraging students to make decisions, teachers own their role and image as leaders who model democratic leadership.

Teachers can begin sharing their power in the classroom and becoming partners in their students learning slowly, using whatever they are comfortable with at first, gradually branching out. For example, student decisions can start with something as simple as a suggestion box moving all the way to learner-driven classrooms where students become full partners in designing the curriculum, the teaching tools and the methods used. A starter kit of other ideas include:

- thoroughly brainstorming all possibilities before routine decisions are made
- developing teacher-student learning contracts
- using simulations and role plays followed by discussion of the character's actions and choices
- employing cooperative learning strategies
- holding classroom meetings

*Notes from the work of Marian O'Malley, Center for Peace Education/NC ESR

- allowing students to take an active role in classroom governance, for example, creating together with the teacher, the groundless for how people should treat each other in the class or developing solutions and consequences for discipline problems
- giving regular feedback to the teacher on lessons taught or input on the way the students would like to go about learning various academic content
- observing and analyzing various methods that groups use to make decisions

SUGGESTED INSTRUCTIONS:
1. Open discussion by asking, "What decisions have you already made today? What decisions do you make by yourself? What decisions does your family make for you? What decisions do you and your family make together? What decisions does the government make for you? What decisions does the school make for you? What decisions do you make together with your friends?"

2. Write a list of the decision-making situations on newsprint. For example:
   - What you eat for breakfast / When you eat breakfast
   - How many miles per hour you can drive on the highway
   - What you do and where you go on a weekend with your friends
   - What math problems you do in class
   - When you eat dinner / What you eat for dinner
   - When you have to be home at night on the weekends
   - When you can get a job
   - Where you apply to college
   - When you learn to drive
   - What you wear in the morning
   - Who your friends are / What you do with your friends
   - What homework you choose to do
   - When school starts in the morning
   - How long you get to use the telephone

   Ask students, "Who's involved in each situation?" and, "Who decides what will happen?" (i.e., you, your family, your friends, the school, the teacher, the government).

3. Point out that all decisions have *constraints* and *limitations.* For example, "What you eat for breakfast" will depend on what's in the house to eat. Ask students what constraints would affect "What are you going to do - where are you going to go this weekend?" (i.e., money, transportation, what you and your friends are allowed to do, etc.) Ask students to quickly write down a list of five things they want to do this

week, this year, this decade! Have students pair up with a partner to discuss the constraints and limitations which might determine whether they actually get to do each activity on the list.

4. Ask students what questions they can ask that would help them make good decisions. Generate a list of these questions to post in your classroom as reminders when students make decisions by themselves, with another person, or as a whole class. **Handout 7:5A Responsible Choices and Decisions** includes a sample list of questions.

5. Identify the situations that you've listed and discussed above that involve groups of people. Ask students to think about ways that groups make decisions (use classroom decisions as examples.) Then pass out copies of **Handout 7:5B Decision-Making Processes**. Have students take turns reading. After reading about each model, do a quick demonstration of the model:

> **I DECIDE or YOU DECIDE (Autocratic)** - One person in class gets to decide music you will listen during quiet reading, the problems you will do for a math assignment, the amount of homework time at the end of class, or another some other decision that affects the whole class.

> **GET INPUT (Participatory)** - Generate suggestions for community service project, a field trip, or some special class activity that students might like to do during the year.

> **VOTE ON IT (Democratic)** - Vote on "Give Me a Break" choices: 1) a designated *No Assignment Night* for the quarter; 2) Dropping lowest quiz grade in the quarter; 3) One *Take the Night Off* chit to be used any time during the quarter.

> **WE ALL AGREE (Consensus)** - Do a "go-around" or a quick "Thumbs up / Thumbs down/ Thumbs in the middle" to see if there is agreement about a specific school policy or classroom rule.

6. Discuss the questions at the bottom of **Handout 7:5B**.

🖋 **Going Further:**
   1. Generate a list of procedural/management/assignment decisions that you and your students can make together in your classroom.

   2. Identify major school decisions, policies, and procedures that matter most to students in your class. Make predictions about who made

specific decisions, the process used to make different decisions, and the reasons/specific circumstances that prompted different decisions. Interview people to check your assumptions and get accurate information. Then make a decision-making "map" which depicts what students learned.

3. Have each student or pairs of students choose to observe a group in the process of making a decision. Brainstorm a list of groups that students might want to observe. Then brainstorm a list of what they want to listen and watch for when they observe the decision making opportunity. Ask students to record their observations and identify the decision making processes they observed. After students have made their observations, have them share their experiences and discuss what they feel were the advantages and disadvantages of each decision making process.

Some groups students might observe:
- family decision making
- clubs or other extra curricular groups who are making plans
- a school board meeting
- a city council meeting
- a design or planning group in business
- a civil court case
- a traffic court case
- a sports team deciding on strategies
- a student council meeting
- a school newspaper or yearbook editorial meeting
- a youth group planning future events
- a neighborhood block meeting or neighborhood association meeting
- planning committees of various civic and business groups
- a co-op, condo, or tenants association meeting
- board meetings of non-for-profit groups
- meetings for local election and referendum volunteers
- legislative hearings or committee meetings
- committee meetings of religious organizations

Responsible Choices and Decisions:
Some Considerations

- ☐ Are people affected by the decision part of the decision making process?

- ☐ Does it respect the rights and needs of people affected by decision?

- ☐ Are people who are supposed to make the decision work involved in making the decision?

- ☐ Do you have what you need (people and resources) to make the decision work?

- ☐ Is it balanced? Does it seem fair to everyone involved?

- ☐ Is it safe?

- ☐ Does it help (not hurt) people?

- ☐ Do people feel good about the decision making process?

- ☐ Does it respect property, public space, and the environment?

- ☐ Is it moral? Is it legal? Is it smart?

Four Decision-Making Processes
Here are four processes we can use to make decisions:

1. I DECIDE or YOU DECIDE (Autocratic Decision-making)
One person *makes the decision alone.* This happens when a person is responsible for making a choice by herself or himself. People make "I Decide" decisions when 1) one person is responsible for the safety and well-being of others; 2) one person is in charge of a situation; or 3) one person needs to act quickly and there's no time to talk to other people.

2. GET INPUT (Participatory Decision-making)
One person or a small group collects all ideas and suggestions, discusses the **+'s** and **-'s** of each idea with everyone, and then makes a decision that includes the best *input from everyone.*

3. VOTE ON IT (Democratic Decision-making)
Everyone generates ideas about what to do and then *everyone votes* on the best idea. Final choices and decisions can be made by selecting 1) the idea that receives the most votes or 2) voting until one idea receives a *majority* vote (At least half + one) or 2/3 vote

4. WE ALL AGREE (Consensus Decision-making)
Everyone participates and has a say before reaching agreement on a *decision that everyone in the group can support.* In consensus, the ideas that people don't like are thrown out or changed before there is a final agreement that is "good enough." Consensus happens when each person in the group finally agrees with the decision.

1. Which process do you think takes the shortest time to make a decision?
2. Which process do you think takes the longest time to make a decision?
3. Which process would you use to decide what to do immediately when somebody is hurt?
4. Which process do we use most often in public decision-making? Why?
5. Which process would you use to decide which movie to see on Saturday with your friends?
6. Which process would a teacher use to decide what math skills to teach?
7. Which process would a teacher and students use to decide on classroom rules?
8. Which process would you use to decide what job offer to take?

Activity 6: Tools For Prioritizing And Building Agreement

PURPOSE: This activity offers four techniques you and your students can use for identifying preferences and making choices that reflect the interests and needs of all participants or for thinking through controversial issues and strong disagreements.

LEARNING STRATEGIES: Group decision making

TIME: Flexible. These techniques can be used any time you and your class are making decisions about what to do.

MATERIALS: Newsprint, markers

SUGGESTED INSTRUCTIONS:

1. Stickering to Identify Preferences

If you are prioritizing options or narrowing possible directions/activities/suggestions/strategies, put list on newsprint. Use red and green stickers to identify the two or three most desirable options (use green stickers) and the two or three least desirable options (use red stickers). Items with mostly red or green stickers will give you a quick read of group preferences. If an item has a significant number of both reds and greens, it's probably one that needs more discussion or clarification. If the group is small, each person can sticker individually. If it's a large group, you might want to divide into groups of five and have each small group talk through choices and reach a consensus about where to place their stickers.

2. 100-Point Commitment - What Are You Really Willing to Do?

Agreeing on priorities isn't worth much if the group isn't willing to make a commitment of time and energy to those priorities. This is one way to get a quick read to see what the group is truly willing to do. If you've narrowed a list to five to ten items, post them on newsprint. Each person has 0 to 100 points to invest. The guideline requires that you can only place points on items that you are willing to work on. You can place up to 50 points on a single item but no less than 25 points on a single item.

3. Reaching Consensus by Talking It Through

When you are trying to reach a consensus decision, have people indicate their level of agreement by raising one to five fingers.

Five fingers--->Complete agreement/enthusiastic support
Four fingers--->It's good enough/can support publicly
Three fingers--->Tentative support with some reservations
Two fingers--->Can't support until a major concern is addressed
One finger--->Fundamentally disagree/can't support at all

Keep talking it through until everyone is a "three", "four", or "five". One option is to form small groups of three students (a #1, a #5, and someone in the middle) which work together to identify one major concern and brainstorm suggestions for compromise and negotiation.

4. Finding Common Ground

This technique is especially useful for thinking through a controversial issue with clearly defined polarizing positions on both sides. This process can help students identify where there might be potential areas of agreement on what to do and how to do it. Use the following format for discussion or writing.

    a. Identify both positions in no more than a paragraph.

    b. Make lists of four or five interests that each position reflects.

    c. Look for concerns and interests that overlap.

    d. Identify specific demands, policies, actions on which there doesn't seem to be room for compromise or negotiation right now.

    e. Reframe common concerns and interests in language that would be agreeable to both sides.

    f. Brainstorm a list of possible actions, policies, agreements, or next steps which could emerge from common ground.

Position	Interests-------------->		<------------Interests	Position
What's your demand? What do you believe? Why is it right?	What do you care about? What worries you? What are your fears? What are your biggest concerns? What do you need? Why does it matter?	**Common Ground** **Mutual Concerns & Interests**	What do you care about? What worries you? What are your fears? What are your biggest concerns? What do you need? Why does it matter?	What's your demand? What do you believe? Why is it right?

Activity 7: When The Group's Not Working.....

PURPOSE: When the group's not working well—when you can cut the tension with a knife—you know it's time to stop what your doing and think and talk about what's going on. This activity offers several ideas for how to get tough and sometimes painful concerns and issues out in the open so your group can move from underground tension and complaining to aboveboard responsible problem solving. These strategies can help turn group conflicts into "teachable moments" that can lead to positive changes in your class or group.

LEARNING STRATEGIES: Personal reflection, structured dialogue, group problem solving

TIME: Flexible, but be mindful that if you've opened up some sore spots, allow enough time for students talk through their thoughts and feelings about the issue.

MATERIALS: Note cards, newsprint, markers

SUGGESTED OPENERS FOR TOUGH CONVERSATIONS:

1. When You're Afraid to Say It Out Loud

Have each person identify one or two issues of concern that affect the group and how it's working together. These should be issues that people think have to be addressed and resolved as a whole group. Write concerns on note cards anonymously. Write all of the responses on newsprint. You may want to combine similar concerns and place a ☑ next to a concern for every time it's mentioned. There are several ways to use this information:

a. Identify broad categories or overlapping concerns as a whole group or let a subgroup do it and present a condensed list to whole group.

b. As a whole group or in smaller groups of four to seven, do a "go-around" in which each person speaks to an important issue or concern on the newsprint that is *not* the one that they wrote down. This is not the time to do back and forth responses. The purpose is to hear what everyone has to say about issues they feel strongly about.   This also helps individuals recognize that others share similar concerns.

c. After identifying the two or three issues people feel are most important to address, divide up in three's for an extended conversation about these issues. (Different groups might choose different issues to address.) You might use some questions to frame a proactive discussion that can lead to suggestions and solutions.

374

2. These Are My Hot Buttons!

None of us are mind readers! Sometimes tensions within a group worsen simply because no one will actually say what's bothering them about how individuals treat each other or how the group does its work together. One way to get at this is to ask individuals to identify one or two hot buttons that they want others to know about----situations or behaviors that students are willing to "red flag" so there is the possibility that the specific behaviors can be reduced or eliminated. A couple of ways to frame this:

"My hot button gets pushed when_____.

"I would like people to consider _____ [an alternative]_____.

"I feel frustrated when_____. I wish instead that

_____ [an alternative]_____."

3. Ouch! That Hurts! Part 1

When back biting, openly harsh criticism, and downright nasty personal interactions are rife within a group, one option is to have everyone in the group hear out loud the things that people say that are creating the tensions and bad feelings. One way to do this is to ask individuals to write down on note cards one or two comments that they often hear which are hurtful, make them very angry, or do damage in a way that prevents the group from being cohesive and effective. Read some or all of the comments out loud to everyone.

After you've read the comments, give students time to think and talk:
- How did it feel to hear these comments?
- What kind of climate do these comments create?
- How do these comment affect how the group works together?
- Where do we go from here?

4. Ouch! That Hurts! Part 2

For most students, there are certain fighting words, slurs, names, put-downs, insults, loaded phrases that immediately trigger anger or hurt feelings. Ask students to give examples (out loud or written anonymously) of some of the words and phrases that upset them. Invite students to explain to others why these words bother them; ask students how they feel when they hear them. You may want to explore the historical and cultural reasons why some words trigger such intense feelings.

Make a list of specific words and phrases that make students upset—words that they think hurt people's feelings or "push people's buttons." These are words that students don't want to hear another student use to describe or refer to them. As a whole group, select about 10 to 15 words or phrases that the class agrees are "fouls"—words that the class agrees should not be used in the classroom. Post these in the classroom as a reminder to everyone in your class.

Brainstorm suggestions for what students can do when they hear someone use these words. One option which can help defuse potential conflict is to remind others that in this class, "That's a foul! We don't say that in here."

5. "That's a Winner!"

Make a classroom list of words and phrases that make students feel like winners. Think about the words and phrases you want to hear that let you know you belong and what you're doing is appreciated.

6. Make a Wacky Wish List

One way to lighten up and move beyond the bad feelings/bad group dynamic is to make an outrageous and ridiculous wish list of wonderful, wacky things you want to happen in your life that can never materialize in this world.

Activity 8: The Newspaper Project: Thinking About Individual, Competitive, And Collaborative Work Styles

PURPOSE: In this activity, students create three design projects in order to explore differences between individual, competitive, and collaborative work styles.

LEARNING STRATEGIES: Individual and group problem solving, written reflection, whole group discussion

TIME: One period for the activity and one period for presentations and debriefing. If you want to focus on collaborative learning only, you can choose to do just Phase 3 of the activity.

MATERIALS:

Each group of five students needs the following materials:

One large bag of newspapers	Colored and white paper
Several colored markers	Stapler and staples
A ball of string	Assorted magazines containing
A roll of masking tape	pictures
Two or three pairs of scissors	One large note card

Each student needs a copy of **Handout 7:8** and a pencil
Five or six small bags of snacks or pencils for prizes

SUGGESTED INSTRUCTIONS:
1. **Preparation for the activity:**
   a. Be sure you use a space that contains enough work spaces (tables or desks and chairs) so that you can divide your students into groups of five.
   b. Collect and organize materials so that you can place a complete set of materials in the center of each group's workspace.
   c. Write directions and questions on separate pieces of newsprint.
      ~Directions for Phase 1
      ~Directions for Phase 2
      ~Directions for Phase 3
      ~Reflection questions to be answered after each phase of the activity
      ~Group debriefing questions
   d. For Phase 2, you need to make a paper hat out of newspaper to have as a model for students to see. Fancy up your hat by stapling or taping on three or four cut-out figures, letters, symbols, or designs (for example, the initials or name of your school, paper snowflakes, hearts, stars, geometric shapes, etc.)

2. **Directions for each phase of the activity:**
   Phase 1:
   a. You will have 12 minutes to make anything you want from the materials on your table.
   b. You will create your project on your own by yourself.
   c. Since this is independent work time, you will not be allowed to talk.

   Phase 2:
   a. You will have 12 minutes to make a paper hat *exactly like mine.*
   b. You will be told how much time you have left every three minutes.
   c. Students who make an exact copy of the hat will receive a prize.

   Phase 3: *(You might want to abbreviate directions depending on your class.)*
   a. Your group's goal: To plan and create something out the materials on your table that meet the following criteria.
      ~ Your project needs to have a purpose. What could it be used for? What does it explain, represent, or symbolize? What is the project's message? How does it work?
      ~ Your project must be sturdy. It must be able to stand or hang on its own.
      ~ Your project needs to be aesthetically pleasing. How have you used pictures, paper, newspaper, color, and form in interesting ways to make your project original and pleasing to the eye?
   b. You will have 5 minutes to plan what you want to do before you work with the materials. Your *whole group* must agree on what you finally decide to make.
   c. You will have twenty minutes to complete your project.
   d. When you have finished your project your group will assess how successfully you met the original criteria by giving yourself 1 to 5 points each (5 being the highest and 1 being the lowest) for *purpose, sturdiness, and aesthetics.*
   e. You need to choose one or two people in your group to present and explain your project to the rest of the group.

3. **Reflection Questions:** See **Handout 7:8 Thinking About Learning and Work Styles**

4. **Debriefing Questions for Whole Group Discussion:**
   • Select questions from **Handout 7:8** to discuss.
   • Which phase of the activity did you like best? least? Why?
   • Say more about the positive or negative feelings that you experienced during different phases of the activity.
   • How was the learning approach different in each phase? How was the teacher's role different? How did the teacher's role affect how you worked? How was the climate/atmosphere different? Which approach worked best for you?

(You will get a rich variety of responses here. Some students really like what they did in Phase 1—open-ended assignments with no clear-cut instructions or outcomes, assignments where they can experiment and try things out; others absolutely hate it. Most kids respond negatively to Phase 2, but some get hooked into the "contest" dynamic and like the pressure and the challenge. Individual reactions to Phase 3 often depend on how well students worked together and how successful the group met the project criteria.)

- *(Explore the kinds of projects students created in Phase 3)* If you had been working by yourself would you have come up with the same project on your own? In what ways were five heads and five sets of hands better than one? How was it helpful to talk over ideas with others? Did you have some false starts before you came up with your final project? Did people take on different roles in your group? Did anyone specialize—i.e., have one thing that s/he was very skillful at doing? What did you contribute that was different than anyone else's contribution?

* *(Explore the advantages and disadvantages of using different workstyles—individual, competitive, and collaborative—to do a job. You may want to point out that innovative work place efforts like Total Quality Management encourage both individual initiative and collaborative problem solving more than a competitive work style because it results in higher satisfaction, productivity, and personal investment. The SCANS Report from the Department of Labor cites "getting along and working well with others" to be one of the top three qualities for effective workers in the 21st century.)*

What work style do you use at school most often? What work style would you like to use more often at school? What kinds of tasks and activities work best if they are carried out *individually/competitively/collaboratively*? What kinds of efforts require people to use all three work styles effectively? What would be some clear mismatches of task and work style?

5. **Step-by-Step Instructions for Teacher:**
    1. Explain to students that they will be creating three different design projects to explore different ways that people work and learn. Let them know that each time they will be able to use any of the materials on their table. Also, point out that you will be playing a different teacher role each time.
    2. Review instructions for **Phase 1**.
    3. Give students 12 minutes to work on their projects. Your role is to be a neutral observer. You don't interact or intervene except to remind students that this is a silent activity.

4. Give students 3 minutes to write in their responses on **Handout 7:9** beneath the Phase 1 heading.
5. Review instructions for **Phase 2**.
6. Give students 12 minutes to work on their projects. Your role is to be the brow-beating criticizer. Keep reminding students that this is a contest, that they can only win if they make an exact copy; point out to the whole class when someone is doing the hat "wrong"; keeping saying how simple it is to do if you only follow the instructions; praise some students openly; keep pressuring students about time.
7. Give out prizes to anyone who made an exact copy of your hat.
8. Give students 3 minutes to write in their responses on **Handout 7:9** beneath the Phase 2 heading.
9. Review instructions for **Phase 3**.
10. Give students 20 minutes to work on their projects. Your role is to be the encourager, giving two kinds of feedback—let students in various groups know what you see and hear that shows that they are working well as a group and give feedback about their projects that indicates that they are meeting the design criteria. Give students a two-minute warning and remind groups to fill out their assessment note cards.
11. Give students 3 minutes to write in their responses on **Handout 7:9** beneath the Phase 3 heading.
12. Clean up the mess before students present their projects.
13. Give each group about two minutes to make their presentations, explaining what they decided to do, describing their project, and giving their "1 to 5" assessments.
14. Leave fifteen to thirty minutes for whole group debriefing.

✏ **Assessment:** Ask students to write about what they learned from this activity. The writing focus could go in several directions:
1. What did you learn about yourself as a worker/learner. Is there a work style that works best for you? How do you know?
2. If you felt that your group worked well together, summarize the key things a group needs to do so that you "get it right."
3. If you felt that your group had a hard time "getting it together", summarize the things that make working as a group very challenging.
4. Think about a project or assignment you've done in the past at school that was a very satisfying experience. Describe what you did and the work style or combination of work styles that you used to successfully complete your project. Why do you remember this experience?
5. Think about yourself at the job. What kind of boss or supervisor would you want to have? What would they do and say that would help you do your best on your job?

THINKING ABOUT LEARNING AND WORK STYLES

Questions:	Phase 1:	Phase 2:	Phase 3:
What did you like about this activity?			
What didn't you like?			
What feelings did you have while you were working? Why?	I felt _____ because	I felt _____ because	I felt _____ because
What was easy to do?			
What was hard to do?			
What did the teacher say and do?			

Activity 9: Collaborative Problem Solving

PURPOSE: This activity offers some guidelines for group problem solving in the classroom.

LEARNING STRATEGIES: Will vary.

TIME: Flexible.

MATERIALS: Will vary problem to problem.

COLLABORATIVE PROBLEM SOLVING involves students and teachers in both creative and critical thinking. What you and your students choose to do will depend on:
- how you frame the questions and pose the problems
- the kinds of problems you choose—problems in the classroom and school community, problems that emerge from academic disciplines, problems from the real world
- the experiences, knowledge, information, data, tools, and resources students already have
- the experiences, knowledge, information, data, tools, and resources students might need to solve the problem

COLLABORATIVE PROBLEM SOLVING INVOLVES THE FOLLOWING STEPS:
1. Posing, defining, and analyzing a problem;
2. Gathering information and assessing the steps necessary to solve the problem;
3. Generating possible solutions to the problem;
4. Choosing the best solution considering constraints, group interests, and the means and resources available to solve the problem;
5. Implementing a plan, strategy, or solution.

One of the benefits of open-ended problem-solving is presenting students a challenge to which there are a number of approaches and solutions. Debriefing problem-solving activities is an excellent opportunity for students to reflect on how they think through a problem and decide what to do.

SOME GUIDELINES FOR EFFECTIVE GROUP PROBLEM SOLVING:
1. Describe the problem in detail.

2. Encourage students to help formulate questions that give them a way in to thinking about possible solutions, for example:
   - Find the best way to....
   - What would be different if....?
   - Given what you have found out, make predictions about....
   - What information do you need to decide how to....?

- How could you reduce/minimize....?
- How could you increase/maximize....?
- How could you do this in another way that is cheaper/faster/more energy efficient/less time consuming....?
- What factors will influence your final choice among alternative solutions....?
- What are the advantages and disadvantages of.................?
- What must the solution do? What should the solution do? What would you like the solution to do?
- What is likely to happen if the problem is solved? What is like to happen if it is not addressed?
- What keeps the situation from getting worse? What keeps the situation from getting better?

3. Set the challenge and set goals. (both social goals and academic content goals)

4. Ensure that students have access to resources they need to tackle the problem comfortably. Brainstorm resources and review the challenge to make sure that students know what they are doing. Encourage students to move beyond "one way thinking" —there are many ways to solve the problem.

5. Set constraints on what groups can and cannot do; limiting resources and materials can often stimulate creative thinking.

6. Set criteria for assessing the quality of students' work, the academic skills they use, and the social skills needed to work together effectively. Make time for students to reflect on what they have experienced and learned. (both content and process)

7. Limit the number in a group; balance groups so that students in each group reflect a variety of skills and interests.

8. Ensure that everyone in a group has a role and a responsibility.

9. Divide time between **planning** (research, brainstorming, and/or strategizing (What do we need to do first, second, etc.?) and **doing** (actual design, solution, construction, etc.)

10. Give instructions in several ways and if appropriate use examples, illustrations, and models to show possibilities.

Activity 10: Frames for Analyzing Conflicts

PURPOSE: The frameworks included here provides students with different approaches to thinking through a conflict with it is an interpersonal, intergroup, community, national, or international conflict.

LEARNING STRATEGIES: Small or large group problem solving

TIME: Will vary according to the conflict you are discussing

MATERIALS: The resources you need will depend on the conflict or problem you are working with.

SUGGESTED FRAMES:

1. Analyzing Conflict by Analyzing Groups

1. One way to consider the complexities of a conflict is to identify all the groups immediately affected by a conflict and all the groups who would be involved in resolving the conflict or implementing a solution. If key constituencies are left out of the decision-making process, conflict is likely to continue and resentments will continue to build. This process will also enable students to appreciate that conflicts are much harder to resolve when many different groups are involved.

GROUPS IMMEDIATELY AFFECTED BY CONFLICT	MOST IMPORTANT CONCERN OF GROUP	WHAT WOULD THIS GROUP WANT TO TELL ALL OF THE OTHER GROUPS?
GROUPS INVOLVED IN RESOLVING THE CONFLICT AND/OR IMPLEMENTING A SOLUTION	MOST IMPORTANT CONCERN OF GROUP	WHAT WOULD THIS GROUP WANT TO TELL ALL OF THE OTHER GROUPS?

It is important, as well, to consider the relationships among groups.

* Are groups unequal in power, status, financial resources, influence, and allies?

* What institutions play a major role in either precipitating the conflict or resolving the conflict and implementing a solution?

* Are there any groups who benefit from continuation of the conflict?

* Which groups are most interested in resolution? Are there any groups who could be allies?

* Which groups seem farthest apart/closest together regarding what they want?

* Do the people most deeply affected or harmed by the conflict or crisis have a voice in decision-making process? If they don't, are more powerful groups committed to resolving the conflict? If not, why not?

2. What Would Happen If?

One way to examine the impact of various solutions on different groups is to create "IF. . . . WHAT WOULD HAPPEN?" questions that recognize that a change for one group necessarily implies changes in status for other groups as well.

For example:
> If the Palestinians were to control the West Bank, what would happen to the new Jewish settlers who have recently moved there?

3. Looking at Winners and Losers

If you are examining past or current conflicts that have resulted in armed conflict, or have been only partially resolved or temporarily diffused, it is helpful to identify all groups affected by the conflict and determine WINNERS and LOSERS in the short-term and the long-term. A deeper analysis of some conflicts may reveal that winners may in fact have lost more than they appeared to have gained.

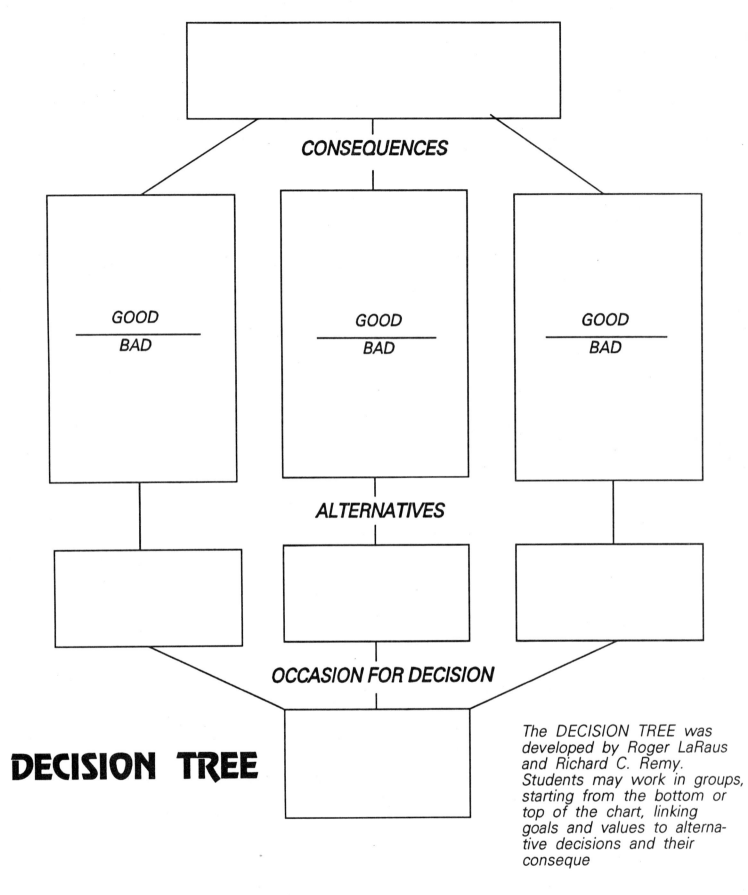

GOALS / VALUES

CONSEQUENCES

GOOD
___
BAD

GOOD
___
BAD

GOOD
___
BAD

ALTERNATIVES

OCCASION FOR DECISION

DECISION TREE

The DECISION TREE was developed by Roger LaRaus and Richard C. Remy. Students may work in groups, starting from the bottom or top of the chart, linking goals and values to alternative decisions and their conseque

Mershon Center, The Ohio State University   Used With Permission

ACTIVITY 11: THE -ATE PROCESSES OF PEACEMAKING*

PURPOSE:
1. Students will become familiar with a variety of peacemaking processes and discuss their use and appropriateness in various interpersonal, community, national, and international conflicts.
2. Students will identify peacemaking processes being used in different examples of conflict situations.
3. Students will examine current conflicts and decide which process might be the best "next step" given the stage of a particular conflict.

LEARNING STRATEGIES: Whole group discussion, reading for understanding, pair problem-solving, and cooperative learning.

TIME: 1 - 2 class periods

MATERIALS: Handout 7:11, magazine articles, videos clips, and/or newsclippings that describe current conflicts.

SUGGESTED INSTRUCTIONS:
1. Write the *-ate words* (See **Handout 11:7: The -Ate Processes of Peacemaking**) on the board or newsprint, leaving a large amount of space around each word. Ask students what they know about these processes—using any of these questions to find out what students know and understand about these terms:
   - Where have you heard these words before? In what context?
   - What do these words mean to you?
   - Can you think of examples where individuals and groups have used these processes? Who was involved? What was happening? What had happened before?
   - Which of these processes have you used before? What was the situation in which you were using this process? What did you want to happen? Did it work?
   - What are some of the differences between the *-ate words*? Do any processes work better in some situations than others?

   Jot down students' responses on the board or newsprint and keep adding information and examples as you continue the activity.

2. Pass out copies of **Handout 7:10** to individuals or pairs of students. Read the handout together, soliciting examples as you read and clarifying the differences between peacemaking processes. One way to "concretize" this discussion is to think of school related examples of each process. Be sure to point out how some processes allow conflicting parties to work things out themselves, on their own terms, while other processes leave disputants with no control over solutions or decisions. Use examples from the end of the activity to review various processes.

387

3. Select 8 to 10 newsclippings that describe various conflicts (from interpersonal to global). Make sure that you select conflicts in which the appropriate next step toward resolution (conciliation, facilitation, negotiation, arbitration, etc.) varies from example to example.

4. Make several copies of each news clipping so that each pair of students can receives several articles. Pass out newsclippings and ask each pair of students to read the article and talk through their understanding of the conflict so that they are able to summarize the present stage of the conflict.

5. For each conflict examined, it may be useful to keep in mind the factors which make a conflict more or less difficult to resolve by the parties themselves. Be sure students consider whether hostilities are too hot for parties to use a voluntary process.

   Factors which may influence process choice:
   * Number of conflicting parties (How does each party define the problem?)
   * Duration, intensity, and history of present conflict.
   * Relevant history of previous peacemaking efforts that may influence present climate.
   * Present climate and relationship among conflicting parties.
   * Familiarity of parties with each other's values, beliefs, and cultural norms.
   * Presence of different cultural styles of negotiating, speaking, and "doing business" that may impede communication.
   * Presence of key influential individuals who seek both a positive change in the relationship and resolution of the conflict.
   * Presence of any fairly obvious solutions that could benefit both parties.

6. Then ask each pair of students decide which process or processes of peacemaking would be the most effective choice given the present stage of a particular conflict. If they were an advisor for this particular conflict what next step would they recommend that might help the conflicting parties work toward resolution of the conflict.

7. Have students describe their conflicts and their process choices with the whole class.

*The idea for the "-ate" words framework is from *Elementary Perspectives*, William J. Kreidler

Examples of the -Ate Processes of Peacemaking

INITIATE

Interpersonal — A student sets up a conference with her teacher to discuss an essay she wants to rewrite.

Community — The Mayor suggests to unhappy city council members that public hearings be held in neighborhoods where residents think that they are not receiving adequate services and street repairs.

International — Former President Jimmy Carter continues to maintain contact with government officials throughout the world.

COMMUNICATE

Interpersonal — Any "mixed-message" between parent and child can lead to miscommunication. A parent casually suggests that Shana needs to do the laundry but never says when. At dinner, the laundry isn't done and Mom is furious. Shana was planning to do it after her homework and didn't realize her brother needed his uniform for practice that night

Community — A large corporation suddenly lays off 400 workers in a local factory without fully disclosing the reasons for the decision. Citizens are outraged and neither group attempts to talk it through.

International — "Citizen diplomacy" exchanges among U.S. and Soviet citizens, scientists, artists, and farmers in the 1980s created opportunities to think beyond stereotypes and gain deeper understanding of each other's cultures and people.

CONCILIATE

Interpersonal — Recurring conflicts between the same two groups of students might require an airing of grievances before students work with a counselor to diffuse the conflict. A facilitator may <u>conciliate</u> a meeting with co-workers who are experiencing ethnic or racial tensions in the work place as a first step toward improving the climate and relationships at work.

Community — Third parties may <u>conciliate</u> a gathering of "old" neighborhood residents (who feel their security and property values are threatened) and "new" immigrants (who just want to live there and don't feel comfortable participating in neighborhood customs).

International — A neutral party convenes a relaxed and informal gathering of "North" and "South" government officials and citizens that has no fixed agenda except to explore differences in values, needs, and interests as well as common concerns.

FACILITATE

Interpersonal — Using a facilitator (a parent, a teacher, or a student) can make a first conversation about where to go and what to do on a family or school trip a productive experience rather than an exercise in frustration. A facilitated process will ensure that one person doesn't dominate the discussion and can help people narrow down choices and possibilities.

Community — When a community or local group of citizens wants to change a policy, decide a new course of action, or collectively plan an event, an impartial facilitator is helpful to avoid perceptions that the person who's running the meeting is not "taking sides" with one group or another.

International—The United Nations must have more facilitators per capita than any other organization on earth! Whether it's the Children's Summit, the Earth Summit, or any of the hundreds of working sessions that various agencies convene annually, the U.N.'s success in different arenas depends, in large part, on its capacity to facilitate constructive, productive dialogue among representatives from over 160 nations.

FORMAL NEGOTIATIONS

Interpersonal — A teacher and student arrive at a mutually acceptable schedule for the student to finish back assignments.

Community — Neighborhood residents agree to let fast food restaurant locate nearby if restaurant builds a fence and plants trees and bushes to reduce noise.

International — Bi-lateral negotiations involve two parties (Example — U.S./Russia START II talks— strategic arms reduction talks involving the elimination of some nuclear weapons, the reduction of others, time table and verification of agreement). Multilateral negotiations involve more than two parties (Example — the Group of 7 [Canada, France, Germany, Italy, Japan, U.K., U.S.A.] working out agreements to eliminate agricultural tariff restrictions).

INFORMAL COLLABORATIVE NEGOTIATIONS

Interpersonal — Family members negotiate (who's going to do what family chores when). These decisions are dependent upon everyone's schedules and individual needs and requests.

Community — A school district agrees to develop a plan for desegregating student populations and faculties within the district. Teachers, school administrators, board members, government officials, students, and community residents develop an action plan that is mutually agreeable to all parties and addresses each groups concerns.

International — Members of groups involved in "the troubles" in Northern Ireland have spent several years of informal negotiations preparing the way for official negotiations among the British and Irish governments and political parties in Northern Ireland. Defining the problem, setting the agenda, and clarifying who will be participants have been so difficult that the aim of future official negotiations may not be to solve "the troubles" (will Northern Ireland remain under U.K. rule or join the Republic of Ireland?) but to explore more incremental steps which diffuse the conflict and improve the civil environment.

MEDIATION

Interpersonal — Mediation is often used by parents and teachers in situations where siblings or students are fighting or quarreling over "stuff" and can't seem to work out the conflict by themselves. When parents or teachers mediate, they are ensuring that the children take responsibility for working out a solution.

Community — Mediation clinics in schools, neighborhoods, and public institutions are places where disputants can bring their differences and work out a mutually agreeable solution in an environment that is safe with a third party who will not "take sides."

International — The 1978 Camp David Accords between Israel and Egypt were mediated by President Carter. Israel agreed to evacuate all its settlements in the Sinai in exchange for an Egyptian guarantee of demilitarization of the region. Both nations agreed to full diplomatic recognition of each other.

ARBITRATION

Interpersonal — Parents, principals, and teachers may be asked to play the role of arbitrator when siblings or students cannot work out their differences by themselves or choose not to work things out in the presence of a mediator. Yet, parents and teachers more often play the role of self-appointed arbitrator rarely asking beforehand if the children or students involved have agreed to follow the binding decision that will be imposed.

Community — Referees at sports events are arbitrators although we seldom think of them in this role. Arbitration is most common in settling labor and business disputes. The arbitration process is used to settle contract disputes between management and labor (over salaries, benefits, working conditions, etc.) as well as between companies that must work our agreements for how they do business together.

International — Arbitration is not a significant practice in the international community because nations would have to agree to the binding decision of the arbitrator. However, many diplomats and practitioners feel that arbitration has a promising future in the settlement of international disputes (over boundaries, fishing rights, treaty violations, etc.) with neutral nations serving as arbitrators.

ADJUDICATION

Interpersonal — Even family members sometimes have their "day in court" when siblings may present their unresolved grievances to Mom and Dad who then decide a fair way to work out the problem. Many schools also have student courts where students accused of school infractions are given a hearing and judged by their peers.

Community — With more lawyers per capita than any other nation, "going to court" seems to be the American way of settling disputes. Because the legal system is an adversarial one (someone wins and someone loses), other forms of conflict resolution (where a satisfactory settlement is agreed to by both parties) have only recently become practical alternatives to the court system.

International — The International Court of Justice is the official judicial organ of the United Nations. The World Court has jurisdiction over cases involving territorial sovereignty, fishing jurisdiction, the right to asylum, and the violation of treaties and conventions. Court decisions are theoretically binding; hence, nations rarely use the Court. On the other hand, decisions are not binding **in fact** because there is no consistent international system of enforcement. Harry Truman once said, "When Kansas and Colorado have a quarrel over the water in the Arkansas River they don't call out the National Guard in each state and go to war over it. The bring suit in the Supreme Court of the United States and abide by the decision. There isn't a reason in the world why we cannot do that internationally."

One success: In 1984, the U.S. and Canada agreed to have a five member chamber of the World Court determine the maritime boundary of the Gulf of Maine. One failure: In 1979, the U.S. began proceedings against the Iran for the seizure of the U.S. embassy. Iran publicly rejected the Court's right to render a decision.

LEGISLATION

International — The body of international law includes treaties, trade and arms agreements, customs, decisions of the World Court, and declarations and conventions of the United Nations. Compliance with international law is voluntary and is not enforceable.

The Universal Declaration of Human Rights, adopted by the General Assembly in 1948, is an example of "law" that will be selectively and inconsistently observed at a nation's convenience.

On the other hand, the "laws" concerning the treatment of prisoners of war and civilian populations under the Geneva Conventions of 1949 are followed by most nations. Perhaps the best example of international law that has almost universal support is the 1982 U.N. Convention on the Law of the Sea. It is a set of rules to govern all uses of the oceans (navigation, fisheries, mineral resource development) and protect and preserve the marine environment and the living resources within it. The framing of this convention is unique in international law. There was a deliberate attempt to include the active participation of the entire international community in drafting this convention.

The -Ate Processes of Peacemaking

	Who controls the decisions? / Who controls the process?	Is the process voluntary? or coercive?	What's the focus? relationships? problem? or both?
Initiate Acknowledging a problem or bringing up a conflict is never easy, but somebody has to go first! One individual or group initiates a conversation or invites the other party to talk. Sometimes this means discussing a problem first with parties not directly involved in the conflict or engaging in unofficial, "back channel" communication to explore how parties might want to proceed and to help them identify the range of issues that they might want to discuss in the future.	Disputants ----------- Disputants	Voluntary	Relationships
Communicate The first step toward violence is often the refusal to listen. The possibilities of misunderstanding another party's values, motives, feelings, and meanings are endless! Effective communication involves: 1) Knowing as much as you can about the other party and her/his perception of the problem; 2) Non-verbal rapport building—respecting and matching the other party's pacing and style; 3) Active listening; and 4) The abilities to respond, question, and exchange information without judgment.	Disputants ----------- Disputants	Voluntary	Relationships
Conciliate Sometimes individuals and groups may feel too hostile or alienated to even talk together by themselves. The term conciliate comes from the Latin *conciliare*, "to bring together." A third party brings two parties together to share concerns and feelings, air grievances, and explain their perceptions of the conflict. The purpose is to build a stronger foundation of understanding and trust, preparing the way for future problem solving. This is especially important for parties with deep differences and deeper resentments and anger.	Disputants ----------- Third Party	Voluntary	Relationships

The Five Processes of Peacemaking

Process	Who controls decisions? / Who controls the process?	Is the process voluntary? or coercive?	What's the focus? relationships? problem? or both?
Facilitate This process is used to assist a group of individuals or many parties with divergent views to reach a goal or complete a task to the mutual satisfaction of the participants. The facilitator functions as an impartial process expert—gathering information; setting agendas; ensuring that all parties are heard and that significant issues are discussed; keeping the group focused; summarizing "where the group is"; taking a group through a decision-making process; tracking time and recording the content of the conversation, class, or meeting.	Disputants ---------- Third Party	Voluntary	**The Problem and Relationships**
Negotiate Both parties agree to try and solve the problem by themselves. People identify their important needs and interests and agree to explore alternative solutions that are different from either party's original demands. **Informal Negotiations** involve a collaborative process that focuses equal attention on the relationships and the problem. Parties choose a solution that is satisfactory to both of them; they also choose to work it out in a way that helps to maintain or improve their relationship with each other. **Formal Negotiations** usually involve more hard bargaining and compromise and less attention to underlying issues and relationships among conflicting parties.	Disputants ---------- Disputants	Voluntary	**The Problem and Relationships**
Mediate Conflicting parties agree to work out a problem but request assistance of a neutral third party to help them resolve the conflict. Mediators do not judge who is right and who is wrong and do not suggest or tell parties what to do. Rather, mediators use a systematic step by step process that enables parties to hear each other's concerns and interests so that they can focus on possible solutions that are mutually agreeable. The conflicting parties (not the mediator) come up with their own solutions and decide how to make their solution work.	Disputants ---------- Third Party	Voluntary	**The Problem and Relationships**

The -Ate Processes of Peacemaking

	Who controls the decisions? / Who controls the process?	Is the process voluntary or coercive?	What's the focus? relationships? problem? or both?
Arbitrate Disputing parties agree to a hearing in which a neutral third party or panel hears both sides of the dispute and makes a binding decision which both parties have agreed to honor. Arbitration is more flexible than a court hearing (adjudication) because parties can choose the arbitrator and set the framework and conditions of the arbitration.	Third Party --------- Third Party	Voluntary	The Problem
Adjudicate (Litigate) Resolving a dispute through a formal court hearing or a trial is the most common form of dispute resolution in the world. In most domestic legal systems, according to civil law, a party who thinks he or she has been treated unjustly can bring another party to court. A judge and/or lawyer will hear the evidence presented by lawyers and decide which party is right according to the law. This is an adversarial, WIN-LOSE process; the dispute is settled in favor of one party at the expense of the other.	Third Party --------- Third Party	Coercive	The Problem
Legislate Laws and rules are the building blocks which help create an ordered society. Laws often emerge from shared values and laws establish common codes of behavior and standards for the treatment of people, property, and the environment. National governments can enforce laws and exercise their authority to punish violators. A government established under the rule of law can adapt to new situations and "right wrongs" in society by changing the law. In the U.S., conflicts among constituencies often involve a "clash of rights". The crafting of legislation which a majority of citizens will perceive as fair particularly involves the democratic art of "building consensus".	Third Party --------- Third Party	Voluntary	The Problem

ACTIVITY 12: Taking Action On A Community Problem

PURPOSE: Conflicts surround students in their own communities. One way for students to get involved is to investigate a conflict or problem that affects them, their friends and families, and their local community. In an action research project, students move from identifying, describing and analyzing a problem to exploring how to affect the changes that will help them achieve their desired outcome.

LEARNING STRATEGIES: Various inquirey and investigation methods and various kinds of performance and presentation assessments.

TIME: Multiple class periods over several weeks.

MATERIALS: Handout 7:12, other resources and materials will depend on the type of project that students choose to do.

SUGGESTED INSTRUCTIONS:

The action research form, **Handout 7:12,** provides a frame for thinking about a community problem. Once your class has decided on a problem it wants to tackle, students can work on this form in small groups and then discuss their ideas with the whole class.

The following examples describe problems which students have identified and the desired outcomes they wanted to achieve:

The Problem	*Desired Goal*	*Specific Outcome*
There are not enough summer jobs for young people in our community.	Increase the number of summer jobs opportunities available to teens	---->Double the number of jobs available for young people in the community by 1995.
There are not enough police patrolling in our neighborhood. There is too much crime.	Identify and implement strategies, policies, and programs which will make our neighborhood safer.	---->Establish a community policing program that includes neighborhood safety programs and better street lighting within the next year.
Our community doesn't have a public recycling program	Develop more recycling opportunities for a variety of materials.	---->Establish a public pick-up pilot recycling program in two neighborhoods by 1995.

Community Action Research Project:

What's the problem? (What's not working? What needs are not getting met?
What is the controversy about?)

_____

_____

What is your goal? What do you want to change? _____

_____

My interest is **How to:**

_____   _____
       (Action Verb)   **(Desired Outcome Expressed**
                                              in Terms of Need & Interests)

Why is this a good idea? Why would people in the community support the outcome
you think is desirable?

_____

_____

1. What is the root causes of the problem? (differences over power and
decision-making; allocation of resources; obstacles to meeting basic needs;
clash of values, beliefs, personalities) _____

_____

_____

2. Who is presently affected by the problem?_____

_____

_____

What is your evidence? How can you document this? _____

_____

_____

Who else may be affected by the problem if it is not resolved? _____

_____

_____

3. What key individuals and groups need to be part of the problem-solving process? What key resources does each individual or group have that could help you? What decision-making power do they each have?

Key Individuals or Groups	Key Resources and Power

4. What information do you need before you engage in discussion with others about this problem?

_____

_____

How will you get the necessary data and information that you need?

_____

_____

5. Identify three key people or groups who could help you achieve your goal. Identify a common interest that you have with each person or group. _____

_____

_____

6. Identify two key people or groups who could prevent you from achieving your goal. What would be their objections? Are there any common interests you have with these persons or groups?

_____

_____

7. What steps do we need to take before we discuss the problem publicly with key individuals and groups ? (documenting the extent of the problem and the need for your solution; developing a survey, proposal, or petition; preparing a presentation; interviewing people who can help you get the facts you need; publicizing a meeting; identifying key decision-makers are who need to approve necessary changes that help you achieve you goal)

Task to be completed	Timeline	Who does it?